AUTHORIZING MARRIAGE?

AUTHORIZING MARRIAGE?

CANON, TRADITION, AND CRITIQUE
IN THE BLESSING OF SAME-SEX
UNIONS

EDITED BY *MARK D. JORDAN,*
WITH *MEGHAN T. SWEENEY*
AND *DAVID M. MELLOTT*

PRINCETON UNIVERSITY PRESS

PRINCETON AND OXFORD

Copyright © 2006 by Princeton University Press
Published by Princeton University Press, 41 William Street,
Princeton, New Jersey 08540
In the United Kingdom: Princeton University Press,
3 Market Place,
Woodstock, Oxfordshire OX20 1SY

Library of Congress Cataloging-in-Publication Data
Authorizing marriage? : canon, tradition, and critique
in the blessing of same-sex unions / edited by
Mark D. Jordan; with Meghan T. Sweeney and David M. Mellott.
p.   cm.
Includes bibliographical references and index.
ISBN-13: 978-0-691-12346-2
ISBN-10: 0-691-12346-2
1. Same-sex marriage—Religious aspects—Christianity.
I. Jordan, Mark D. II. Sweeney, Meghan T. III. Mellott,
David M.

BT707.6.A98 2005
261.8'35848—dc22   200504863

British Library Cataloging-in-Publication Data is available

This book has been composed in Galliard

Printed on acid-free paper. ∞

pup.princeton.edu

Printed in the United States of America

10 9 8 7 6 5 4 3 2 1

CONTENTS

CONTRIBUTORS

Daniel Boyarin is the Taubman Professor of Talmudic Culture in the Departments of Near Eastern Studies and Rhetoric at the University of California at Berkeley. His books include *Carnal Israel: Reading Sex in Talmudic Culture*, *Unheroic Conduct: The Rise of Heterosexuality and the Invention of the Jewish Man*, *Dying for God: Martyrdom and the Making of Christianity and Judaism*, *Border Lines: The Partition of Judaeo-Christianity*, and the anthology *Queer Theory and the Jewish Question* (with Ann Pellegrini and Daniel Itzkowitz).

Steven Greenberg is Senior Teaching Fellow at the National Jewish Center for Learning and Leadership. He first came to wide attention under the pseudonym "Yaakov Levado," which he used when describing the situation of gay and lesbian Orthodox Jews. Since then, he has published numerous articles and the book *Wrestling with God and Men: Homosexuality in the Jewish Tradition*.

Laurence Paul Hemming is Dean of Research Students for Heythrop College, University of London, and a former guest professor in the Faculty of Theology of the Catholic University of Louvain. He is the author of *Heidegger's Atheism: The Refusal of a Theological Voice* and has contributed to collections reflecting on the relationship between theology and philosophy. His latest book, *Postmodernity's Transcending: Devaluing God*, is a genealogy of the aesthetic sublime.

Mark D. Jordan is the Asa Griggs Candler Professor in the Department of Religion at Emory University. His research interests include the history of Christian teachings on sex, the relationship between Christian theology and power, and the varieties of theological rhetoric. His recent books include *Ethics of Sex*, *Telling Truths in Church: Scandal, Flesh, and Christian Speech*, and *Blessing Same-Sex Unions: The Perils of Queer Romance and the Confusions of Christian Marriage*.

Dale B. Martin is the Woolsey Professor of Religious Studies at Yale University. He specializes in New Testament and Christian origins, including attention to social and cultural history of the Greco-Roman world. His books include *Slavery as Salvation: The Metaphor of Slavery in Pauline Christianity*, *The Corinthian Body*, and *Inventing Superstition: From the Hippocratics to the Christians*. Martin has published several articles on topics related to the ancient family, gender and sexuality in the ancient world, and the ideology of modern biblical scholarship. He is now working on issues related to gender, sexuality, and biblical interpretation, including an analysis of contemporary interpretation theory and its relationship to current uses of the Bible.

Saul M. Olyan is Professor of Judaic Studies, Professor of Religious Studies, and director of the program in Judaic Studies at Brown University. He is the author and editor of numerous articles and books, including *Biblical Mourning: Ritual and Social Dimensions, Rites and Rank: Hierarchy in Biblical Representations of Cult, "A Thousand Thousands Served Him": Exegesis and the Naming of Angels in Ancient Judaism*, and *Asherah and the Cult of Yahweh in Israel*. Olyan is a coeditor of the monograph series Brown Judaic Studies.

Susan Frank Parsons is Special Lecturer in Ethics at the University of Nottingham. Her books include *The Cambridge Companion to Feminist Theology, Feminism and Christian Ethics*, and *The Ethics of Gender*.

Eugene F. Rogers Jr. is Professor of Religious Studies at the University of North Carolina at Greensboro. His books include *Thomas Aquinas and Karl Barth* and *Sexuality and the Christian Body: Their Way into the Triune God*. Rogers has also edited the wide-ranging anthology of classical and contemporary texts *Sexuality and the Christian Body*.

Kathryn Tanner is Professor of Theology in the Divinity School, University of Chicago. She does constructive Christian theology in the Protestant tradition, with the intent of meeting contemporary challenges to belief through the creative use of both the history of Christian thought and interdisciplinary methods such as critical, social, and feminist theory. Her books *God and Creation in Christian Theology* and *The Politics of God* discuss the coherence and practical force of Christian beliefs about God's relation to the world. *Theories of Culture: A New Agenda for Theology* explores the relevance of cultural studies for rethinking theological method. Her latest work, *Jesus, Humanity, and the Trinity*, sketches a systematic theology that centers on the incarnation.

Mary Ann Tolbert is the George H. Atkinson Professor of Biblical Studies and the executive director of the Center for Lesbian and Gay Studies in Religion and Ministry at the Pacific School of Religion. Her writings on the gospel of Mark, including *Sowing the Gospel: Mark's World in Literary-Historical Perspective*, have established her as a leading voice in the interpretation of the New Testament. Her research also focuses on feminist hermeneutics and social location. She is a coeditor of *Reading from This Place*, which includes the volumes *Social Location and Biblical Interpretation in the United States* and *Social Location and Biblical Interpretation in Global Perspective*, and *Teaching the Bible: The Discourses and Politics of Biblical Pedagogy*.

INTRODUCTION

Mark D. Jordan

American Political debates over same-sex unions are punctuated by appeals to a "Judeo-Christian tradition of marriage." When the appeals are rejected, it is often with an argument about the separation of church and state—as if the only error in them were the application of religious reasoning to the legislation of a pluralistic democracy. The appeals ought to be much more generally troubling, because they reduce complex Jewish and Christian traditions to mere slogans. The slogans presuppose any number of confusions and reductions. They conflate Jewish with Christian, of course, even though the two groups of religious teachings and practices, diverse in themselves, typically differ in their assumptions about marriage or their prescriptions for it. (To see the mistake in claiming that the "Judeo-Christian tradition" has always prohibited marriage except between one man and one woman, it is enough to read the Book of Genesis.) The appeals further presume that "marriage" was essentially the same over the disparate cultures and several millennia traversed by the two religious traditions. They make it seem, finally, if only in their self-assurance, that all Jewish or Christian reasoning about family or sanctifying sexual desire must come down against same-sex unions. The essays in this volume show that religious traditions are more complicated—and more provocative.

For this volume, the authors were asked to consider some hard questions: Do the canonical scriptures of Judaism and Christianity offer any justification for blessing same-sex unions, whether as marriages or as some other form of erotic union? Could such justification be found in traditions of scriptural interpretation, religious law, or liturgical practice? If not, can contemporary exegesis or theological critique legitimately construct justifications for offering those blessings to couples of the same sex?[1]

Their responses to these questions took different forms. The arrangement of essays here represents only one way of grouping them. The first three papers are concerned with biblical interpretation. Saul M. Olyan reviews passages from the Hebrew Bible that often figure in debates over same-sex desire, but he is most interested by a phrase in David's famous lament over Jonathan that suggests a homoerotic and possibly sexual relationship between them. Dale B. Martin considers a larger number of passages throughout the New Testament that make a strong case against marriage of any kind. Mary Ann Tolbert concurs with Martin, adding alternative readings and additional passages, but her main concern is to argue that the canonical texts offer an ideal of friendship that contemporary same-sex couples can find affirming and helpful.

The next group of essays takes up categories and principles from Greek philosophy that resonate with both Jewish and Christian thinkers at various times. The two essays converge on Plato's *Symposium*. In a revision of his earlier views, Daniel Boyarin argues from Diotima's speech not only that Platonic love has nothing to do with physical touch, but that it is much closer than might be imagined to some versions of Rabbinic Judaism. In dialogue with Aristophanes' speech, Laurence Paul Hemming undoes the simplistic binary logic deployed in so many condemnations of same-sex coupling that invoke other-sex "complementarity."

The next two essays are concerned not so much with marriage as with weddings—with the liturgical rites that inaugurate and sometimes define a marriage. Steven Greenberg rehearses the historical function of the elements in a traditional Jewish wedding and then suggests how they might be revised or replaced in a liturgy for same-sex couples. I take up the best cases for the historical existence of rites for same-sex pairs—of lovers, of friends—in order to analyze the fallacies in the search for liturgical precedents. In different ways, Greenberg and I have one eye on history and another on the ambiguities of contemporary practice.

The volume concludes with three essays that provide theological assessments of the contemporary debates. In a deft retrieval of Richard Hooker, Kathryn Tanner argues that "conservative" Episcopalian opposition to same-sex love is in fact a new Puritanism that undoes principles of Anglican polity. Susan Frank Parsons points beyond opposition to homoeroticism from natural law or purpose to a theology of a created relationship called into the future. Placing himself squarely between critics of marriage and critics of same-sex desire, Eugene F. Rogers Jr. argues that same-sex couples should be blessed in order to recognize that they are means of sanctification for those called to be within them.

These brief descriptions are meant not to summarize the essays but to show one way in which they fit together to make a whole. After reading them, you will see how many other patterns they make—and how silly it is to reduce any of them to a single point or position. For example, the essays cannot be sorted simply as between exegesis of sacred texts and modern revision or reconstruction. The most constructive essays refer to scriptural passages, and the most exegetical attend to questions of contemporary application. The authors are all accomplished textualists of one sort or another and none of them advocate throwing over traditional texts in some fantasy of pure invention or utopian revolution. Nor do the essays divide neatly as between historians and theologians. In this volume, there is no tidy contrast between an inert past and a lively present—or between a sacred past and a decadent present.

What may be more interesting, the essays do not fall out along religious or denominational lines. Certainly some essays concentrate on the Hebrew scriptures, rabbinic interpretation, and contemporary Jewish liturgy and others interpret the New Testament, Christian theologians, and the rites of Christian communities, but the conclusions they draw are not, to my eye, deeply opposed or even significantly segregated along that line. There are no predictable denominational divisions among Protestant, Anglican, and Roman Catholic authors. Unexpected agreements can be found in the experience of many ecumenical and interreligious groups in recent decades. Here they may suggest how quickly debates over same-sex unions cross all the old lines.

Nor can the essays be neatly classed as "left" or "right," "liberal" or "conservative." Some readers will no doubt judge the conclusions or sympathies of the majority of contributors as appallingly "liberal," but then they will immediately have to concede that the term *liberal* is no longer meaningfully opposed to *conservative*. Many of the essays that argue in favor of "liberal" conclusions about same-sex unions do so with arguments in the classic manner from scripture and tradition. They are seriously engaged with interpreting and applying religious traditions. If they are not immediately labeled "conservative," that is because the label now has less to do with conserving traditions than with agreeing to a certain list of answers, some of which may be quite alien to tradition.

The contributions do agree, on my reading, in resisting reductions. They insist that authoritative texts, and especially canonical texts, should never be simplified according to the taste of one or another contemporary polemic. This resolution entails resisting conceptual or philosophic reductions built into the frames within which texts about anything sexual are now interpreted. The belief that sex supremely determines the character of human persons or their relations is hardly the invention of same-sex advocates. It is a much more general feature of American discourse. It motivates both proposals for blessing same-sex unions and defenses of heterosexual marriage. It appears as much in the latest versions of sexual liberation as in the (highly untraditional) assumption that heterosexual Christian marriage ought to guarantee a certain minimum of sexual satisfaction, even experimentation. American "muscular Christianity" of the nineteenth century seems to have been succeeded by a hygienic-therapeutic Christianity in the late twentieth, according to which sexual pleasure is the right of every Christian couple—though not of their children.

The contributors also agree, on my reading, in multiplying conceptions of sex and gender—or of sex, sexuality, and gender—or of whatever overly neat scheme one tries to impose. The conceptions sometimes turn to obvious and yet easily suppressed links, as between misogyny and the angry rejection of same-sex love. Traditions that restrict or formerly restricted the participation of women are also traditions that severely repress same-sex desire, at least between men. The same point could be made by noting that almost every traditional condemnation of same-sex desire carries with it a derogatory reference to women.

Resistance to reduction is also evident when the essays deal with the possibilities for liturgical innovation and the loud demands to refuse any. The memory for liturgy in many religious groups is notoriously short. If some textual or symbolic elements of the rites do quote much older ceremonies, the whole of even the most traditional rite is often framed, performed, or understood with quite contemporary sensibilities. The same might be said of arguments over liturgical change. It is often noted that the quarrels over the smallest detail of liturgy can quickly become ferocious, even (or especially) when the detail in question is of rather recent origin. The same reaction is frequent enough in that unruly mixture of religious, familial, communal, economic, and reproductive considerations that surrounds most marriage rites. Those attending many Jewish or Christian weddings would be astonished to learn the origin or early significance of many of the central liturgical elements—and yet many resist changing what they learned (often without understanding) as children.

The essays that follow range widely, but they hardly cover every topic or vantage point on Jewish and Christian marriage. Some topics were excluded by the original questions posed to the contributors. The emphasis on constructive engagement with the traditions' authorities did not particularly invite sociological or anthropological studies—though one may notice how those issues play at the border of some of the essays here. The original emphasis also did not solicit strategic plans for changing the official policies of religious groups or rewriting current legislation (in those groups that distinguish legislation or canon law from theological and liturgical traditions). Nor will the essays here be recognized immediately as pastoral (to use the Christian metaphor), if *pastoral* refers to a fairly narrow range of practical guidelines. In another and more traditional sense, all of the essays are eminently practical and pastoral because they treat urgent questions of contemporary religious living. Nor, finally, do the essays pretend to treat the authorities of the hundreds of religious traditions not mentioned by them, including some important varieties of modern Judaism and Christianity.

Some readers may feel a more important exclusion. They will conclude that some important voices are missing—voices representing ethnic, racial, national, and class identities or sexual roles beyond lesbian and gay. Will it be any consolation to say that strenuous efforts were made to invite a diverse group of contributors? Some of those invited declined because of the usual hazards of individual obligations. Others who should have been invited may have been missed through the limits of acquaintance. But it should also be admitted that not all the limitations were individual. To state the obvious: Some groups are significantly underrepresented in academic circles, and therefore the few scholars who have established themselves are inundated by invitations. What is just as important for this volume, the number of scholars willing to write about same-sex issues varies tremendously from one religious group to another. It is much easier— much safer—to speak publicly about same-sex unions in Reconstructionist Judaism or liberal Protestantism than in Roman Catholicism or Orthodox Judaism, especially if one holds a religious office. It is safer to speak about these issues as a Jew or a Christian than as an adherent of some other religions—or so the responses to invitations would suggest.

Polemicists often speak as if the world were swarming with "liberal" scholars in every field ready to take up the least detail of queer life with uninhibited explicitness. This is simply not true. The triumph of queer studies has been greatly exaggerated even in most secular fields. Outside a few famous departments, scholars working on homosexual topics often find themselves battling to teach courses or secure students—and to keep their jobs. The situation is more perilous in religion or religious studies than in many other fields. To be able to write affirmatively about same-sex topics in religion, one has to be employed either in a secular school (where the study of religion is often suspect) or in one of the dwindling number of "liberal" seminaries or religious institutions. Even for those who have such happy appointments, the pressures that can be brought to bear are often formidable. Several contributors to this volume have had to consider carefully what they could say in print without costing themselves or their home institutions much trouble. Anticipations of consequences have weighed so heavily on some potential contributors that they decided they could not participate. No one should judge their decision who has not been subject to such pressures.

The missing voices would weigh more heavily if this volume pretended to be representative. It does not. Indeed, it does not pretend to be complete in any way. Its aim is much more modest. The essays collected here mean to show at least two things. The first is that the question of recognizing or blessing same-sex unions is much more complicated as a religious question than is typically admitted in public debate. This is because—the second point—religious marriage itself is much more complicated than most debaters want to admit. The two points are important enough to be worth demonstrating. They are demonstrated here quite fully, if from a necessarily limited selection of evidence. It is particularly important to demonstrate them because they seem to be forgotten week after week, year in and year out, no matter how many other topics advance and retreat through the public debates.

The essays that follow say much more beyond these two points. They offer startling readings of scripture. They uncover the philosophical questions underneath the apparently solid floor of religious debate. The essays disconcert assumptions about the fixity of gender or the importance of sex. They make something so familiar as this weekend's wedding ceremonies appear suddenly alien. The one thing they refuse to do is to pretend to answer all the important religious questions about same-sex unions.

"SURPASSING THE LOVE OF WOMEN"

ANOTHER LOOK AT 2 SAMUEL 1:26 AND THE RELATIONSHIP OF DAVID AND JONATHAN

Saul M. Olyan

The love of Jonathan for David reported in the biblical text has been the focus of much attention from both nonspecialist commentators and professional biblical scholars. Many nonspecialists, and some biblical scholars, have claimed that texts such as 1 Sam. 18:1–3 and 2 Sam. 1:26 suggest that David and Jonathan shared a homoerotic love, with some arguing that this love was expressed sexually.[1] At the same time, most specialists addressing these texts have ignored or dismissed both sexual and nonsexual homoerotic interpretations. Instead, biblical scholars have often argued that the relationship of Jonathan and David is best understood as a close friendship, with a number of commentators underscoring the political dimensions of the love of Jonathan for David. According to these scholars, the rhetoric of love found in the biblical materials describing the relationship of Jonathan and David is clearly a manifestation of ancient West Asian covenant discourse, in which loyal partners in a political relationship—whether equal or unequal in status—are said to love one another, and refer to one another using the terminology of kinship (e.g., "brother" in parity relationships; "father" and "son" in treaties of unequals).[2] Though there can be no doubt that covenant discourse has indeed shaped the descriptions of Jonathan's relationship to David, are the majority of specialist commentators correct to dismiss or ignore the homoerotic interpretation entirely? My purpose in this essay is to explore whether or not the biblical text may also suggest a homoerotic—and possibly sexual—relationship between Jonathan and David alongside the obvious covenant bond attested in both the prose narratives of 1 Samuel and in the elegy of 2 Sam. 1:19–27. The focus of my interest is the curious claim of David's Lament with respect to Jonathan: "Your love for me was wondrous, surpassing the love of women" (2 Sam. 1:26). At the end of this investigation, I will consider briefly the implications of a homoerotic interpretation of 2 Sam. 1:26 for contemporary debate regarding gay marriages and same-sex unions.

Though rarely recognized by nonspecialists, the covenantal dimensions of the Jonathan/David materials are quite explicit and have been well elucidated for the most part by scholars in the biblical field.[3] 1 Sam. 18:1 states that "the soul of Jonathan was knit to the soul of David, and Jonathan loved him as himself"; in v. 3, we learn that "Jonathan and David cut a covenant (*berit*) because he [presumably, Jonathan] loved him as himself."[4] 1 Sam. 20:14–15 speaks of David's covenant loyalty (*hesed*) owed to Jonathan and his descendants and v. 17 mentions an oath of Jonathan prompted by his love for David. In David's speech to Jonathan in 1 Sam. 20:7–8, he uses the language of a subordinate treaty partner in relation to Jonathan, referring to himself as Jonathan's "servant" (*eved*) and mentioning the treaty context explicitly: "You will be loyal in covenant (literally, "do covenant loyalty") to your servant, for you brought your servant with you into the covenant of Yhwh." In contrast, although 2 Sam. 1:19–27, David's Lament for Saul and Jonathan, does not mention a covenant directly, it speaks nonetheless of Jonathan as David's "brother," a treaty term native to the discourse of allies.[5] The mention of "cutting a covenant" (*karat berit*), "doing covenant loyalty" (*asah hesed*), and the swearing of an oath in the David/Jonathan narratives suggest clearly that the love that accompanies these actions, and even prompts them, is covenant love. Similarly, the use of the terms *servant* in 1 Sam. 20:7–8 and *brother* in 2 Sam. 1:26 also suggests a covenant setting, though the texts apparently disagree on the nature of the treaty relationship between Jonathan and David, with 1 Sam. 20:7–8 casting David as the subordinate partner, and 2 Sam. 1:26 suggesting a treaty of equals.[6]

The language of love is native to covenant settings, a commonplace not only in biblical texts concerned with covenantal relations but also in extrabiblical West Asian treaties and related correspondence.[7] In such contexts, *to love* means to establish a covenant bond or to conform to treaty obligations.[8] Biblical examples of the love idiom used in the covenant between Yhwh and Israel include the command to Israel to love Yhwh: "You shall love Yhwh your god with all your heart, with all your soul, and with all your might. And these words, which I command you this day, shall be upon your heart" (Deut. 6:5–6). A second such example is Yhwh's statement in the Decalogue that he is loyal in covenant to those who love him (that is, to those who keep his commandments) while punishing those who hate him (that is, those who break covenant) and their descendants: "For I, Yhwh your god, am a jealous god, visiting the iniquity of parents upon children to the third and even the fourth generation of those who hate me, but doing covenant loyalty for the thousands, for those who love me and keep my commandments" (Exod. 20:6; Deut 5:10). The rhetoric of covenant love is manifest also in texts that describe treaty relationships between kings, between a king and his people, or between other individuals. One example of such a use of love language is the description of David's loyal treaty partner Hiram, the king of Tyre, as a "lover of David" in

1 Kings 5:15. In 1 Sam. 18:16, all Israel and Judah are said to be "lovers" of David, because he led them in war; in 18:22, it is the servants of Saul who are said to love David. The speech of Joab to David in 2 Sam. 19:7 refers to David's loyal army as "those who love" him, and to his enemies, led by his rebellious son Absalom, as "those who hate" him. In all of these cases, love means loyalty in the context of a covenant bond, whether it be between a deity and a people, a king and a fellow king, or a king and his army.

The fourteenth century BCE Amarna archive of diplomatic correspondence between Pharaohs Amenhotep III and IV and their allies and vassals illustrates a comparable use of the rhetoric of love in extrabiblical treaty contexts. In a number of Amarna letters, the Pharaoh's ally King Tushratta of Mittani uses the love idiom to describe his relationship with the Pharaoh, his treaty partner, or the relationship of his forebears with those of the Pharaoh. An example is Amarna letter 17:24–28: "My father loved you, and you in turn loved my father. In keeping with this love, my father [g]ave you my sister."[9] In Amarna letter 19:1–2, Tushratta addresses the Pharaoh as "[my] brother, my son-in-law, who loves me, and whom I lov[e]," thereby combining love language with that of brotherhood, as would be expected in a parity treaty context.[10] Similarly, the rhetoric of love is used in the letters of vassals to the Pharaoh, and the love is mutual: Just as the vassal loves his lord, so the Pharaoh loves his vassal. In Amarna letter 53:40–44, Akizzi of Qatna states that he and several other vassals love Pharaoh, their lord; "all of these kings," writes Akizzi, "are my lord's servants."[11] Amarna letter 121:61–63 assumes that the suzerain should love his vassal, meaning in this context to act on his behalf against a common enemy.[12] As in the letters of allies preserved at Amarna, to love in the letters of vassals means to be loyal to the treaty partner. Other West Asian diplomatic texts of the second and first millennia BCE bear witness to similar uses of the love idiom and other technical covenant language. Correspondence between the Hittite king Hattusili III and the king of Babylon speaks of the kings as "affectionate brothers," their relationship as "brotherhood," and their interactions as loving.[13] In the first millennium BCE treaties of Esarhaddon and Ashurbanipal of Assyria, vassals swear to love their suzerain, and loyal vassals are described as those who love their lord.[14] In all of these cases, both biblical and extrabiblical, use of the love idiom indicates either the establishment of a political relationship or, more commonly, its perpetuation through the loyalty of participants, as a number of scholars have pointed out.

Though the covenant interpretation accounts well for the love rhetoric in the prose narratives of David and Jonathan and for the use of the term *brother* to describe Jonathan in David's Lament (2 Sam. 1:26), it does not effectively explain the Lament's love comparison (2 Sam. 1:26). In this poem, a dirge probably composed at the time of the deaths of Saul and Jonathan, possibly of Davidic authorship, and attributed to David in the prose framework, Jonathan's love for David is compared to the love of women and found to be superior: "Your love for me was wondrous, surpassing the love of women."[15] Though various scholars have maintained that this statement too concerns covenant love, they have not recognized that the comparison is extremely peculiar in a covenant context, given what we know of love comparisons made by treaty partners in other West Asian texts. For love comparisons in treaty contexts are of two types: the covenant love of treaty partners is compared in one of several ways, or covenant love itself is likened to another, analogous love type that, like covenant, requires fidelity. In both types of love comparison, loyalty or disloyalty to the obligations of the covenant bond is the issue that gives rise to comparison in the first place. Yet the comparison of 2 Sam. 1:26 fits neither pattern, though it shares characteristics with both. The fact that it likens Jonathan's love to the love of women—generally understood by scholars to be a reference to sexual or sexual-emotional love—suggests that a noncovenantal interpretation of 2 Sam. 1:26 is likely, one in which fidelity is not the focal issue.[16]

The first type of love comparison native to covenant settings likens one treaty partner's love in covenant to that of another treaty partner of the same class (e.g., an ally's love is compared to that of his ally) or compares two different manifestations of a treaty partner's love (e.g., an ally's love for his ally is likened to his love of his ally's predecessor). The comparison may be constructed in one of the following ways: "the love of x is like the love of y," "the love of x is greater than the love of y," or "the love of x for y is greater than the love of x for z." In each example of this type of love comparison, fidelity to treaty obligations is clearly the focus of concern. In Amarna letter 17:24–26, Tushratta, the king of Mittani, states the following concerning the relationship of his father to the Pharaoh, his treaty partner: "My father loved you, and you in turn loved my father."[17] This statement illustrates one type of comparison mentioned, as the love of each partner is comparable. The following examples illustrate another type, in which the love of one partner for his ally is said to be greater than his love for his ally's predecessor. In Amarna letter 19:12–13, Tushratta states that the Pharaoh, his treaty partner, has loved him ten times more than he loved his (Tushratta's) father.[18] In Amarna letter 26:30–34, Tushratta, writing to the Egyptian queen mother, states that he demonstrates ten times more love for her son the king than he did for her dead husband, his predecessor.[19] In these and other cases, the love of a king in a treaty context may be likened to the love of a fellow king, his ally and treaty partner, or different manifestations of a king's covenant love may be compared. The comparison may suggest equality of love or superiority of love, but the thing compared is always another example of covenant love.[20]

The second type of love comparison attested in covenant settings likens covenant love to another love type to which it can be compared because the latter type also requires fidelity. This kind of love comparison is associated in particular with descriptions of a metaphorically female Israel's relationship to her (male) god. Thus, according to Jer. 2:2, the love of Israel for Yhwh during her early days was like the love of a young bride for her husband:

> I remember the loyalty (*hesed*) of your youth
> The love of your betrothal
> Your following me in the wilderness
> In a land not sown . . .

The defining characteristic that each love type has in common is fidelity; this is the focus of the comparison and what makes comparison possible. Israel is likened to a young bride precisely because Israel was loyal in covenant in her "youth," according to Jer. 2:2, just as an idealized young bride is loyal to her husband and does not stray.[21] Hosea 3:1 is similar in its comparison of Hosea's love for an adulterous woman to the love of Yhwh for a disloyal Israel that worships other deities, thereby violating covenant obligations: "Go, love a woman who is loved by another and who is an adulteress; [it is] like the love of Yhwh for the children of Israel. As for them, they turn to other gods and are lovers of raisin cakes." In this example, the basis for the comparison is disloyalty rather than loyalty, but as with Jer. 2:2, Israel's loyalty to Yhwh, or lack of same, finds an analogue in the loyalty or disloyalty of a wife to her husband. Just as an adulteress lacks fidelity to her husband, so too does Israel with respect to her god. A third example of this type of love comparison is found in Amarna letter 24:121–123. Here it is said that the love of allies for one another ought to be like the love of a person for his patron god: "As man loves Shimige on seeing him, so do we want, between us, to love one another."[22] In this instance, as in the others, fidelity is the basis for the comparison: the loyalty (= love) of human treaty partners for one another ought to be like the loyalty (= love) of a worshiper for his patron deity. In each of these examples, the two types of love that are compared are similar, and therefore comparable, because fidelity is expected to characterize each love type.

How is the comparison of 2 Sam. 1:26 similar to the two types of love comparison characteristic of treaty contexts and how does it differ from them? First, it should be noted that the comparison of 2 Sam. 1:26 shares a "love of x is greater than the love of y" structure with some of the comparisons that liken the love of one treaty partner to that of another of the same class. And like comparisons of covenant love to an analogous love type, 2 Sam. 1:26 likens one type of love (Jonathan's love for David) to another (the love of women). That said, one must also observe that 2 Sam. 1:26 does not compare the love of one treaty partner to that of another of the same class. Rather, it likens Jonathan's love to "the love of women," an expression generally understood by scholars to be a reference to sexual or sexual-emotional love.[23] If 2 Sam. 1:26 were concerned with covenant love, we might expect it to say something like "your love for me was wondrous, surpassing the love of other brothers" (= partners in a parity treaty), or "surpassing my love for you." Such formulations would compare the love of treaty partners of the same class (e.g., the love of other allies for David or that of David himself for Jonathan). This kind of comparison would make sense in a context in which parity treaty language is used elsewhere in the same verse of the relationship in question ("my brother Jonathan"). Also, unlike comparisons of covenant love with another love type, the two love types of 2 Sam. 1:26 do not share a basis for comparison if Jonathan's love for David refers to covenant love. For in other examples of this type of comparison, covenant love is likened to another kind of love sharing a central characteristic: fidelity to a set of obligations. An example of this, as noted earlier, occurs in Jer. 2:2. There, Israel's love for Yhwh in its early days is like the love of an idealized young bride on account of the fidelity common to both types of love. In 2 Sam. 1:26, however, Jonathan's love for David is compared not to another love type that is characterized by fidelity, but apparently to the experience of sexual or sexual-emotional love with women as a class. Were we to translate the Hebrew *ahavat nashim* as "the love of wives" instead of "the love of women," it seems at first blush that one could make a case that fidelity to obligations is at issue, since the wife must not commit adultery, and men such as David had multiple wives.[24] But even comparison to "the love of wives" would be odd in a human covenant context such as this, given that the relationship in question involves two men, that male-female love as constructed in biblical and other West Asian texts consistently has a sexual component, even if it is only potential, and given that male-female love is typically hierarchical in its casting, in contrast to the fraternal covenant language found elsewhere in the verse, which suggests parity.[25] Thus, there are serious difficulties raised by understanding the Hebrew expression *ahavat nashim* as "the love of wives," and by arguing that fidelity to obligations is the basis for the love comparison. It is more plausible to translate the expression "the love of women," as virtually all commentators and translations do, and investigate possible bases for the love comparison other than covenant loyalty. The comparison of 2 Sam. 1:26, though it shares characteristics in common with both kinds of love comparison made in treaty contexts, differs from both types in important ways. Though it uses love rhetoric, it is likely not a statement about fidelity to a treaty.

To what, then, might the love comparison of 2 Sam. 1:26 refer? It seems impossible to ignore the potential significance of the sexual or sexual-emotional interpretation of the expression *the love of women*. As mentioned earlier, this understanding is commonplace among scholarly commentators on this passage, and certainly seems defensible, though the expression itself occurs nowhere else in the Hebrew Bible.[26] As is frequently observed, the Hebrew root *to love* (*ahev*) and its derivatives can have a sexual or sexual-emotional meaning in certain contexts, particularly when associated with the relations between men and women. Hosea 3:1 is an excellent example of the sexual usage ("Go, love a woman who is loved by another and who is an adulteress"), as is 2 Sam. 13:1, 4, 15, verses that describe, using derivatives of the root *to love*, the sexual desire of David's son Amnon for his half sister Tamar, whom he violates. In 1 Kings 11:1, Solomon is said to have "loved many alien women," with a list of foreign wives and concubines following. The association of *love* and eroticism or sex in biblical descriptions of the relations of men and women is equally true of the few texts that describe a woman as the lover rather than the object of love. Prov. 5:19 speaks of a man's wife as "doe of love" and advises: "Let her breasts satisfy you at all times / With her love, may you be intoxicated always." Even if an emotional component is evident in such love, as it certainly is in a text such as 1 Sam. 18:20, which describes the love of Michal for David, the sexual component remains ever-present, at least potentially if not explicitly.[27] If "the love of women" refers to the sexual or sexual-emotional love women offer a man, the comparison of Jonathan's love to it suggests that the two types of love have something in common, a basis for comparison. Because it seems as though fidelity is not likely to be that basis, the sexual or sexual-emotional component of love itself could well be. Like love comparisons of the covenant type, those of the sexual or sexual-emotional type are attested in biblical materials. An example is Gen. 29:30, where Jacob's love for Rachel is compared to his love for Leah in a manner not unlike the love comparison of 2 Sam. 1:26: "He came also to Rachel and he loved Rachel more than Leah."[28] Thus, the elegy may be suggesting through its comparison that Jonathan's love for David was of a sexual or sexual-emotional type and that it was more wondrous than the same such love David had experienced from women.

If David's Lament suggests that Jonathan's love for David is of a sexual or sexual-emotional type rather than a covenantal type, why would treaty terminology ("my brother, Jonathan") be used by the poet in the same verse of the composition? As I have observed, the language of brotherhood and the love idiom are at home together in covenant discourse, as are love comparisons that make a statement about fidelity. In fact, the use of fraternal terminology before the love comparison in 2 Sam. 1:26 sets up the reader to expect a love comparison focused precisely on the issue of loyalty in covenant, but such does not come to pass. It may be that the poem's author (David?) drew purposefully on the vocabulary and rhetorical conventions of treaty discourse in an intentionally subversive way, manipulating such familiar forms to communicate an unexpected and even startling observation about Jonathan's love: Although the two were bound by a parity treaty, there was more to their relationship than simply a covenant bond. The suggestion that covenant idioms were manipulated in order to communicate such an assertion is strengthened by the observation that David is portrayed as a nonconformist and even a manipulator of ritual and social conventions in the prose narratives about him. One example of this is his behavior at the death of his infant son, described in 2 Sam. 12:20–23. Having undertaken petitionary mourning rites in an attempt to save his child's life, David, upon hearing the news of the child's death, abandons his mourning posture and, through a series of ritual reversals, returns to quotidian life, baffling his servants by so doing. When confronted by his courtiers about his nonconforming ritual behavior, he answers their query in a way that suggests that he believes mourning after death to have no purpose whatsoever, because the dead cannot be brought back again. And because it has no purpose, he refuses to meet social and ritual expectations by enacting it. A second example of David as ritual and social nonconformist is 2 Samuel 19, the narrative describing the aftermath of his army's vanquishing of Absalom, his rebellious son, and Absalom's followers. Instead of rejoicing with the army, as is expected after victory, David privileges his own, private feelings, mourning the death of his son. David reverses this nonconforming ritual behavior only after he is warned that he will lose the army's support entirely if it continues. In 2 Sam. 3:31–37, like 2 Sam. 1:19–27 a part of the apologetic "History of David's Rise,"[29] David manipulates mourning rites to achieve political ends at the death of Abner. I acknowledge that it is odd indeed to find anything subversive or even unconventional in a dirge such as 2 Sam. 1:19–27, characterized as much of it is by idealization of the dead and conventional, gendered imagery.[30] Nonetheless, verse 26, however it is interpreted, departs from convention, and David is portrayed as a manipulator of ritual and social norms in the "History of David's Rise" and other narratives of 1 and 2 Samuel, particularly norms associated with mourning. In short, whether or not David authored the dirge attributed to him, its manipulation of treaty discourse is not inconsistent with the portrayal of David's ritual behavior in the narratives describing his career.

A number of scholars have pointed to alleged impediments to a homoerotic and sexual interpretation of 2 Sam. 1:26, and I shall consider these presently. Markus Zehnder, followed by Steven L. McKenzie, argued that the statement about Jonathan's love in 2 Sam. 1:26 is best characterized as "poetic exaggeration" ("dichterischer Übertreibung"), not intended to be understood in a literal, possibly erotic, sense.[31] Though Zehnder did not provide an argument directly in support of this assertion, McKenzie defended it by drawing on Zehnder's later assertions regarding the whole complex of materials about David and Jonathan: "Homosexual acts were condemned in Israelite law (Lev. 20:13). So David's apologists would hardly have described him as homosexual or included a piece that described him that way."[32] Aside from McKenzie's problematic projection of contemporary, Western categories on the ancients ("homosexual"/ "heterosexual"), a practice that has been well critiqued by others,[33] his assumption that (all?) homoerotic acts were condemned by Israelite legal tradition and his argument that, therefore, David's apologists would not include a text such as 2 Sam. 1:19–27 if it suggested a sexual relationship between David and Jonathan, are unconvincing for a number of reasons. First, unless one is reading the biblical text canonically, something a historian does not do, one cannot make a case that the surviving biblical legal corpora in general oppose same-sex sexual acts between males; only Lev. 18:22 and 20:13 voice any opposition. And furthermore, as I have argued elsewhere, these laws, which are part of the Holiness legislation and date very likely to a period long after the composition of 2 Sam. 1:19–27, only oppose anal intercourse; they have nothing at all to say about other potential sexual acts between men.[34] In contrast, earlier legal materials, such as the "Book of the Covenant" (Exod. 20:22–23:33) or the legal collection in Deuteronomy 12–26, do not even touch on the issue of homoerotic sexual acts. Therefore, McKenzie's argument that David's apologists would have been reluctant to make use of a text that included a homoerotic statement because of Lev. 20:13 lacks cogency. For it cannot be shown that any community in Israel ever opposed all homoerotic sexual acts, nor is it evident that consensual anal intercourse between males was proscribed by any circle before the Holiness School interdicted it at a time likely long after the composition of David's Lament.[35] In short, it is not at all clear that the tenth-century BCE apologists responsible for the "History of David's Rise" would have been particularly bothered by a homoerotic meaning of the love comparison of 2 Sam. 1:26. What is clear, however, is that a central priority of the apologists responsible for the "History of David's Rise" is to show that David was innocent of the deaths of Saul, Jonathan, Abner, Eshbaal, and other Saulides who stood in the way of his ascent to the throne.[36] Inclusion of the Lament underscores the narrative's insistence on David's innocence with respect to Saul's and Jonathan's deaths. Not only does David not serve the Philistines in battle against Israel at Mt. Gilboa, he and his men mourn publicly at the report of the deaths of Saul and Jonathan and Israel's defeat, in effect switching sides and declaring an affiliation with Israel and Saul rather than with Achish of Gath, David's overlord, and the other Philistines.[37] The Lament functions in its immediate narrative context almost like a proof text for David's true loyalty to Saul and Israel: he mourned for them, as allies do, and even composed this lament on their deaths.[38] In a word, the inclusion of the dirge by the apologists responsible for the "History of David's Rise" cannot be used in a convincing way to determine the meaning of the love comparison of 2 Sam. 1:26, because the lament as a whole so beautifully serves the apologetic purposes of the compilers, no matter what v. 26 may suggest. Any conclusion drawn about the meaning of 2 Sam. 1:26 must therefore emerge out of an analysis of the statement itself.

If David's Lament suggests that a homoerotic and possibly sexual relationship existed between Jonathan and David, what are the implications for contemporary debate over gay marriages and same-sex unions? Marriage and marriage-like unions generally assume sexual relations of some kind, and the laws of Lev. 18:22 and 20:13, as well as other biblical texts, have been cited by various religious conservatives as an impediment to state and community recognition of same-sex unions or gay marriages. I have argued elsewhere on philological grounds that the laws of Lev. 18:22 and 20:13 prohibit anal intercourse specifically; they have nothing to say about other forms of same-sex sexual activity between men and nothing whatsoever to say about such activity between women.[39] If this interpretation is correct, then the Hebrew Bible, even read canonically as a single work, only limits rather than proscribes sexual relations between men, and allows them between women. Such a reading of biblical law opens up the possibility of justifying the blessing of gay marriages and same-sex unions in religious contexts that embrace the authority of the Hebrew Bible in some sense, because the sexual activity normally associated with such marriages or unions would not necessarily violate scriptural law. In addition, a homoerotic relationship between Jonathan and David, especially a sexual one, would provide an example in the biblical text itself of the sexual-emotional linking of two men in a context free of condemnation, though not a direct model for a formalized union or marriage, as the ancients in question apparently had no notion of such a coupling. For such a direct model one must look elsewhere than in the biblical text.[40]

FAMILIAR IDOLATRY AND THE CHRISTIAN CASE AGAINST MARRIAGE

Dale B. Martin

Contemporary Christianity in the United States—whether Protestant or Catholic, liberal or conservative—has so closely aligned the basic message of Christianity with the family and "traditional family values" that it is currently in a state of idolatry.[1] Increasingly, whether they are religious or not, people in America tend to equate Christianity with the family and "family values." It is not just that gay and lesbian people have largely left their churches; single people in general often feel out of place in churches. And other people in non-"traditional" family structures—whether divorced, cohabiting, or in partial nuclear families—tend to be much less active in churches. The reason is that American churches have so identified themselves with the modern, heterosexual, nuclear family that people without such families feel less at home in most churches.[2] The religious term for the identification of anything but God at the center of Christian faith is *idolatry.* And the idolatry of contemporary American Christianity is the familiar idolatry of the church's current focus on the family.

Not only is contemporary Christianity idolatrous in its focus on the family and marriage; it is also hypocritical. It either explicitly states or assumes that its current values are the obvious expression of Christian scripture and tradition. Though most Christians assume that the current centrality of marriage and family represents a long tradition in Christianity, it is actually only about 150 years old. One could even make the argument that the current focus on the heterosexual *nuclear* family dates back only to the 1950s.[3] In this essay I pass over the long tradition of Christianity, although it also provides little support for the modern family. Rather, I concentrate mainly on the New Testament and the writings of the early church. Contrary to most contemporary opinion—Christian as well as non-Christian—there are many more resources in Christian scripture and tradition to *criticize* the modern family than to promote it.

The Historical Jesus

Jesus of Nazareth was not a family man. Though we could debate the construction of the historical Jesus—and all "historical Jesuses" are in fact hypothetical constructions based on the flimsiest of evidence—according to all our available evidence, Jesus never married. This could have been an accident of history. It was not unusual for men in the ancient world to put off marriage, if they married at all, until their thirties. If Jesus was about thirty years old when he began his ministry, as suggested by some traditions (deriving from Luke 3:23), he could have been unmarried just because he had not gotten around to it. But there are other indications that he rejected marriage and family ties and taught his disciples to do likewise. Whatever the historical Jesus taught about sex, about which we have no real evidence, his message apparently included a severe critique of the traditional family, including marriage.

One of the sayings of the Gospels that must be historical is Jesus' response when told that his mother and brothers (and sisters according to one source, a textual variant at Mark 3:32) wanted to see him. Jesus answers, "Who is my mother and who are my brothers? . . . Whoever does the will of God, that one is my brother and sister and mother" (Mark 3:34–35; cf. Matt. 12:46–50; Luke 8:19–21). Jesus refused to identify with his traditional family and instead substituted for it the eschatological community that shared his vision of a new, divinely constituted family.

Indeed, all our Gospels present Jesus as creating and living in an alternative to the household: an itinerant group of men and women unrelated to one another by blood or marriage, most of whom had also apparently separated from their families. Jesus called his disciples away from their households. Although perhaps teaching that the commandment to honor one's parents should still be obeyed (the evidence is either nonexistent or inconclusive), he told one man not even to bury his father—a teaching that would have been perceived as an incredible and offensive affront to family values in ancient Palestine (Luke 9:59–60; Matt. 8:21–22).[4] In another saying, as passed on by Luke, Jesus says, "If anyone comes to me and does not despise [or hate: *miseo*] his own father and mother and wife and children and brothers and sisters, and yes his own life, he is not able to be my disciple" (Luke 14:26). Most modern Christians prefer to remember the saying in its Matthean version, where in place of "despise" or "hate," the author has Jesus say merely that one must not "love more" one's family than Jesus (Matt. 10:37). But the Lukan use of "hate" has support from the Gospel of Thomas 55, which may well be an independent witness to an early tradition. And it is more likely, many scholars believe, that the Lukan form better reflects an earlier, Aramaic source.[5] Moreover, Matthew would more likely have altered a "Q" saying to the less offensive "love more" in order to make Jesus' teaching fit his own high regard for the law of Moses.[6] Thus, the more radical version passed on by Luke and the Gospel of Thomas has the stronger claim to authenticity. A clearer indication that the historical Jesus taught the rejection of the traditional family can scarcely be demanded.

But doesn't Jesus' teaching about divorce, as contained mainly in Mark 10:6–12 and Matt. 19:4–9, imply the support of marriage? Here Jesus forbids divorce even though the law of Moses had allowed it. Wouldn't this imply that Jesus, if the saying is historical, supported marriage and the traditional family at least to the extent that the law did? Not really. After all, Matthew includes Jesus' forbidding of divorce but then follows it up with his saying about those who have "made themselves eunuchs for the sake of the kingdom of God" (Matt. 19:12). The saying is admittedly difficult to interpret and may not be historical—it is found only in Matthew, after all—but its most likely meaning is that the avoidance of procreation and marriage is preferable. The combination of the sayings is evidence that a writer could be opposed to divorce without advocating marriage and family. That possibility is clearly upheld by almost all the Church Fathers, who almost without exception coupled a severe critique of marriage, in some cases all but forbidding it for truly pious Christians, with an even stronger prohibition of divorce.[7] Even if Jesus did forbid divorce, therefore, that cannot be taken as evidence that he advocated marriage.

What was the meaning, though, of Jesus' rejection of marriage and the family for himself and his disciples? One clue comes from his saying about the resurrection and marriage. Jesus says, "In the resurrection of the dead, people neither marry nor are married, but they are as angels in heaven" (Mark 12:26; Matt. 22:30). Thus far the saying as in Mark and Matthew. Luke, perhaps realizing that the saying was too cryptic, expands it, having Jesus explain it this way, "For they [that is, the resurrected dead] are no longer able to die, for they are equal to the angels and are sons of God, being sons of the resurrection" (Luke 20:36). Luke's version may be epexegetical, but it probably does correctly portray the basic meaning of the saying about angels. A common understanding among ancient Jews and Christians was that angels are androgynous, or perhaps completely male. They need not, in any case, reproduce themselves the way human beings do because they are not subject to death. The understanding throughout much of the ancient world was that marriage was for the purposes of legitimate and controlled procreation, which was necessary only because of the fact of death. Marriage, therefore, was completely implicated in the dreaded cycle of sex, birth, death, and decay, followed by more sex, birth, death, and decay. As John Chrysostom put it many years later, "Where there is death, there is marriage."[8] In the resurrection, Jesus taught, that cycle will have been broken. Marriage will be obsolete and even offensive in the kingdom of God. Jesus' rejection of the traditional family and his creation of an alternative community signaled the imminent, or perhaps incipient, inbreaking of the kingdom of God.

All our evidence pointing to the historical Jesus, therefore, indicates that he not only avoided marriage and family himself, but also taught people to forsake those institutions and enter into an alternative, eschatological society. The household was part of the world order he was challenging. It, along with other institutions of power, would be destroyed with the coming kingdom. The household, moreover, represented traditional authority, which he was challenging at every turn. The household was implicated in the cycle of death. Indeed, the household, as the site of procreation, birth, and burial, was the very technology of life *and death* in the ancient world. For the historical Jesus, the rejection of marriage and the family was as necessary as the proclamation of the resurrection and the eternal kingdom of God.

The Gospel of Luke and the Acts of the Apostles

Different Christians in the early church took these early Jesus traditions in different directions. We have already seen that Matthew toned down Jesus' antifamilial teachings somewhat, apparently uncomfortable with having Jesus speak of "hating" one's family. As we will see, later Christians actually turned the gospel around so that it supported rather than challenged the traditional household. Still other Christians carried on the antifamilial tendencies of the historical Jesus. The author of the Gospel of Luke and the Acts of the Apostles laces his entire narrative with the theme.

First, we should note how he himself may have edited the saying I have already quoted about "hating" one's family. Only Luke includes "wives and children" in the list of those a disciple is supposed to "despise." Although Thomas also uses the word "hate" or "despise," Thomas's account agrees with Matthew in *not* including wives in the list. It is possible, therefore, that Luke added "wives and children" to a list of family members he found in Q. This suggestion is supported by an analysis of the rest of the Gospel.

There occur a few small details special to Luke's Gospel that tip his hand about his stance on the traditional family. Only Luke contains Jesus' teaching that people should *not* invite their friends and family to a dinner they host, but that they should instead invite the poor, outcasts, those who cannot return the favor (14:12–14). A few sentences later, in the parable of the great banquet, only Luke has a character decline the invitation because he is about to be married (14:20), an excuse not found in Matthew's version.[9]

Other details in the early portions of Luke's Gospel, details usually overlooked, can also suddenly appear significant when seen in a larger context of Luke's critical stance toward the traditional family. Luke portrays the birth of Jesus, for example, as a very "public" event, not at all a "family affair." And toward the close of that narrative, Luke ominously adds that Mary "pondered in her heart" all that had happened (2:19). The next ominous foreshadowing concerning Mary occurs just a few verses later, when Simeon prophesies that a sword will pierce Mary's soul (2:35). And then, only a few verses later, things become more explicit. At the age of twelve, Jesus in the Temple, though "obedient" to his parents (2:51), clearly expresses his ultimate independence from his fleshly family. He names God as his "father" and his "business" as God's "business" (2:41–51). The Greek here—*en tois tou patros mou*—could refer to the "matters" or "business" of the father (so the King James Version?), the "household" of the father (thus the Revised Standard Version?), or even the "people" of the father (if taken to be masculine).[10] In any case, the contrast between Jesus' traditional family and the household of God is here early highlighted. Mary's soul is already being pierced.

The author of Luke-Acts then constructs his narrative to emphasize this contrast between the community of Jesus and the traditional family. In Luke 8:1–3, we are informed about Jesus' entourage, which includes the twelve male disciples, Mary Magdalene, Joanna, Susanna, and "many other" women. Jesus' "household" now consists of twelve men and several women, none of whom is mentioned as traveling with a spouse or family. It is no surprise, therefore, when a few verses later Jesus gets explicit about his substitution of this new community for his traditional family (8:19–21). Those who travel with him, not the nuclear family of his birth, are his family. In the next chapter Jesus tells the young man to forget burying his father and to follow Jesus instead (9:59–62), which is followed a few verses later by a description of the intimacy of Jesus with his true father: "Everything has been given to me by my father. No one knows who the son is except the father, and who the father is except the son and whomever the son chooses to reveal it to" (10:22). The contrast is thus made between the disruption Jesus brings to "normal" father-son relations and the intimacy of Jesus' own relation to his heavenly father.

Even clearer contrasts occur in the narrative of Acts. At the beginning of the book, for instance, the communal life of the disciples in Jerusalem is described (Acts 2:42–47). They meet in the Temple and in different houses all together. They share belongings and common meals. They hold all things in common (*eichon apanta koina*, 2:44). To make sure we get the point, the author rehearses the account two chapters later. He says that the disciples were all happily united; no one claimed any private property, but they rather held all things in common; whoever owned land or houses (think "households") sold them and delivered the proceeds to the whole group, to be administered by the apostles, who gave to each according to need. Joseph, an apparently single man called "Barnabas" by the apostles, is cited as a particular example: he sold a field and gave the entire proceeds to the community (4:32–37).[11]

Immediately and in direct contrast to this description of communal life, the author introduces the negative countertype: the married couple Ananias and Sapphira, to this point the only married couple mentioned in Acts.[12] In fact, they are the only married couple explicitly mentioned in Acts apart from Prisca and Aquila, who are themselves anything but the "normal," traditional married couple.[13] Note how the actions of Ananias and Sapphira are described (5:1–11). They are Christians with their own private possessions. But instead of doing as the others have done, they sell their possessions and bring only a portion of the proceeds to the church. Twice in the text, the author emphasizes that the two *conspire together* to deceive the church and avoid the communalism of the others (5:2, 9). As usual, the author of Acts presents Satan as the instigator of actions opposite to those demanded in the kingdom of God, and also as usual, the actor on the side of the church is the Holy Spirit, to whom, Peter says, the couple has actually lied (5:3).[14] When Ananias and Sapphira die, we are told that they are carried out and buried by "young men," a detail repeated twice that is hard to explain but may represent the "new" thing happening in this eschatological community of the future (the Greek word for "young men" builds on the Greek word that may also be translated "new"; 5:6, 10; cf. 2:17). Finally, the text emphasizes that the couple is buried together, the wife "right by her husband" (*pros ton andra autes*; 5:10), together now in death as they were together in their conspiratorial marriage that sought its own interests before the communal interests of the spirit-led church.[15] Then, at the end of the story about the married couple, the narrative returns our vision once again to the (nonhousehold) community, telling us that "great fear fell on the whole church and on all those who heard about these events" (5:11).

I think it cannot be an accident that a married couple, one of only two named in the book of Acts, serves as the negative countertype to the nonhousehold, eschatological community of the first part of the book, a community clearly foreshadowing and representing the coming community of God that will replace the traditional family for good. The solidarity of the married couple represents the old, self-serving order of the traditional family and familial solidarity, with its concern for economic stability, inheritance, and continuity, in contrast to the new, young, growing, communal, eschatological household, whose procreation is a miraculous gift of the spirit and whose survival is assured by common solidarity and the gifts of God, a household of brothers and sisters rather than husbands and wives, fathers and mothers. Or to use another early and fundamental social metaphor for the church, the traditional couple is opposed to the *ekklesia*, the "town gathering," the new polity of the gathered people of God that outgrows, transcends, and ultimately rejects the traditional family.

More such examples of the Christian critique of marriage and the family from Luke and Acts could be given, but I will mention only one. It has not often been noted that there is no explicit condemnation of divorce in Luke, though there is in both Matthew and Mark. Luke, unlike Matthew, does not appropriate the material from Mark 10:2–12, in which Jesus explicitly prohibits divorce. The only place where the subject comes up explicitly in Luke is in his quotation of a Q saying, but its precise wording should be analyzed carefully. According to Luke's wording, Jesus said, "Everyone who divorces his wife and marries another commits adultery, and any woman who has been divorced from her husband and marries another commits adultery" (Luke 16:18; compare Matt. 5:32; 19:9). According to most interpretations, this is read as a prohibition of *both* divorce *and* remarriage. But that, I argue, is to read the Lukan passage under the influence of the explicit prohibitions of divorce in Mark and Matthew. Luke's statement could easily be read as a prohibition only of the *combination of divorce with remarriage*. And that is the way I think it must be read. After all, we have already seen that Jesus in Luke, in contrast to the accounts in Matthew and Mark, *urges* his disciples to "hate" their wives. In Luke, Jesus demands that his disciples give up wives and children as well as their other family members in order to follow him. If Luke had Jesus forbid divorce or separation (and we must remember that for most people in the ancient world there was no real difference between divorce and separation)[16] while implying that his disciples must leave behind their wives, he would be caught in an obvious contradiction. But there is no contradiction if we assume that what Luke believed Jesus was prohibiting here was not divorce, but remarriage after divorce. This would also explain why he would *not* want to reproduce Mark 10:2–12 in his Gospel. Thus, Luke leaves out of his Gospel any prohibition of divorce; he has Jesus allow divorce but forbid remarriage. This fits perfectly with the other indications in Luke and Acts that the author took marriage and the traditional family to have been not just "relativized" but actually rejected by the gospel. Luke presents the church as replacing, not supporting, marriage and the family.[17]

The Revelation of John

Luke is not the only New Testament author who dreams of an eschatological community in which marriage and the traditional family are replaced by other social formations. The Revelation of John offers a similar vision, though it is also different in significant ways. The most obvious difference lies in the place assigned to women in the two different texts. Whereas the Christian community in Luke-Acts includes women, sometimes even in central roles, John imagines an exclusively male community, a kingdom of male priests and prophets who have "not been defiled by women" (Rev. 14:4). There is no room in Revelation for actual, human women or for "normal" marriage and family.

John's world is ruled by God, the *Pantocrator*, the ruler of all, a designation for the emperor appropriated by Christians for God. Jesus is also the "ruler of the kings of the earth" (1:5), another imperial title. John and his fellow Christians themselves constitute "the kingdom" (1:6). For John, Christians are priests serving God in the kingdom-empire ruled by God and Christ. John's universe is populated mainly by males. In his vision, he meets twenty-four male elders, four male beasts (4:4–7), two male prophets (11:3ff), and Michael, a male angel who leads an army of apparently male angels (12:7–9). John and his fellow Christians play several different roles in his universe: they are most often designated as fellow-slaves with the angels and brothers of one another, but they are also priests, prophets, and even kings (see 20:6). This is an entirely male community: God is father and Jesus is the eldest son, who is also repeatedly portrayed as a huge, vicious, violent, bloody, horned Lamb. The other members of the household are all brothers and fellow slaves—an all-male household.

The first time we encounter a female figure in Revelation is with the appearance of Jezebel, the false prophet who seduces Jesus' "slaves" in the church at Thyatira (2:20). She is depicted as an adulteress and is promised a violent end along with those who have had sex with her, that is, those led astray by her from the strict ascetic Christianity advocated by John. There are only two or three other female figures in Revelation, according to how one counts. The starring role is played by Babylon, the great Whore, Rome, who spreads her legs for any king who wants her (Rev. 18:3, 9). The other two female figures are the woman who gives birth to the male child in Revelation 12 and the Bride of the Lamb, who appears at the end of the book, but some have speculated that these two figures perhaps overlap in the confusing and fluid symbolism of the Apocalypse. At any rate, they are completely passive figures; they are acted on but scarcely act. The woman of chapter 12 gives birth to a male child (apparently representing Jesus as the Messiah: 12:5), is persecuted by the dragon, and is eventually saved by being put out of the way in "her place" prepared by God in the desert (12:13). Unlike her male child, who is snatched up to sit with the male God on the heavenly throne, she apparently does not get to go to heaven but spends the rest of the book in "her place" in the desert.

The last female character of Revelation is, of course, the Bride. She is prepared by the father God to marry his son the Horned Lamb (19:7). She is clothed in pure, clean linen, in contrast to the filth and blood and gore of the Whore; in fact, her clothing is actually *composed of* the "righ-teous deeds of the saints," that is, John and his fellow brother-slaves (19:8). At the end of the vision, we discover that she is the New Jerusalem (21:2, 10), which is of course populated by the male, servile household of God, including the twelve male apostles of the Lamb (21:14) and the twelve tribes of the *sons* of Israel (21:12). Thus, although the Horned Lamb marries a female figure, her body and clothing are actually com-posed of male deeds and bodies, the population of the divine household, the eschatological city, the finally victorious kingdom and empire.

We see here that although actual sexual intercourse is supposed to be absent from the eschatological community, desire and the erotic, especially the erotic of the eye, is everywhere.[18] First, there is the voluptuous though gruesome seductiveness of Jezebel and the Whore—both of whom are depicted as promiscuous and dangerous. But John and his slave-brothers have resisted that seduction. And they have certainly resisted the seduction of normal marriage and family. They have, remember, "not been defiled, or polluted, by women" (14:1–5). The seduction they have apparently not been able to avoid is a certain erotic of homosocial male bonding that pervades the vision. We have the image more than once in Revelation of God the father and Jesus the Horned Lamb both sitting on the heavenly throne. Jesus also makes this promise to John, "The one who is victorious I will give to sit with me on my throne, as I was victorious and sat with my father on his throne" (3:21; see also 12:5). It is hard to avoid the image, once we actually picture it, of a bunch of men scrambling all over one another and sitting on one another's laps on a huge throne in the sky; perhaps God the father is on bottom, then the Horned Lamb on his lap, and then John and all his slave-brothers on their laps. Furthermore, it is curious that although there is a marriage in Revelation between a male and a female, the female's body and clothing are, as we saw, made up of male bodies. John and his brothers, in the person of the Bride herself, actually in the end *do* get to marry the Horned Lamb.

It is as if, for the author of the Apocalypse, there is no room for "nor-mal" marriage and family in his world. The enemy, Rome, is not a "wife" but a whore who has slept around with every important man in the known world. Jesus is the bridegroom who is about to wed his bride. Christians are slave-brothers who serve in the great household of God and have no contact with women. In fact, they must not do so because they constitute the body of the bride of the Horned Lamb. They keep themselves pure (and John is obsessed with dirt, filth, and cleanliness, as well as with sex)[19] so they can be properly clean for their nuptial copulation with the Horned Lamb. How, in this universe, could Christians find a place for "normal" marriage and family?

In very different ways, therefore, Luke and John the Seer both envisioned Christian community as displacing marriage and family and replacing them with new eschatological social formations. And they may in fact have been inspired, as we have seen, by the teachings of Jesus himself. I now turn attention, though, to an obvious source for early Christian thinking about marriage and family: Paul and Paulinism.

The Apostle Paul

I have dealt at length with Paul's own position on sex and marriage elsewhere, so let me briefly summarize those findings here.[20] As we can see from 1 Corinthians 7, Paul was no proponent of marriage or the traditional family. He preferred that all Christians follow his example and remain unmarried. But he believed that some Christians, perhaps even most Christians, would be too weak to avoid the dangers of desire without sexual activity in marriage. So he allowed Christians to be married, in fact encouraged them to be married, if they were too weak to avoid desire otherwise. Note, however, that Paul never gives any indication that he believed marriage was the proper arena for the *expression* of sexual desire. Rather, his language makes it clear, I have argued, that he viewed marriage as the vehicle for the *avoidance* of desire. According to Paul, Christians do not *express* desire by means of marital sex; they *preclude* it. "It is better to marry than to burn" (1 Cor. 7:9). Because "burning" is a reference to sexual passion and desire, and Paul does not say that it is permissible to "burn" just a little, to "simmer," Paul's statement means that he viewed sex within marriage as the technique that would allow Christians to avoid the experience of sexual desire—ironically, from our perspective, through sexual intercourse performed within marriage but devoid of desire.

This interpretation is borne out by a careful examination of what Paul says in 1 Thess. 4:3–8. Paul tells the newly converted brothers in the church in Thessalonica (for whatever reason, he addresses only men) that each of them should "possess" or "control" his "thing" or "vessel," probably referring either to their genitalia or their wives, "in holiness and honor, not in the passion of desire like the Gentiles who do not know God" (4:4–5). Sexual passion, for Paul, is something that these Christian men should no longer experience; it is part of the Gentile world they have left behind. Marriage is the arena in which they should be able to have sex but avoid desire.

Whether or not one accepts my admittedly controversial interpretations of these passages, it must be admitted that Paul clearly preferred celibacy to marriage for Christians. He had no interest in the "propagation of the species," making babies, or raising families. He cannot be enlisted as a supporter, certainly in the romantic, modern sense, of marriage and family.

The "Profamily" Paul

But he has been so enlisted, not least by his disciples and probably not long after his death. The letter to the Colossians, which I take to be pseudonymous, does not actively promote the family, but it does assume it in the so-called household code proposed to maintain hierarchy and order in the household (3:18–4:1). Wives are told to submit to their husbands "as is fitting in the Lord"; husbands are told to love their wives and not treat them bitterly. Children are told to obey their parents in everything "for this is pleasing in the Lord"; fathers are told not to provoke their children or render them despondent. In the only admonition that exceeds a couple of phrases, slaves are then addressed with a full paragraph. Basically, they are told to serve their masters as if they were serving Christ, and that any misbehavior on their part will be severely punished not only by their earthly masters but even, it is implied, by Christ himself. Then, in a return to the short phrase, masters are told to treat their slaves equitably, realizing that slave-owners themselves have a heavenly master.

Here in the name of Paul, the hierarchy of the ancient patriarchal household is reinforced in a way it never was in the authentic letters of Paul. True, Paul never advocated the abolition of slavery or the true equality of women, but his letters contain nothing really like this.[21] The position of this writer is nonetheless understandable. In the ancient world, if you were going to encourage marriage and the traditional household at all, you did so by placing the household in the structure of the universe, in a descending hierarchy with God on top, then male heads-of-households, then wives, then children, then slaves. The disproportionate attention given here to keeping slaves obedient and submissive works to make their slavery even more secure by inscribing it into their hearts and minds, and into their relationship even to God and Christ. When early Christian authors encourage marriage and family, without fail they do so by reinforcing the patriarchal ideology of their society.

The author of Ephesians, writing later and also in Paul's name, elaborates the household code from Colossians. The author of Ephesians, though, makes the male, patriarchal ideology even more insidious by conflating the superior male's role with that of God and Christ in relation to the church. As Christ is head of the church, so the man is head of the woman; as the church is submitted to Christ, so wives must submit to husbands and women to men in everything (5:21–24). Perhaps it should be noted that the Greek terms here for husband and wife are those also for man and woman. We in English have to decide how we will translate them, but we should not forget that the husband-wife hierarchy is but an instance of the universal male-female and man-woman hierarchy. The Greek ambiguity (are we talking about just husbands and wives or all men and women?) nicely preserves the universal ideological "truth" that enforces the household-gender hierarchy.

In the next few verses, the role of the husband is expanded, but significantly the comparison of the husband to Christ ends up allowing Christ and his activity to take over the context: "Husbands, love your wives, just as Christ loved the church and handed himself over for her, in order that he might make her holy, cleaning [her] by the washing of water of the utterance, in order that he may present to himself the glorified church, not having any stain or wrinkle or any such thing, but in order that she might be holy and blameless" (5:25–27). Note how the gendering of dirt is introduced. The gender duality makes the male the active agent: the male brings holiness, cleanness, blamelessness, glory, and spotlessness to the profane, dirty, stained, wrinkled, guilty, *female* principle.

Furthermore, the superior male agent is the *only* active agent. Besides "cleaning up" their wives, husbands also feed them, warm them, nourish them, as they do their own bodies. Women, on the other hand, do not do much of anything for their husbands except obey and fear them (5:33). Likewise next with the relationship of children to parents. Children are told simply to obey and honor their parents, but fathers (not the parents in general, note) are to nourish, educate, and admonish their children (6:1–4). Women and children are not told to "love" their husbands and fathers, just to obey, honor, and fear them. And they provide nothing for their men, but are themselves provided for. As in all ancient patronal ideology, the superior is the benefactor, the one who supplies the lack experienced by the inferior, whether of cleanliness, holiness, or nourishment. The patriarchal ideology of the ancient world becomes more pronounced and explicit the more the traditional household is encouraged.

This trajectory becomes simply more explicit and pronounced in the later Paulinism of the Pastoral Epistles. The author of 1 and 2 Timothy and Titus (not by Paul, but a Christian writing in his name many years later) goes to greater lengths to reinforce and encourage the presence of the ancient family in the church and the structuring of the ancient church itself to resemble the hierarchical household and state. Early in 1 Timothy, for instance, the readers are instructed to pray for "kings and all in authority" (1 Tim. 2:2). (It is hard to imagine John making any such statement in his Apocalypse, just as it is hard to imagine him encouraging marriage and household economy as this author does.) In the Pastorals, women are not even allowed to pray or speak; they must learn "in silence and all submission" (2:11). They may teach younger women, but they are to have no authority over men whatsoever (2:12). This is justified because of their implication in the deception and sin of Eve. Their main role is as childbearers, through which they may be saved if they behave themselves properly (2:15).

Not only is the patriarchal household strengthened within the church; the church itself—no longer a "town meeting"—is forced into the mold of the patriarchal household (3:5). Thus women without husbands become a particular problem for this author. The author, anxious to allow neither young nor old women to escape the confines of the household, urges that the younger women be encouraged to find themselves husbands. For the older women, for whom that would not usually be a practicable solution in the ancient world, the author must figure out some way to insert them into the household of the church. They cannot be allowed to be independent or outside patriarchal authority. They therefore are inscribed in roles within the church family under the authority of its male leaders (5:3–16). It goes without saying that slaves in these letters are similarly dealt with: they are told not to expect any relief from Christianity for their servitude (6:1–2).

The familial hijacking of the apostle Paul, therefore, began early in Christianity. Paul was made to support marriage and the traditional family. But not surprisingly, that meant that Paul became a stronger proponent of social, cosmic, and ecclesiastical patriarchy and hierarchy than he had been in his authentic letters. In the ancient world, to promote marriage and the family necessarily meant to promote patriarchal ideology. And Paul was put to service to that end.

The "Antifamily" Paul

If the canonical disciples of Paul worked to enlist the apostle in their pro-family agenda, other followers of Paul in the ancient church made him their spokesman for an antifamilial Christian message, a message that eventually proved to be more powerful and dominant in the Christianity of late antiquity than the profamily version. One of the most popular of ancient ascetic tracts was a short document known to modern scholars as *The Acts of Paul and Thecla.*

The story of Thecla recounted in the document is fascinating for the way it appropriates many of the elements of the Greek romantic novel in order to promote a Christian ascetic message. Ancient Greek novels are highly eroticized and romanticized narratives in which two young people struggle throughout the long narrative to consummate their love. The characters are usually separated at the beginning of the story and seek to be reunited. They are placed in all sorts of tragic and traumatic situations of love and danger. They cry about their fate, weep, mourn. Though their virtue is continually assaulted, they are usually able to remain loyal to one another, and they are eventually reunited and married. The ancient novels actually worked to teach quite conservative notions about the value and eternity of marriage and the traditional, elite Greek household.[22]

The Acts of Paul and Thecla plays on these themes and disrupts them at the same time. The heroine, Thecla, is an upper-class woman who becomes enamored of the ascetic message of the apostle Paul, which teaches young people and women to keep themselves absolute virgins, to avoid sex entirely, to reject marriage, to devote themselves to complete and pure celibacy. According to Paul in this text, the only way to keep the flesh pure and experience the resurrection and eternal life is to remain virginal and celibate. Thecla's attraction to Paul and his message is narrated in the tones of the desire and passion of the novels: her desire for Paul is provoked simply by hearing his voice or seeing him teaching (§7); like a love-struck heroine, she wastes away when apart from him and is "taken captive" by him (§§8–9); she experiences her love for Paul as a disease (§10). When she is finally allowed to come into his presence, she kisses his fetters and rolls herself around in the dust where he had earlier been sitting (§§18, 20). Throughout the narrative, moreover, the exceptional beauty of Thecla is emphasized; she is even repeatedly portrayed as naked and exposed to the voyeuristic public and authorities (§§33, 34). The emphasis throughout the narrative on the absolute necessity of celibacy is surpassed only by the story's highly charged eroticism. Thus, although the Christianity presented by the text is one of complete sexual renunciation, it is scantily clothed in the obviously erotic rhetoric of the ancient romantic novel.

The ultimate "enemy" of the narrative is the household. Over and over again, the story sets up a conflict between the male heads-of-households— *patres familiae*—along with the male political authorities, on the one hand, and the vast majority of the women, on the other. When Thecla is arrested or condemned to torture, it is the women of the city who pray for her, beg for her release, and bemoan her fate. But interestingly, the wives are not the only ones who side with Thecla against their own husbands. They are joined by the "young men and women" of the towns and cities. And in one scene of torture, a lioness, meant to attack Thecla, ends up siding with her. The lioness attacks the male lion and eventually gives her own life in battle against the *male* beasts in order to save Thecla. Conflict in the story pits male heads-of-households against all other potential members of households—women, girls, and young men—on the other side with Thecla. The men understand perfectly what is at issue: they themselves insist that if Christianity and Thecla succeed, that will mean the destruction of their households (§§10, 15–16).[23]

In the end, Thecla triumphs. She baptizes herself (in a huge vat of killer seals, which are all miraculously killed by a lightning bolt before they can eat Thecla); she promises to cut her hair like a man's; she dresses herself like a man. At the end of the story, she is given a fortune by a rich widow so that she and her mother(!) can become independent and self-supporting. Thecla no longer needs a man even for financial support. Totally freed from the family and household, financially and spiritually independent, she leaves even Paul, becomes an apostle *like* Paul, and goes off to spread the Christian message of the destruction of the ancient household and to establish alternative communities of erotic Christian ascetics. Traditional marriage is rejected in favor of erotic asceticism.

The Acts of Paul and Thecla appropriates the authority of the apostle Paul to promote a woman-centered, though admittedly androgynous, form of ascetic Christianity set up in direct opposition to the male-dominated, traditional hierarchical household as promoted by other early Christian documents such as the Pastoral Epistles. Though it must be admitted that Thecla plays the starring role in the narrative, Paul also becomes here a radical opponent of the family. The story seems to recognize what we had surmised when reading the pseudepigraphical Pauline texts: if you want to challenge the male-dominated authority structures of ancient culture, you must reject marriage and the family.

The Jovinian Controversy

Though there were some early voices, such as the author of 1 and 2 Timothy and Titus (examined earlier), who promoted ancient "family values," the opposite point of view, which valued celibacy over marriage, gradually became the more dominant position in late ancient Christianity, at least among the church's leaders and as portrayed in its writings. As J.N.D. Kelly has put it:

> From the second century onwards a widening stream of such [ascetic] essays [he is here referring first to Jerome's Letter 22, really a treatise denigrating marriage and advising celibacy] had been published by Christian writers. . . . They all draw on a common fund of ideas and expound, though with widely differing nuances, what is essentially the same doctrine. This is that marriage is, on the most favorable interpretation, a poor second best; virginity is the original state willed by God, and sexual intercourse came in only after the Fall. The underlying presuppositions are that the sexual act is intrinsically defiling, and that indulgence in it creates a barrier between the soul and God. If one is mar-

ried, it is better to abstain from intercourse; a second marriage betokens regrettable carnal weakness.[24]

By the late fourth century, it was difficult to find a church leader with a different opinion.[25]

Difficult, but not impossible. In fact, the issue came to a head in a controversy centered around a Roman Christian named Jovinian, who, sometime around 390, began teaching, not the *superiority* of the married state, but that those who married and had sex were no worse in the eyes of God than virgins or celibates. Jovinian based his argument on a "high" view of baptism. He taught that all baptized Christians were and would continue to be of equal spiritual and moral status whether they were married, widowed, or virgin. Christians who fast are not superior to those who eat with thankfulness. And at the last judgment, all Christians who have preserved their baptism faithfully will receive equal reward regardless of whether they have been ascetics or not.[26]

Jovinian was quickly and firmly condemned. In probably 393, the bishop of Rome, Pope Siricius, called a synod, which promptly rejected Jovinian's views and excommunicated Jovinian and eight of his associates. Siricius announced the excommunication in a letter to Italian bishops, in which he called Jovinian and his friends "the authors of a new heresy and blasphemy." They were, he says, "wounding Catholics, perverting the continence of the Old and New Testaments, interpreting it in a diabolical sense; by their seductive and deceitful speech they have begun to destroy no small number of Christians and to make them allies of their own insanity."[27] David Hunter has noted the historical significance of the letter: "Siricius's letter marked the first time in the history of Christianity that the superiority of celibacy over marriage was officially defined as doctrine, and conversely, that its denial was labeled as 'heresy.'" Though the sentiment had long been held by at least the vocal leadership of Christianity, it had not before been explicitly affirmed as the only permissible Christian view. "Siricius's letter, therefore, marked a distinctive hardening of boundaries in the later fourth century, the moment at which a previously implicit Christian consensus about marriage and celibacy reached a consequential degree of explicitness"—by means, that is, of an explicit statement declaring the inferiority of marriage as doctrine.[28]

In the wake of the condemnation, Jovinian and his friends betook themselves to Milan, but the famous and powerful bishop there, Saint Ambrose, also convened a synod of his own and confirmed both the condemnation of Jovinian's views and the excommunication. Both the pope and one of the most respected of the Church Fathers had condemned as "heresy" the opinion that the married state could be held to be of equal virtue with celibacy.

The most vocal opponent of Jovinian, however, was Jerome, one of the most prolific and famous of early Church Fathers and biblical interpreters, who wrote a fairly long treatise refuting Jovinian's claims point by point and besmirching his reputation. Never one to rise above personal invective and misrepresentation, Jerome exaggerates Jovinian's arguments and claims that Jovinian had disparaged celibacy, for which there is absolutely no evidence. Jovinian had simply argued that celibacy was not a *superior* state when compared to marriage.[29] Jerome's main concern is to maintain hierarchy of virtue and reward. He ranks virginity highest, followed by marriage, with fornication ranking below both. Elsewhere, he ranks virginity highest, followed by widowhood, and then marriage. Or he can combine widows and those who avoid sex even though married, and place them above sexually active wives, but below virgins.[30]

Jerome *claims* that he is not condemning marriage or sex completely (e.g., *Against Jovinian* 1.3). When he is careful, he writes that "the Church does not condemn marriage but makes it subordinate."[31] But Jerome gets carried away in his disgust for sex and marriage, and many of his readers, ancient and modern, have felt that Jerome does in fact come very close to condemning marriage. Jerome argues that sex is permissible *only* for procreation (*Against Jovinian* 1.20). He argues that since abstaining from sex with one's wife "honors" her, having sex with her is equivalent to "shaming" her (1.7). Throughout, he portrays any kind of sexual activity, even that in marriage, as impure and polluting to the participants: *all* sexual intercourse is "unclean" (1.20). Finally, Jerome also (though he had apparently not by this time heard about the official condemnations of Siricius and Ambrose) calls Jovinian's view of the equality of marriage and virginity "heresy" (2.37).

Saint Augustine somewhat later also came out with publications against Jovinian's view of the "equality" of marriage. Augustine thought that Jerome had gone too far, making sex and marriage sound not only "second best" but even sinful. Augustine seems to have altered his views about sex and marriage at different stages of his life. Generally, at any rate, Augustine ended up advocating that marriage was indeed a "good" and that sexual intercourse within marriage should not be condemned if done under the right conditions and with proper attitudes. The main purpose of sex is to produce children, and so sex within marriage should be indulged only for purposes of procreation. Thus, couples should not indulge if the woman is already pregnant.[32] Yet against Jovinian, Augustine affirms the superiority of celibacy: "For this reason it is a good to marry, since it is a good to beget children, to be the mother of a family; but it is better not to marry, since it is better for human society itself not to have need of marriage."[33] Augustine's position would be the one to become *the* view of the church until the Reformation and the beginnings of modernity.

This debate should not be simply ignored as "ancient history." Jovinian's view—and remember that he was advocating simply the *equality* of marriage, not its superiority—was declared heretical by a pope and three of the most honored Church Fathers and saints: Ambrose, Jerome, and Augustine. Whereas Jovinian seems to have been motivated by notions of equality that remarkably resemble modern Christian sensibilities, the "orthodox" Christian leaders were all concerned to maintain strict hierarchies both in this life and in the life to come, hierarchies of virtue and reward in which perpetual virginity occupied the highest position, with celibacy, then abstinence in marriage, then sexual activity in marriage occupying positions of virtue in a descending grade. That was the view that was considered the Christian view for most of Christian history. It is highly ironic that promoters of modern Christian "family values" and the centrality of marriage and family for Christianity portray themselves as the supporters of Christian tradition. In fact, they would be considered heretics by the "orthodox" Church Fathers.

The Puritan Revolution

The long history of the "orthodox" position on marriage and family came under challenge beginning in the sixteenth century and reached a new height with the writings of Anglicans and especially Puritans in the seventeenth century. Some precursors to the Protestant Reformation had already challenged the critical view of marriage and sex of the previous centuries. "Humanist" scholars began proclaiming the superiority of the married state to celibacy. Erasmus may have been influenced by his contact with English humanists in his writing of *Encomium Matrimonii*, in which he praised the married state in comparison to celibacy. The Council of Trent, however, condemned Erasmus's views, and *Encomium Matrimonii* was placed on the index of prohibited books in 1547.[34]

Though the movement was encouraged by the Reformers Luther and Calvin, it was in England, no doubt as a result of the English Reformation and the abolition there of monasteries and the allowance of clerical marriage, that a change of doctrine became increasingly popular. As Lawrence Stone explains, "The medieval Catholic ideal of chastity, as a legal obligation for priests, monks and nuns and as an ideal for all members of the community to aspire to, was replaced by the ideal of conjugal affection. The married state now became the ethical norm for the virtuous Christian."[35] The very notion of what constituted a proper Christian churchman changed. In the words of Christopher Hill, "The monasteries, nunneries, friaries and chantries disappeared, and the priest, set apart by his celibacy and mediating the sacraments of the universal Church, yielded place to the parson as good family man."[36]

We must recognize that this was not simply a "reform" of previous corrupt practices or a "purifying" of the Church along the lines of acknowledged orthodoxy. It was, rather, a radical *reversal* or *overturning* of previous Christian teaching about the superiority of celibacy over sex and the family.[37] And it was happening among Puritans and Anglicans alike. The theme of "holy matrimony" pervaded Protestant sermons throughout the sixteenth century.[38] Puritans increasingly took the concept further, and it is not difficult to see why: especially after the Restoration of the monarchy and the re-"Establishment" of the Church of England in 1660, Puritans were forced to rely on "separated" churches, and these were constructed as voluntary associations of "pure" and "holy" households. For the Puritans, the separated church made up of pious households replaced the parish as the true locus for religious observation.[39]

The seventeenth century saw the publication of many books of advice for the householder, informing him how to arrange and manage his family in a productive and pious manner. But they also sounded the new note of approval for marriage and sex, and explicitly valued marriage over celibacy. William Perkins, at the beginning of the 1600s, provided readers with his sage recommendations on the subject "Of Christian Oeconomie, or Household Government," and though he sounds reserved about marriage compared to the unrestrained encomia of our own day, he insists that it is the superior state: "Mariage of it selfe is a thing indifferent, and the kingdome of God stands no more in it then [*sic*] in meates and drinkes; and yet it is a state in it selfe, farre more excellent, then the condition of single life."[40] Puritans in the New World read these manuals and wrote their own. They repeatedly insist that God had ordained marriage for everyone, and that sex in marriage was essential.[41]

As we have seen, a few early Christian writers, most notably the author of 1 and 2 Timothy and Titus, offered the household as model for the structure of the church. Puritan authors, in a sense, reversed the direction of influence: in work after work of the sixteenth and seventeenth centuries, they admonish their readers to make their home into "a little church." It is as if the household comes to replace the church as the primary locus of religious activity, certainly as the primary ideological model for piety and observance. The male head of the household assumes the role of priest or pastor. In a commentary on the conversion of the jailor's household in Acts 16:34, Thomas Taylor preached, "Let every Master of Family see to what he is called; namely, to make his house a little Church, to instruct every one of his Family in the feare of God, to containe every one of them under holy discipline, to pray with them, and for them: that there may be a draught or Modell of a Church in his House."[42] In a regularly recurring theme of the entire period, authors told their readers, here in the words of William Gouge in the early seventeenth century, "a family is a little Church, and a little commonwealth."[43] It is not surprising, therefore, that the period, according to Levin Schücking, saw the development of home Bible study as a Protestant invention emphasized even more by Puritans. In fact, the era saw the rise of the "family Bible" in homes.[44]

Lest this portrait sound too much like the "family" of our own day, we should emphasize that we are speaking here not of the modern, private, nuclear family but of the "household." Though the nuclear family certainly became more visible in this period, perhaps sociologically as well as ideologically, and it may even be true that most Puritans experienced household as predominantly nuclear (that is, it may be that many households *did* include only husband, wife, and immediate children), the kind of household that we see in literary remains of the period, including legal records and the like, was not *presented* mostly as the nuclear family. These advice books, for instance, always have large sections on how to deal with one's servants, sounding as if they assumed their presence in any "normal" household. The ideal Puritan household in New England included apprentices and servants, who would live with the family, and sometimes children from other homes who had been "sent out" to live with another family for any number of reasons. Moreover, New England colonies and communities were officially and legally constructed as collections of households, not individuals. Therefore, the authorities made repeated attempts in some locales to keep single adults from living alone or together outside a "normal" household. Single adults, even males, were forced to live within other existing family units. There were, therefore, all sorts of experiments attempting to incorporate "all stray bachelors and maids under the discipline of a real family governor."[45]

Furthermore, there was no expectation in New England communities that the family was "private" or immune from governmental interference or "social engineering." Modern conservatives may argue that "it doesn't take a village to raise a child; it takes a *family*." But their Puritan forefathers were ready to interfere when they felt that a householder was not fulfilling his role properly. The "state," therefore, had control over who would be a householder and who not, and over their behavior. In the early and mid-1600s, if a householder was not behaving as the governing authorities thought he should, they could disband his household, take away his children and servants, parcel them out to other households, and force him to become a member of another household himself.[46] The Puritan household was a far cry from the nuclear family free from governmental interference so central to modern conservative romance.

The Puritan family was also firmly patriarchal. New England communities did have laws limiting the rights of husbands and providing protection for wives and children. Communities, according to recent studies, did sometimes side with women against their husbands. Some scholars have argued that Puritan women experienced better situations than women of previous eras in Europe. Yet the Puritan household was staunchly hierarchical, with the "master" firmly in charge, at least ideologically.[47] No modern notion of egalitarianism in marriage made its way into the Puritan family. Rather, it is as if what we saw to be the case in early Christianity was true also in Puritanism: the more the family is emphasized, the more patriarchy and hierarchy are strengthened.[48]

Modern Christians, if they paused long enough to look at the actual history rather than their American romanticizing of it, should think twice before calling on their Puritan "forefathers" to support their own ideology of the family. First, they must admit that the Puritan revolution was, by the standards of earlier Christianity, "heresy." When modern gay and lesbian Christians urge the recognition of same-sex marriages in churches, they are actually asking for a change much less radical than that already accomplished by the Reformers and the Puritans, who completely reversed doctrines and ethics of fifteen hundred years of Christian tradition and made the married state not only equal to singleness but superior to it. In comparison, simply valuing gay and lesbian relationships on a par with those of their heterosexual neighbors is a modest innovation. Second, modern advocates of "traditional family values" should admit that their notion of the (usually) egalitarian, private, nuclear family is not a true continuation of the Reformation or Puritan household after all. The irony, or rather hypocrisy, of modern appeals to "tradition" or the "religious heritage" of American "forefathers" to support the modern notion of family should be obvious.

The Christian Legacy of the Family

There were certainly voices in ancient Christianity, as throughout its history, that have *interpreted* the gospel to support and promote traditional family values, whether those be understood as the values of the ancient household or the modern nuclear family. But I would argue that the vast majority of the resources of scripture and Christian tradition until the modern period lend themselves much more readily to a critique of marriage and the family than to advocacy of them. Though the Christianity of the vast sweep of history from the Church Fathers until the Reformation did not go so far as to condemn marriage outright, it consistently assigned an inferior position to marriage and to those Christians who married. The "higher calling" was most often understood to be the avoidance of marriage, certainly in much of the New Testament and for almost all of late ancient Christianity.

It is thus ironic, though not really surprising, that American Christianity, especially Protestantism, has reversed the traditional valuations of Christianity. Coupled with the obscene emphasis on patriotism and nationalism, the emphasis on the family in American Christianity and popular culture approaches idolatry. "Family values" are practically the only values, along with perhaps nationalism, that seem universally recognized as "Christian values" in American popular culture, including most churches.

This essay has had as one of its goals to highlight how wrong modern Christians are when they claim that their own ideology, and idolatry, of the family is "the biblical" or "the traditional" position. If they were true to the historical meaning of the texts and the tradition, they would have to admit that their high valuation of marriage and the family runs *counter* to the teachings of Jesus, the authors of the Gospels, Paul, and other biblical writers, as well as most of the Church Fathers, popes, and saints. Furthermore, their own promotion of marriage and their adoration of the family run counter to the longer tradition of Christianity, at least of "orthodox" Christianity, and represent a rather radical and recent innovation in Christian doctrine and ethics.

Another goal of this essay, therefore, is to point out the many texts available to queer Christians that may be used to criticize the modern idolatry of marriage and family. Though I support to some extent the extension of state recognition of same-sex unions on a par with heterosexual marriage—gay and lesbian couples should have all the rights and privileges recognized by the state for heterosexuals—I am deeply ambivalent about pursuing same-sex marriage as a solution to the injustices of homophobia. I believe that both the state and the church should get out of the marriage business.

There are many excellent reasons why people in general and Christians in particular should *not* want to give the state the power to recognize and regulate marriage. When we give the state the right to legitimize one kind of sexual relationship or social formation, we automatically give it the right to render all other relations illegitimate.[49] Surely, the church should never cede its own prerogatives to the state—especially a state as bloodstained and beholden to the interests of the powerful as ours is. But *all* people should realize this: when you marry, you give power to the state over your sexual relations, your person, the most intimate details of your life and body. To agree to marriage is to agree that the modern, violent, bureaucratic state has the right to control your life in its most intimate realms, public and private, personal and sexual, individual and collective. Not to put too fine a point on it, marriage cedes to the state or the church your genitals.

The modern emphasis on marriage and the nuclear family, moreover, fools people into thinking that the modern family can do what it cannot do. The modern family simply cannot bear the weight placed on it; it cannot deliver all the goods demanded of it, whether social, economic, emotional, or psychological. Conservatives and liberals who focus on the family, therefore, are allowing the state to shirk its own responsibilities.[50] They are attempting to push off onto the fragile modern family the responsibilities that only the state in the modern world can really bear: for universal child care and education, health care, care for the elderly and disadvantaged. The state should get out of the marriage business and get to the tasks that are its true responsibilities: caring for its citizens.

But I believe the church should also get out of the marriage business. Marriage is an exclusive and exclusionary technology for control.[51] Modern churches legitimate one kind of social and intimate bonding and therefore declare illegitimate all others. *This* relationship is good—in fact, "divine." All others are bad or at best inferior.

This exclusionary technique can be seen also in the connection of marriage to procreation. Though the stigma and shame associated with births "out of wedlock" have gradually diminished, they are still present—as is proven by the fact that cohabiting couples so often decide to marry when they become or decide to become expectant parents. Marriage legitimates childbirth. But it necessarily therefore declares other births illegitimate. Why should the church want to allow *any* of its children to be thought "illegitimate"? *Our* cry, rather, should be "No bastard children!" Bastard children are not created by the absence of marriage, but by marriage itself. Marriage makes bastards by making the category possible. For these and many other reasons we could give, both the state and the church should get out of the marriage business.

Yet queer Christians need not stop with the simply negative task of critiquing marriage and the family. Another goal of this essay is to provoke contemporary Christians into thinking about different ways of reading Christian scripture and tradition. Queer Christians (whose queerness may manifest itself in all sorts of unexpected ways) should use their imaginations to allow scripture and tradition to inspire new visions of Christian community free from the constraints of the modern, heterosexual, nuclear family. We could imagine traveling bands of erotic followers of Jesus, or spirit-filled "town meetings" sharing things in common, or lively communities of men or women living together, or lively communities of men *and* women living together. We could imagine "households" of new construction, representing in their own adventuresome lives together hopes for new communities of the future. Eschatological communities. Communities in which single people are not second-class citizens, in which there are no "bastards," in which sexual orientation does not in itself stigmatize, in which varieties of households are nurtured. Alternative models to the traditional family are ready to hand in rich Christian scripture and tradition.

The texts of scripture and tradition I have analyzed bring both problems and possibilities. Some of them offer alternative visions of human community but at the price of an asceticism that renders desire and sex shameful or even sinful, a course we must also reject. Others are built on ideologies that despise the body or women. There will be no resource in Christianity or any other tradition, however, that is not to some extent problematic. All human models are tainted. There are no clean words. But these resources may also be used for retraining our imaginations both to see the inherent evils in the modern idolatry of marriage and family and to develop visions of alternative, eschatological, forward-looking communities. Rather than looking to scripture and tradition to justify the recognition of same-sex unions and marriage, we should attempt to recover and revise resources from a forgotten Christianity vouchsafed to us in scripture and premodern traditions: the long and valuable history of the Christian case against marriage.

MARRIAGE AND FRIENDSHIP IN THE CHRISTIAN NEW TESTAMENT

ANCIENT RESOURCES FOR CONTEMPORARY SAME-SEX UNIONS

Mary Ann Tolbert

Contemporary marriage in the Western world of the twenty-first century is a different institution altogether from the practices and purposes of marriage in Greco-Roman antiquity.[1] Today, mutuality, intimacy, lifelong companionship, shared economics, and sexual pleasure are generally listed as central values for marital relationships. Over the past several centuries in the Western world, the need for families themselves to produce the material means for survival, such as food, shelter, and care in sickness and old age, has been drastically reduced, depriving marriage of many of the most important roles it fulfilled throughout most of human history. In the absence of supplying this needed material support, modern marriage has focused instead on providing emotional and psychological support for the couple. Romance, intimacy, mutuality, and emotional and sexual compatibility have replaced fertility, wealth preservation, and family alliances as the primary justifications for modern marriage. Even the creation of progeny is not as high a value in many discussions—especially Protestant discussions—of contemporary marriage as mutuality and intimacy have become. Because some married couples in our seriously overpopulated world have made the moral choice to forgo childbearing, and because marriage between people incapable of childbearing, such as the elderly or impotent, is still valued and encouraged, the production of offspring as the sine qua non of marriage has dropped out of many discussions of contemporary marital values, even Christian marital values. However, the production of legitimate heirs for the preservation of family assets within a decorously ordered household was the most important function of marriage in antiquity. Moreover, many of the values attributed to modern marriage, such as mutuality, fidelity, intimacy, companionship, and sexual pleasure, are in the main not found at all or not found in the same way in ancient constructions of marriage and are certainly not values associated with marriage in the Christian New Testament. Indeed, the writers of the

Christian New Testament were not greatly in favor of even the ancient institution of marriage, as we shall see.

In looking for theological resources in the New Testament for blessing alternative unions, such as same-sex unions, one immediately runs into two seemingly intractable problems: first, marriage in the New Testament and in Mediterranean antiquity generally was constructed for purposes and embodied values quite different from contemporary understandings of marital unions; and second, even that very different kind of marriage is at best a grudgingly permitted institution in the New Testament, far inferior to the almost universally recommended path of celibacy. In other words, finding supportive, much less enthusiastic, views about marriage in the New Testament is a challenge,[2] and the type of marriage that is even modestly allowed is strikingly different from what people understand marriage to be and do for individuals and society today.

In order to explore these problems with marriage in the New Testament more deeply and also to locate other potentially more useful resources for both contemporary heterosexual unions and same-sex unions, I propose to review briefly the purposes of marriage as they are discussed in the Christian New Testament and then investigate where the values of mutuality, intimacy, fidelity, interdependence, and companionship—the values most often related to contemporary marriage—can be found in New Testament texts. I intend to suggest that the ancient topos of friendship, as it appears in the New Testament, may form a useful theological resource for developing contemporary understandings of the value of blessing same-sex unions, or indeed, of blessing any form of mutual commitment and love.

Sources for the Discussion of Marriage in the New Testament

In discussing the purposes of marriage in the Christian New Testament, I will look particularly at references to marriage in the gospel tradition and also more briefly to Paul's understanding of marriage in his letters. Both of these sets of writings provide enough material on marriage to develop some hypotheses about their views of its purpose. I will not be discussing the regulations for ordering marriage relationships that are found in the so-called household codes of the Deutero-Pauline letters of Ephesians and Colossians, or in 1 Peter. In this discussion I am less interested in how marriage relationships should be internally ordered (an extremely important point for any feminist analysis of Christian marriage) than I am in what the purpose and status of marriage was in the eyes of most New Testament writers.[3]

By way of introduction to these issues, let me say that I will be arguing that in the gospel tradition, marriage is primarily understood as a way of establishing lifelong kinship (or flesh-and-bone) relations, but because the new community that Jesus initiated inducts followers into a very different set of lifelong relations, marriage as a cultural institution became less important or even a hindrance to the life of this new community. For Paul, too, marriage is problematic for those "in Christ" in large part because it distracts from the important work of spreading the gospel in this short time before the return of the Lord. But Paul also develops a quite distinct understanding of the function of marriage from discussions of that institution present in the writings of other Greco-Roman moralists. Finally, given that both Paul and Jesus were, as far as we know or, more to the point, as far as the materials in the New Testament represent them, both unmarried adult men, it has always been profoundly problematic for Christians to argue from a New Testament perspective that marriage is somehow necessary for human wholeness or even for social cohesion within a society or group. The very source of the Christian revelation of the divine in the human, the model for humanity, was an unmarried man, and, consequently, we should not be especially surprised that the New Testament celebrates the path of celibacy as the best option for any who would follow that man.

Marriage in the Gospel Tradition

Discussions of marriage in the gospel traditions are fairly rare. There are only three clusters of material in which marriage is mentioned: first, the teachings on divorce and remarriage in Mark 10:2–12, Matt. 5:31–32 and 19:3–12, and Luke 16:18; second, the teachings on resurrection in Mark 12:24–25, Matt. 22:30, and Luke 20:34–35; and third, the marriage feast (*gamos*) settings of a few of Jesus' parables, teachings, or miracles (Matt. 22:2, 25:30; Luke 12:36, 14:8; and John 2:1–11). There are also a few scattered references to husbands or wives, but because Greek, like Hebrew, has no special word for "husband" or "wife" aside from the general terms for man and woman, the decision concerning whether marital relationships are being cited in a text is dependent on the interpreter's assumptions about the particular context of the saying (e.g., in Luke 14:26, "If one comes to me and does not hate his own father and mother and *wife* and children and brothers and sisters . . . he cannot be my disciple," the translation "wife" is appropriate because of the familial relationships being listed). Aside from these references, the very important Jewish and Greco-Roman institutions of marriage in antiquity are absent from the New Testament stories of Jesus. Because the third set of materials, the marriage feast settings of some of Jesus' teachings and miracles, seems mainly to indicate that marriage was a common cultural institution in the New Testament period,[4] I am going to concentrate my comments on the first two of these three clusters of material in the Gospels.

In each of the three synoptic Gospels, Jesus presents a teaching on divorce and remarriage. In Mark and once in Matthew (19:3–12), those sayings are framed as a test put to Jesus by some Pharisees concerning the issue of divorce. In Luke 16:18 and Matt. 5:31–32, a version of the saying is present without the narrative frame of the "test." In all of these instances, Jesus' words concern not only divorce, but also, and often more centrally, remarriage. Indeed, in my reading, Jesus' comments in Luke, clearly, and in Mark, arguably, do not prohibit divorce at all, but instead remarriage.[5] In all of the texts, it is remarriage that, according to Jesus, results in adultery, a violation of one of the Ten Commandments. Because, as both Mark and Matthew allow the Pharisees to point out, Moses in Deut. 24:1–4 clearly permits divorce and remarriage to another person, Jesus' position challenges the rather clear meaning of the received scriptural tradition. To support his view of divorce and remarriage as adultery, Jesus cites two verses in the Genesis creation accounts, Gen. 1:27, "he made them male and female," and Gen. 2:24, "a man shall leave his father and mother and be joined to his woman and the two shall become one flesh" (Mark 10:6–8; Matt. 19:4–5). Jesus' use of these parts of the creation accounts to refer to marriage has had a major impact on arguments about marriage among Christians throughout church history and certainly in the present discussion concerning same-sex marriage.

It is not at all obvious that either of the two Genesis verses quoted, or the longer creation accounts from which they come, ever had marriage in their purview. Indeed, even the apostle Paul apparently did not understand Gen. 2:24's statement that "the two shall become one flesh" as a description of marriage, since he uses the phrase in 1 Cor. 6:16 to describe what happens when a man visits a prostitute. For Paul the phrase appears to be a description of what happens with any act of sexual intercourse, whether within marriage or not within marriage. Moreover, much of the Hellenistic Jewish and later Christian traditions denied that marriage or sexual relations took place in the Garden itself, preferring to set the moment of true sexual marriage relations at Gen. 4:1 when the birth of Cain is announced.[6] The book of Jubilees, written in the second century BCE, is an interesting example of this pattern. At first its rendition of the creation story in Jubilees 3 seems to buck the nonmarital trend by having Adam "know" Eve as soon as God brings her to him; however, it then goes on to confirm the trend by indicating that the creation of the man and woman and the animals actually occurred outside of the Garden. Indeed, after their initial sexual encounter, Adam had to wait forty days and

Eve eighty days before being allowed to enter the Garden itself (Jubilees 3:1–14). Philo, the first-century CE Alexandrian Jewish writer, who was a near contemporary of the New Testament authors, even describes the newly created woman as appearing to the man's gaze as sisterly kin.[7] Consequently, seeing marriage relations in these Genesis texts was much less common in antiquity than is often assumed today.

Nevertheless, by placing the quotations from Genesis 1 and Genesis 2 on Jesus' lips as his justification for claiming divorce and remarriage as adultery, the gospels of Mark and Matthew opened the way for generations of later Christian interpreters, especially many present interpreters, to read marriage into the creation accounts and on that basis to claim marriage as essential to God's good creation. Jesus, of course, never makes that greater claim about marriage; to the contrary, in Matthew's version of this test with the Pharisees, Jesus goes on to recommend not marriage as the best path to the kingdom, but instead making oneself a "eunuch for the sake of the kingdom of heaven" (Matt. 19:12), a saying that many modern commentators take as a metaphor for celibacy but which at least some early Christian men believed to be a direct command for Christians to practice self-castration.[8] Why Jesus would claim these verses, and especially Gen. 2:24, as evidence that divorce and remarriage constitute adultery, is clarified if we recognize that the Genesis text is developing an argument for how two non-blood-related people could unite to form a blood or kinship-related unit. Gen. 2:21–24 indicates that both the man and woman are created by God from the same single body, the same flesh. Thus when Adam says to the woman, "this at last is bone of my bone and flesh of my flesh," he is actually doing nothing more than stating the obvious. It is this "sameness" of the man and woman, being created from the same one body, that makes them fitting companions for each other. In fact, the Genesis Rabbah, one of the earliest of the exegetical midrashim of Rabbinic Judaism, actually depicts the creation in Gen. 1:26–27 as one of a single androgyne who is then split into two halves in the second creation story in Gen. 2:21–25: "When the Holy One, blessed be he, came to create the first man, he made him androgynous, as it is said, 'Male and female created he them and called their name Adam (Gen. 5:2).' Said R. Samuel bar Nahman, 'When the Holy One, blessed be he, created the first man, he created him with two faces, then sawed him into two and made a back on one side and a back on the other'" (Genesis Rabbah 8:I).[9] Philo also views male and female as "divided halves, as it were, of a single living creature."[10] In arguing for an original androgynous human creature who is later divided into separate genders, both Philo and the early Rabbis may have been influenced by the fairly well known Greek myth of the three original androgynous creatures split by the gods and forever seeking reunion as male/male, male/female, and female/female, a myth related for posterity by Aristophanes in Plato's *Symposium*.[11]

Whatever influenced their views, their purpose in positing an original single being with two aspects who was then split into male and female later in the Garden is both to harmonize the two different accounts of the creation of humanity found in Genesis 1 and 2 into a single, intelligible account,[12] and to emphasize the kinship and similarity of the male and female, coming as they do from the same flesh and bones. The narrative introducing the creation of separate genders in Genesis 2 compels a similar reading of the crucial importance of their "sameness." So, in Gen. 2:18–20 the animals God had created turned out not to be fitting companions because of their "otherness," their difference from Adam. Evidently, only ones who share exactly the same bone and flesh make fitting companions. As far as Genesis 2 is concerned, then, it is sameness, not difference—or "complementarity"[13]—that marks the special relationship between the man and the woman. Reading the creation accounts in their own ancient context makes it clear that the privileging of difference is a modern value, not at all an ancient one.

It is also the "sameness" of sharing "bone" and "flesh" that elsewhere in the Hebrew Bible is used to denote kinship relations. For example, in Gen. 29:14, Laban greets Jacob as his kinsman by saying, "Surely you are my bone and my flesh," and similarly David, in 2 Sam. 19:12–13, appeals to the elders of Judah as his brothers, "his bones and his flesh." (See also Judg. 9:2; 2 Sam. 5:1; and 1 Chron. 11:1.) Understanding Gen. 2:24 as the affirmation of kinship, or bone and flesh relations between a man and woman, illuminates the way Mark and Matthew portray Jesus using this verse in his confrontation with the Pharisees. If marriage (or in Paul's case, just intercourse) establishes a bone and flesh bond between man and woman like the bond of bone and flesh between kin, it cannot be dissolved until death. Brothers and sisters, mothers and children, cousins, uncles, nephews and nieces, all other kinship bonds remain inescapably in place throughout life; no matter how much one might wish to "divorce" one's siblings, they remain one's siblings until death. In the same way, Jesus reads Gen. 2:24 to indicate that a similar lifelong kinship relationship is established by marriage. Death alone breaks that kinship bond; no writ of divorce can do it. Thus, remarriage constitutes adultery because it has to be understood as violating the kinship bond established by bone and flesh.

The second set of material mentioning marriage in the Gospels, the resurrection controversies in Matt. 22:23–33, Mark 12:18–27, and Luke 20:27–40, seems to bear out this kinship reading of marriage. When the Sadducees ask Jesus whose wife a woman married serially to seven brothers will be in the resurrection, Jesus castigates their ignorance about the power of God, for in the resurrection, he says, there is no marriage. The kinship bonds of this world have no relevance in the resurrection, where everyone will be like angels in heaven, and bone and flesh will have melted away. Indeed, Luke has Jesus imply even more: that those of this age who wish to be worthy of resurrection in the future do not marry (Luke 20:34–36). That marriage establishes lifelong kinship relations makes marriage a hindrance for those whose hopes are on the age to come and who want to join the new "family" of Jesus, which depends not on bonds of bone and flesh, but on doing the will of God (Mark 3:35).

Marriage in Paul's Letter to the Corinthians

In his letters, Paul also thinks marriage will prove a painful distraction from the life of faith "in Christ" that believers are called to live, so his ardent wish is that all people could be as he is, evidently joyfully unmarried. For Paul, the better path is always to remain celibate. In his longest discussion of marriage (in 1 Corinthians 7), however, Paul develops a rather novel view of its possible function for Christians. Just as Jesus told the Pharisees that Moses had permitted divorce as a concession to their weakness, Paul similarly posits marriage as a concession to those Christians too weak to be able to control their own passions by self-will alone. For Paul, as for many Jewish and Roman moralists of his time, passion and desire were unruly traits of the body that had to be severely controlled, or better yet excised, in order to live a morally respectable life. Paul suggests that for those Christians whose passions are too strong (1 Cor. 7:36) for their own will to control, marriage is an acceptable path for channeling and ultimately, perhaps, destroying passion. In other words, for Paul, marriage becomes a kind of remedy for lust. This suggestion makes more sense than may at first appear. In the first-century Mediterranean world, free men of some means married primarily for lineage and offspring, not for passion. They were completely free to satisfy their passions and desires outside of marriage with prostitutes, courtesans, mistresses, and all the other classes of available sexual laborers, slave and free, as this famous quotation from Demosthenes makes clear: "This is what it means to be married: to have sons one can introduce to the family and the neighbors, and to have daughters of one's own to give to husbands. For we have courtesans for pleasure, concubines to attend to our daily bodily needs, and wives to bear children legitimately and to be faithful wards of our homes."[14] Consequently, to limit sexual passion and desire only to the one marriage partner was for a free man a severe sexual curtailment, which might well result in the eroding of passion altogether.

Although he does not encourage the establishment of real families and certainly not the production of progeny, Paul nevertheless often uses the language of family to describe the fictive family of Christians who are united in kinship in the one body of Christ. This metaphorical employment of familial terms such as *brother, sister, father,* and *children* for relationships among members of the Christian community, which can be found throughout Paul's letters, has the effect of redefining the family into a new spiritual fellowship by subverting traditional kinship ties.[15] Binding that fellowship together are the sacrifice of Jesus' bone and flesh on the cross and the community's willing choice to become the "bride" of the risen Christ. In this light, Paul's ambivalence about marriage, which he still declares is not a sin, arises because of marriage's potential to reassert a human bone-and-flesh bond in place of the spiritual one provided by Christ. Nevertheless, however torn Paul may be concerning the value of marriage, he is not at all ambivalent about sexual passion. It is always dangerous and damning, not only because it results in a loss of manly control, but also because it has a high tendency to destroy the bonds of the new fictive family and pull one away from its saving embrace. When and if marriage serves to encourage the development of such passion, it should be avoided. However, if passion is already running strong, then channeling it solely into the marriage bed, especially a Christian marriage bed, may provide a powerful control on the damage it can cause to the new spiritual family "in Christ."[16]

Although there are certainly a few other New Testament texts we could explore about the purposes of marriage, from what we have seen in the Gospels and Paul, it is clear that marriage in the New Testament, always a second-rate lifestyle choice at best, was regarded quite differently then than it is today, when it is lauded for its intimacy, mutuality, love, companionship, and fidelity. Where, if anywhere, does the New Testament locate these contemporary values for intimate relationships?

Friendship in the New Testament

I suggest that the ancient cultural institution of friendship, the "mutually intimate, loyal, and loving bond between two or a few persons"[17] not related by bone and flesh, is the New Testament context in which many of today's often-cited marriage values can most easily be found. While friendship was highly valued in classical Greece,[18] it is also recommended in the Jewish wisdom tradition as early as the writings of Ben Sira in the second century BCE.[19] Like the Genesis 2 creation story's characterization of sameness as the basis of the fitting companionship between man and woman, likeness or sameness is the bedrock of true friendship. Indeed, Ben Sira alludes to the creation of male and female in the image of God in Gen. 1:27 as establishing the likeness between divine and human that allows for friendship between them (Sir. 13:15).[20] Even the faithfulness of friends was for Ben Sira simply a reflection of the faithfulness of God (Sir. 1:15; 37:15). Moreover, a friend was to be carefully selected and then tested for fidelity and truthfulness, according to Ben Sira. Friends shared their most intimate confessions with each other and faithfully kept those confidences secret (Sir. 27:16–21). True friends did not desert each other in troubled times, and in good times could be counted on always to speak truth instead of flattery. Friends loved each other faithfully until death. The mutuality and sameness that grounded friendship did not mean, however, that friends were always equal in power, prestige, or wealth, although for Ben Sira, at least, the most trustworthy friendships matched rich to rich and poor to poor (Sir. 13:15–23). In Roman times, particularly, friendships often flourished between wealthy men and their circle of often less-fortunate companions. In those situations, the ability to sort out true friends from false or "fair-weather" friends was the subject of considerable ethical and philosophical writing and reflection.

Many of Ben Sira's views on friendship are echoed later in the first-century CE writings of Philo, although Philo's understanding of friendship probably owes primary allegiance to Stoic views. For Philo, friends should be impartial because they care only for their friend's welfare, and are frank speakers, not flatterers; they should share all things in common and be so near and dear to each other that it is as if they share the same soul.[21] Like Jesus' redefinition of family as those who do God's will in Mark 3:33–35, Philo argues that true friendship, the kind that binds the two into one, arises from honoring "the one God."[22]

In the New Testament, friendship language and values can be seen in many texts but particularly in the Gospels of Luke and John, and in Paul's letters. John 15:12–15 is an especially excellent example of the concept. Jesus tells his disciples that they are to love one another because of his love for them, and "greater love has no one than this, that one give up one's life for one's friends." In addition, Jesus says that they are his friends, not his slaves, but his friends, because he has shared his deepest knowledge and understanding of God with them; he has chosen them and tested them, and now he will die because of his love for them. As this passage illustrates so clearly, friendship establishes mutual dependence, intimacy, freedom of association, and love—even to death—as its most important qualities.[23]

The language and values of friendship, found throughout the New Testament and many other writings in the Greco-Roman world, provide, I believe, the closest parallels to many of the functions and values Christians and others assert for marriage today. Marriage partners share all things in common, as did ancient friends; marriage should be a relationship marked by mutuality and reciprocity, as was ancient friendship; marriage promotes honesty and intimacy, the faithful keeping of secrets and confidences, as did ancient friendship; marriage partners are each other's soul mates, as were ancient friends; and marriage binds the two into one until death, as did ancient friendship. Although many forms of eroticism were part of the practice of ancient friendship, genital sexual relations probably were not, at least not in the stated ideal of friendship. Yet, marriage today incorporates values far beyond those of sexual intercourse and the production of progeny. Those personal and social values find remarkably close parallels in ancient discussions of friendship. And, for the purposes of this essay, it is also important to point out that the language of friendship in the ancient world and most often in the New Testament, as in the case of Jesus with his disciples in John 15:12–15, occurs between and among people of the same gender. Although a few Greco-Roman texts suggest that men and women can be friends, the vast majority of the references insist on the similarity of gender for true friendship to occur. Ancient soul mates were most often people of the same sex.

In our time, the institution of friendship is greatly undervalued and unsupported socially and culturally. By *friends* we mostly mean passing acquaintances who move in and out of our lives. To think of giving up our lives for a friend seems incredible. In a speech during the opening session of Emory University's conference on "Sex, Marriage, and Family and the Religions of the Book," Jean Bethke Elshtain asserted that people are willing to die only for "faith, family, and freedom"[24]—friends were not part of that equation. Yet in the New Testament, it is friendship that binds non-bone-and-flesh-related people together in love, intimacy, and interdependence. Jesus in John's Gospel is willing to die for his friends, not his faith, his family, or his freedom. It may be that the crisis of marriage that so many commentators today bemoan so loudly is not related to the undervaluing of heterosexual marriage but rather, at least in part, to its overvaluing. Perhaps because its importance for the material sustaining of life has waned so greatly, marriage has been hyped by its proponents as the pinnacle of all human emotional and psychological growth. Heterosexual marriage has become the be-all and end-all of life, to the exclusion of all other loving and intimate relationships. Moreover, the present loud cries defending marriage against the "attack" of lesbians and gay men who simply wish to join in the marital state has pushed the current rhetoric on heterosexual marriage to apocalyptic levels: we are told that if same-sex marriage is permitted, civilization as we know it will collapse. Although that dire prediction does not appear to be finding fulfillment in the State of Massachusetts' present experiment with same-sex marriage, the valuation bestowed on marriage in civil and ecclesiastical discourse has rarely been higher. Indeed, some Christian proponents even claim that one cannot be a whole person without the experience of opposite-sex "complementarity" in marriage,[25] an exceedingly odd claim coming from a tradition whose founders, Jesus and Paul, were unmarried adult men. If heterosexual "complementarity" were required for spiritual wholeness, what theological sense would we be able to make of Paul's wish in 1 Cor. 7:7 that all Christians could be as he was, single and evidently without sexual desire? In the New Testament, at least, marriage is more a potential hindrance to discipleship than an essential foundation for society.

We expect so much from heterosexual marriage today because we are encouraged socially, culturally, and religiously to demean, deride, or trivialize all other forms of intimate, mutual, lifelong bonding, whether in same-sex couples or in other faithful, loving relationships. Maybe we need to listen to the New Testament more carefully and take its downgrading of marriage and valuing of friendship much more seriously than most Christians currently do. Such a move would, at any rate, be more faithful to what the Christian New Testament actually says about marriage and other forms of intimate relationship than is presently found in much contemporary Christian sentimentalized rhetoric about the unique importance of marriage for the continued well-being of society. It seems that we need to be reminded that the New Testament does not by any stretch of interpretation promote marriage, heterosexual or not, as the bedrock of Christian community. What the New Testament really promotes is quite different: "Greater love has no one than this, that one lay down one's life for one's friends" (John 15:13).

WHY IS RABBI YOḤANAN A WOMAN?
OR, A QUEER MARRIAGE GONE BAD

"PLATONIC LOVE" IN THE TALMUD

Daniel Boyarin

Prologue: Divine Intercourse-Between Rabbis

I will begin by citing a startling, even shocking, text from the Babylonian Talmud:

תלמוד בבלי מסכת עירובין דף נד עמוד ב

מאי דכתיב +משלי ה'+ אילת אהבים ויעלת חן וגו' למה נמשלו דברי תורה לאילת? לומר לך: מה אילה
רחמה צר , וחביבה על בועלה כל שעה ושעה כשעה ראשונה - אף דברי תורה חביבין על לומדיהן
כל שעה ושעה כשעה ראשונה

What is it that is written, "Let her be as the loving hind and pleasant roe etc." Why have the words of Torah been compared here to a hind? To teach you: Just as the hind has a narrow vagina and is beloved by her lover at each and every time, just as at the first time, so the words of Torah are beloved by their learners at each and every time, just as at the first time. (Babylonian Talmud, Eruvin 54b)

This sensational, even disturbing, figure is crucial for understanding late ancient Jewish bodies and pleasures, desires, fulfillments, and frustrations. A look at the whole context of the verse being cited (including the bit hidden, as it were, in the "etc." of the text) will be illuminating:

Let thy fountain be blessed: and rejoice with the wife of thy youth.
Let her be as the loving hind and pleasant roe; let her breasts satisfy thee at all times; and be thou ravished always with her love.
And why wilt thou, my son, be ravished with a strange woman, and embrace the bosom of a stranger? (Prov. 5:18–20)

As frequently the case with rabbinic midrash, the interpretation that the Talmud gives is a combination of the very plausible (to us) and the outrageous (to us). On the most obvious level, the verse seems to be speaking of a human wife, giving a piece of straight and ordinary wisdom, not different from that of Kohellet 9, "Enjoy life with a woman whom you love." Seen from that perspective, the interpretation given by the midrash seems outrageous not only in terms of the boldness of its imagery but also as interpretation. The broader context of the verse suggests, however, that it is not so wild an interpretation after all.

The chapter of Proverbs is clearly a polemic for marriage, for family values, if you will. On that straight reading, there are two women with whom a man might wish to be intimate, his wife and a "strange" woman. The chapter, in its Wisdom, counsels strongly faithfulness to the "wife of your youth" as the only way to happiness. Yet there is another meaning encrypted here as well, one in which it is Wisdom herself, Dame Wisdom, who is the legitimate wife of one's youth, and the "strange woman" is some foreign and impure knowledge or ignorance:

> My son, attend unto my wisdom, and bow thine ear to my understanding:
> That thou mayest regard discretion, and that thy lips may keep knowledge.
> For the lips of a strange woman drop as a honeycomb, and her mouth is smoother than oil:
> But her end is bitter as wormwood, sharp as a two-edged sword. Her feet go down to death; her steps take hold on hell. (Prov. 5:1–5)

We see here a rich ambiguity in the syntax of these verses. It is the wisdom imparted by the father that counsels the young man to stay with a legitimate wife and not go astray with a strange woman, but clearly, wisdom *is* the wife of his youth, and folly, of one sort or another, is the stranger.[1] The whole context of these early chapters of Proverbs, with their hymns of love to Wisdom, suggests such a reading.[2] On this reading, this chapter of Proverbs incorporates a brilliant allegory, in which both the *mashal* and the *nimshal* function equally. "The wife of one's youth," Wisdom, according to the Rabbis, can be understood by them, then, only as Torah. Hence our midrash: Rejoice in the wife of your youth, Torah, and delight in her as in a female deer.

What shocks, then, is not the allegoricality of the reading but the concrete vivid sexual direction in which they take it. Words of Torah provide erotic, even sexual, pleasure, analogous only to the pleasure of inserting one's penis into a tight place. This pleasure, as is well known, is sought and found in the company of men, and even, most exquisitely, in the study pair of two men who learn Torah together, sometimes for years (or even longer) on end.

My own suggestion is that this wild rabbinic analogy opens up to a productively queer reading of the institution of Torah-study itself, the concept of queer here being taken from the work of the founding diva of queer theory herself, Eve Sedgwick. Sedgwick has elucidated how in a "heterosexual" economy of desire, shared female objects (principally women) provide the medium of erotic exchange between men. She refers to this desire as homosocial.[3] The Torah is the authorized female object of erotic, straight desire between Rabbis, in their own powerfully eroticized relationships with one another, particularly through the medium of the study-pair, the *havruta*.

To explore this suggestion, I will be taking a new look at another Talmudic text that I have looked at several times in the past but always under the sign of a gender studies, not a sexuality or queer, analysis. Then I was primarily interested in the construction of masculinity involved in this text. Now it is the issue of desire and its fulfillments that concerns me, as well as the ideology of marriage. This new reading, moreover, suggests quite a different way of relating late ancient Jewish sexual culture to that of antiquity.

Resh Lakish Reducks

The legend is found in a remarkable sequence of narratives about the beautiful Rabbi Yoḥanan, surely one of the paradigmatic culture heroes of Rabbinic Judaism (Baba Metsia 84a ff.). The extraordinary beauty of Rabbi Yoḥanan, described in terms of his radiance, is surely to the point in understanding the narrative:

> Said Rabbi Yoḥanan, "I have survived from the beautiful ones of Jerusalem." One who wishes to see the beauty of Rabbi Yoḥanan should bring a brand new silver cup and fill it with the red seeds of the pomegranate and place around its rim a garland of red roses, and let him place it at the place where the sun meets the shade, and that vision is the beauty of Rabbi Yoḥanan.

Given all this, it is no wonder that:

> One day, Rabbi Yoḥanan was bathing in the Jordan. Resh Lakish saw him and thought he was a woman. He crossed the Jordan after him by placing his lance in the Jordan and vaulting to the other side. When Rabbi Yoḥanan saw Rabbi Shimon the son of Lakish [Resh Lakish], he said to him, "Your strength for Torah!" He replied, "Your beauty for women!" He said to him, "If you repent, I will give you my sister who is more beautiful than I am." He [R.L.] agreed. He [R.L.] wanted to cross back to take his clothes but he couldn't. He [R.Y.] taught him [R.L.] Mishna and Talmud and made him into a great man.

From at least one point of view, this is a narrative of the formation of a marriage, a story told in Babylonia about Palestinian Rabbis. As such, although layered, the primary context for reading it is the Babylonian one.

Michael Satlow has argued for a fundamental difference between Palestinian and Babylonian marriage ideologies. Noting that Babylonian sources almost never, if ever, speak of the *oikos* as a value in itself, whereas Palestinian texts do ubiquitously, he argues compellingly that the whole issue of marriage was quite differently configured for the Palestinians than the Babylonians, with the former representing "Stoic" positionings of marriage as necessary for the good ordering of society, his prime example being Antipater of Tarsus.[4] On the other hand, according to Satlow, the greater Babylonian ambivalence about marriage, particularly in its relation to Torah-study, is closer to the Cynic position of Diogenes.[5] Without, of course, ascribing a mapping of the Palestinian onto the Stoic position or the Babylonian onto the Cynic one (nor does Satlow do so), the analysis of the Talmudic text presented here (and not considered by Satlow in this context at all) would bear out his suggestion that Babylonian rabbinism, more exclusively the product of a scholastic social formation, is closer to the "Cynic" (in my reading, Platonic) view of marriage.

In the Talmudic story, we find a doubling of the female Torah by a human woman shared between men—à la Sedgwick—as the sign of the triangulation of desire that saves, as it were, the phenomenon of queerness. The narrative is ambiguous at several crucial points that powerfully inscribe it within discourses of desire. First of all, in the text that I have cited (from the Hamburg MS) we find explicitly that the object of Resh Lakish's desire, a nude and beautiful man seen from a distance, was misprised by the desiring subject as a woman. (In other manuscript traditions, it should be emphasized, Rabbi Yohanan's gender—or Resh Lakish's "mistake"—is not mentioned at all, promoting much more strongly the homoeroticism of Resh Lakish's precipitous desire.) In both cases, Resh Lakish's move is an allusion to King David—that other rough and ruddy warrior—who sees Bathsheva immersing herself nude in the Siloam Pool and swoops down on her from the roof.

But there is another crucial ambiguity in the text, beyond the possible ambiguity of Rabbi Yohanan's own gender. After discovering the "truth" of Rabbi Yohanan's gender and having been told that his own strength should be devoted to the hetero pursuit of that tight vagina, the Torah, Resh Lakish comes back at Rabbi Yohanan by retorting that his beauty is for/should be devoted to women. If we follow the syntactic parallelism implied by Rabbi Yohanan's original gibe, this ought to mean "Your beauty should be devoted to the pursuit of women," but the text allows another possible reading as well, namely, "Your beauty is wasted on a male body and belongs on a female one." On either reading, the contest and contrast between a depreciated bodily desire for sex with a woman versus an exalted highly homoeroticized desire for Torah could not be more marked in the text. Rabbi Yohanan makes an offer to Resh Lakish that the latter finds impossible to refuse: "He said to him, 'If you repent, I will give you my sister who is more beautiful than I am.'" There is a literal corporeal meaning here. Rabbi Yohanan does have a "real" sister who will marry R.L. and bear him children, but at the same time the whole context of the story suggests as well that the "sister" is a figure for the Torah that the two men will study together. "My sister, my bride" is, as is understood on rabbinic readings of the Song of Songs, a figure for Torah as well. Resh Lakish is to be lured into the rabbinic version of a *philosophia* via an appeal to his carnal desire for a physical lover. Going just a bit further with this line of thought, we can impute the following meaning to Rabbi Yoḥanan's "offer." You, Resh Lakish, by vulgarly desiring that my body be a female one, are showing the low level of your development. I will offer you what you think you want, my sister, but in reality will teach you that what you really desire is the homoerotic fellowship of the sacred band of those who live with the true "sister-bride," the Torah! Resh Lakish takes the bait, and sexually disempowered—he can no longer vault over the river on his lance—becomes nevertheless a "great man," that is, a great scholar in Torah and fellow of Rabbi Yoḥanan.

In order to get a better grasp on a possible reading of this story—which I am figuring as the question: Why is Rabbi Yoḥanan a woman?—I suggest that a somewhat new answer to the question: Why is Diotima a woman? (to which my title alludes) may be apposite.

Why Is Diotima a Woman?

In previous work, I read this Talmudic legend as formative for Jewish male gendering practices and only hinted at its significance for thinking about sexuality.[6] Reading Resh Lakish as a representation of a Jew who inhabits a stereotyped "Roman masculinity" and then becomes socialized into an equally stereotyped "Jewish"—or at least, rabbinic—one, I had turned my attention more to the oppositions between rabbinic and classical constructions of masculine gender. In contrast to a putative Greek norm in which male-male (homoerotic) socialization is into the warrior-hoplite culture, I read then the Talmudic narrative as invoking similar patterns of desire and (presumably sexless) practice in order to socialize males into a "hoplite" culture of Talmudic dialectic rather than physical warfare. (Indeed, in many Talmudic texts, the Rabbis are referred to as hoplites—literally, shield-bearers.) In the current context, I have quite a different end in mind, for the narrative marks several different vectors of erotic desire, differently inflected for gender, and can be read, I suggest now, in ways that bring it much closer to a differently putative Greek culture, the culture of philosophic eros that we find in Plato's *Symposium*. In other words, I suggest that reading Greek culture itself as a fractious and heterogeneous thing will help to bring new nuance and depth to our readings of Talmudic culture also.[7] On the one hand, I propose now that the antithetical eros of this text, with its transmutation of corporeal Ares and corporeal

Eros into spiritualized doubles of themselves is close, quite close, to the philosophical eros constructed by Plato. This text, at any rate, is not simply antithetical to Platonism. On the other hand, Greek culture itself is much more riven than I would ever have imagined, with Plato himself only a small corner of it (and perhaps for centuries, at any rate, a nearly negligible one), and there are aspects in this Talmudic legend that match up better with anti-Platonic aspects of Hellenism, as well. My goal is not to point to Greek "influence" on the Rabbis of Palestine or Babylonia, but through these comparisons to show them as much more ordinary denizens of the late ancient Mediterranean world—with all the possible permutations of ideas—than previously imagined. In fact, the consideration of Proverbs as earlier in this essay suggests that traditions of desexualized homoerotic Wisdom go back much further in that same Mediterranean *Kulturgebiet*.[8] On the other hand, although I am certainly not in a position to draw any historical conclusions yet—or even to imagine historical hypotheses—about actual connections between Talmudic material and Greek/Hellenistic thought, it is important to mention that this narrative, which I examine here by itself, is deeply embedded in its own Talmudic context(s). The current reading puts forth—implicitly—the proposition that this narrative is both synecdochical and perhaps even emblematic of a dialectic that is much more widespread within the rabbinic literatures of Palestine and Babylonia, as well as within Hellenistic culture at large.

A much more nuanced reading of Greek culture itself, however (I think now), will lead us to a richer understanding of the place of the Talmudic narrative within a larger Mediterranean history of sexuality. In pursuit of that end, I am going to reinstate a certain very traditional reading of Platonic love as a forerunner of the spiritualized or sublimated love celebrated by ancient Christianity—that is, not just a swallow, but the spring. However, I hope in so doing to innovate, as well, in two respects: first, by disrupting a more recent (Foucauldian) scholarly consensus inclined to place Plato's theory of eros on more of a continuum with (rather than in opposition to) classical Athenian pederastic practice, and second, by placing the Rabbis and their theories and practices of love closer both to Plato and contemporaneous Christians than they are usually seen to be.[9] The locus classicus for discussing this topic is, of course, Plato's *Symposium*.

Although in recent years it is certainly the speech of Aristophanes (about the round people of three sexes) that has excited the most interest in scholarship of the *Symposium* centered on the history of sexuality or queer studies,[10] Socrates' recounting of Diotima's speech is at least equally important, certainly if we are to understand continuities between ancient Greek and Judeo-Christian cultural formations.[11] In a compelling discussion, David M. Halperin has argued that Diotima is, in fact, a woman because she represents/substitutes for a "real" woman, Aspasia (the much-cherished lover of Pericles) about whom there was a strong, persistent pre-Platonic tradition that she had been Socrates' instructor in matters erotic. Although I endorse Halperin's account of Diotima as a "cover" for Aspasia and his perhaps startling conclusion that she is a prophetess because she is a woman (and not the other way around), I think that this conclusion could be restated more trenchantly. Halperin puts it this way: "[Aspasia] would be quite out of place in the *Symposium*, where Plato clearly wants to put some distance between his own outlook on *eros* and the customary approach to that topic characteristic of the Athenian demimonde."[12] Agreeing with the first clause, I quite sharply disagree with the last: It is not the Athenian demimonde from which Plato wishes to distance himself (or not only that) but the Athenian polis and its everyday life of marrying, having sex (with boys *and* wives), procreating, and being involved in politics. It is not so much Aspasia as *hetaira* or courtesan that would be so problematic as Aspasia as the "wife" and mother of Pericles' children and even Aspasia as an at least behind-the-scenes politician, as well.[13] To be sure, "Plato had a primary reason for preferring a woman, any woman, to be the mouthpiece of his erotic theory." So far, so good. However, Halperin goes on to say: "But in order to replace Aspasia with another woman who was *not* a *hetaira*, Plato had to find an alternate source of erotic authority, another means of sustaining his candidate's claim to be able to pronounce on the subject of erotics. . . . [I]n the *Symposium*, however, he looks to religious sources of authority, to which some Greek women were believed by the Greeks to have access."[14] Although going on to more complex explanations of Diotima, Halperin does not reject the Diotima as Aspasia in priestess-drag account. Halperin allows that the Diotima-replaces-Aspasia substitution may be true enough but maintains that it does not at all explain why Plato remains invested in that tradition.[15]

On my reading, the relationship to Aspasia is crucial for understanding the political eros of the *Symposium*. Not only is Diotima a prophetess from Prophetville (in Halperin's delightfully jeu-ish translation of *Mantinea*) and thus a source of authority, but also, as such, she is totally out of the corporal politico-erotic economy of the city. Her Peloponnesian origin is not beside the point. This notion of Diotima as doubly marked "outsider" (as an apparently celibate woman[16] and as a non-Athenian) is key to my reading of the *Symposium*.[17] If, following Halperin's very attractive suggestion, Diotima is a replacement for Aspasia, more of an attempt to account for Aspasia's place in Platonic discourse seems necessary in order to understand Diotima—and this seems to be the part of the argument most neglected in the literature. The place to look for that is in the *Menexenus*, in which Aspasia is the major character.[18]

Plato, in this, one of his most unusual dialogues, gives us a Funeral Oration, presented as having been written by Aspasia, Pericles' lover and the mother of his children. Although it is not an uncontroversial point in interpretation, many scholars have seen this piece as a parody of Pericles' own funeral oration, among them such notables as E. R. Dodds and Nicole Loraux.[19] In the *Menexenus*, Socrates does not hesitate to treat us to his view of funeral orations in general and encomiastic rhetoric—and remember that the *Symposium* is an anthology of encomia:

> Actually, Menexenus, in many ways it's a fine thing to die in battle. A man gets a magnificent funeral even if he dies poor, and people praise him even if he was worthless. Wise men lavish praise on him, and not at random but in speeches prepared long in advance, and the praise is so beautiful that although they speak things both true and untrue of each man, the extreme beauty and diversity of their words bewitches our souls. For in every way, they eulogize the city and those who died in battle and all our forebears, and even us who are still alive, until finally, Menexenus, I feel myself ennobled by them. I every time stand and listen, charmed, believing I have become bigger, better-born, and better-looking on the spot. (234c)[20]

The contrast between seductive, flattering, beautiful language that is untrue and spontaneous, unbeautiful language that carries truth is already very familiar from the *Symposium*, another work in which Gorgias's rhetoric and encomia in general are explicitly thematized and attacked. Menexenus gets the joke, of course, and remonstrates with Socrates for always making fun of rhetors. In the *Menexenus*, Aspasia is charged with having written Pericles' own funeral oration and now of having composed one of her own out of the "leftovers" from that one (236b). R. E. Allen, following a couple of hints in Aristotle, which he takes to represent the view of the Academy, suggests that "rhetorical flattery is the theme of the *Menexenus*."[21] Aspasia is thus the very emblem of all that Plato hates about Athens, physically erotic, physically procreative, and rhetorical, whereas Diotima is everything that he admires, Laconian, spiritually procreative, and dialogical.

Given the place that Aspasia occupies in Plato's political/philosophical symbol system and the persistent traditions (in the earlier Socratic literature) that it was this virtual wife (and mother) who had instructed Socrates in matters erotic, it seems quite possible to read the substitution of Diotima for Aspasia as a highly marked Platonic intervention into the Socratic tradition, but even more, as a highly marked comment on the Athenian politico-erotic economy in toto. This reading is strongly consonant with but expands the scope of Halperin's second major point as to the femaleness of Diotima, namely, that since Plato has supplanted the Athenian "male" model of eros as acquisition of the beautiful with a "female" one of procreation of the beautiful, it is appropriate that the "mouthpiece" be a woman. Halperin writes: "What Plato did was to take an embedded habit of speech (and thought) that seems to have become detached from a specific referent in the female body and, first to *reembody* it as 'feminine' by associating it with the female person of Diotima through her extended use of gender-specific language, then to *disembody* it once again, to turn 'pregnancy' into a mere *image* of (male) spiritual labor, just as Socrates' male voice at once embodies and disembodies Diotima's female presence."[22] The precise choice of woman, or better put, the remarkably absent woman, the absent *real* woman, Aspasia, the woman who was not there, is an essential aspect of the overall rhetoric of the piece. Because Plato is adopting a procreative model of erotic desire but is contemptuous of the physical procreation of corporeal children, the teacher cannot be a *gyne* (woman) but must be a *parthenos* (virgin). Diotima may be a female, but in Greek, I think, she is not (quite) a woman. She is, however, on this reading a real (if fictional) female. On this reading, the substitution of the Mantinean mantic for the Athenian partner, lover, politician, mother (not *demimondaine*) was a very marked one indeed. If Aspasia is the female version of Pericles, Diotima makes the perfect female version of Socrates, the anti-Pericles. Diotima has to be a woman, on this account, in order to negate Aspasia and all that she means.

The *Symposium* links up, as has already been seen, with a highly significant passage from *The Republic*:

> That leaves only a very small fraction, Ademantus, of those who spend their time on philosophy as of right. Some character of noble birth and good upbringing, perhaps, whose career has been interrupted by exile, and who for want of corrupting influences has followed his nature and remained with philosophy. Or a great mind born in a small city, who thinks the political affairs of his city beneath him, and has no time for them. . . . Our friend Theages has a bridle which is quite good at keeping people in check. Theages has all the qualifications for dropping out of philosophy, but physical ill-health keeps him in check, and stops him going into politics. . . . Those who have become members of this small group have tasted how sweet and blessed a possession is philosophy. They can also, by contrast, see quite clearly the madness of the many. They can see that virtually nothing anyone in politics does is in any way healthy. (*The Republic* 496 a–c)[23]

The opposition between the life of a philosopher and the life of the polis could not possibly be clearer than it is in this passage. The philosopher is an alien by birth or even by virtue of the ill-formedness of his body, which keeps him out of the erotic/political commerce described, for example by the symposiast Pausanias, or is one who is blessed with a certain mantic ability, as Socrates is. Diotima has all three of these characteristics: She is certainly a very marked sort of alien, a physical disability does keep her out of politics (Aspasia is the interesting negative counterexample), and she is a Mantinean mantic to boot. Andrea Nightingale has already connected this passage in *The Republic* with the *Symposium* at exactly the point at which it is of interest to my argument here. She writes: "What is the nature of this new brand of alien [the philosopher]? . . . One of the most prominent aspects of Plato's definition of the philosopher is the opposition he forges between the philosophic 'outsider' and the various types of people who made it their business to traffic in wisdom." Nightingale then goes on to remark that "the clearest and most explicit enunciation of this phenomenon in the Platonic corpus" is perhaps "the *Symposium*'s handling of the exchange of 'virtue' for sexual favors."[24]

Instead of Pausanias's description of a heavenly eros from which virtue flows in exchange for semen (or better put, perhaps, in which semen is the material within which virtue flows), Diotima inscribes an eros that is entirely spiritual in nature, outside the circulation (the traffic) of the sociality of the polis.[25] I wish to emphasize the parallel between rhetoric, sophism, traffic in wisdom, and Pausanian pederasty, on the one hand, and philosophy, alienated wisdom, and Diotima's desire, on the other.

Socrates' treatment of Agathon ("the good/beautiful") in the *Symposium* is meant as an acting out of what he takes to be proper pederasty, as opposed to that of Pausanian heavenly eros—Agathon being the beautiful boy with whom Socrates would love to have conversation. The same relations of power and hierarchy apply: Agathon must assent to Socrates' reasoning, but the realm is not of the body but of the soul. By analogy with the pederasty of demotic Athens (whether "vulgar" or "ouranian"), there is a clear hierarchy in the relationship. If Agathon the *eromenos* gratifies the need of Socrates the *erastes* to penetrate his mind with logos, then, presumably Agathon will receive some of the same things that the ordinary *eromenos* is supposed to receive from his gratifying the need of his *erastes* to penetrate his body with phallus.[26]

This reading puts, I think, quite a different spin on this philosophical eros than Halperin's with its idealizing description of perfect mutuality in the relations of philosophical *erastes* and *eromenos*.[27] As in the erotic exchanges in the Talmud between Rabbi Yoḥanan and Resh Lakish, we can find here in philosophical dialogue, Platonic-style, a strong model of male-male desire, as spiritualized and as intense as the male-male desire of a Byzantine monastery.[28]

My reading thus raises problems for one of Halperin's explanations for Diotima's genitalia, as it does for Foucault's similar insistence on the mutuality of the Platonic "dialectic of love."[29] However, it clearly assimilates Plato's pedagogical ideal to pederasty in the clear asymmetry of the penetrator penetrated, taking the pederastic model of Athens at its best, as represented by Pausanias's speech, and turning it on its head from its bottom, as it were.[30] It is that transfer from anus, vagina, and womb to pure mind that explains why Diotima is not Aspasia. She is neither the possessor of a vagina for pleasure nor a womb for physical procreation; both, in her, are purely spiritual entities, metaphors that help us grasp the proper eros. Ideal eros, for Plato, is entirely a mind-fuck.[31]

Socrates completes his ventriloquistical peroration by insisting: "Such, Phaedrus, is the tale which I heard from the stranger of Mantinea, and which you may call the encomium of love, or what you please." By enacting in the discourse the substitution of dialectic (philosophy) for encomium (rhetoric), Diotima has matched in the form of her expression the form of its content as well, the replacement of the physical eros and the rhetorical, political, ethical socialization that is attendant on it—Pausanias's "heavenly love"—with an even more heavenly love that does not belong to the world of getting and spending at all (pun intended).

It seems to me, then, that Jowett was exactly right in his conclusion that Diotima

> has taught him that love is another aspect of philosophy. The same want in the human soul which is satisfied in the vulgar by the procreation of children, may become the highest aspiration of intellectual desire. As the Christian might speak of hungering and thirsting after righteousness; or of divine loves under the figure of human (compare Eph. "This is a great mystery, but I speak concerning Christ and the church"); as the mediaeval saint might speak of the "fruitio Dei"; as Dante saw all things contained in his love of Beatrice, so Plato would have us absorb all other loves and desires in the love of knowledge. Here is the beginning of Neoplatonism, or rather, perhaps, a proof (of which there are many) that the so-called mysticism of the East was not strange to the Greek of the fifth century before Christ.[32]

My reading affirms the defensibility (if not more) of Jowett's conclusion that the *Symposium* already strongly avows what will be a Christian (or, more broadly, late ancient) theory of sexuality. Both Dover and Foucault are right in asserting that Platonic love is not grounded in a "law" in the sense that it will be for Jews and Christians.[33] However, much more important, in my view, is the essential positing of a spiritual love that is not only not physical but in important ways directly opposed to the physical. The bottom line of the *Symposium* is that Greek eros has been entirely transformed from the attraction to beautiful bodies into the interaction of souls through dialogue. Once again, rhetoric has been marked by Plato as the space of the specious, while Socrates' dialogue, which is equally a "power play," has replaced pederasty. The break with the patterns of socialization in the Athenian polis is total.[34] For Plato, it would seem, the body's beauty, as well as language's beauty, and the beauty of the community of ordinary human beings sharing views and reaching conclusions and decisions, as well as sharing bodily fluids and sometimes making babies, all belong to the realm of the false-seeming, the realm of appearance, the dreaded *doxa*, and all of them together are to be replaced by the eros of love of the Forms, *episteme*. Whether or not this has anything to do with "the mysticism of the East," it does, I think, have everything to do with the conceptions of the relations of the political body to the spiritual one in late ancient Judeo-Christianity.

This break that Plato makes with customary Athenian erotic mores is as sharp as the most pious Victorian scholar could imagine, indeed sharper, because many of them did not have clearly in their minds the physicality of that non-Platonic Athenian love. Greek love and Platonic love thus need to be clearly distinguished. Platonic love, while eros it is, has nothing to do with physical touch, but such love is intended only for a particular elite. For those blessed few, it is understood that from the very beginning their desire will be for the noncorporeal pleasure of seeing the beautiful person and thence it will develop finally into contemplation of the form of Beauty itself. Thus, contrary to at least some generally held contemporary readings of Plato, I believe that Platonic love is, indeed, a matter of complete celibacy, and as such, I will argue elsewhere, had a more profound effect on Christian mores than is currently imagined.[35] This analysis should help us keep clearly separate the two different Christian ideals, procreationism for the many, celibacy for the elite. Finally, it should help us see the Talmudic narrative of Resh Lakish and Rabbi Yoḥanan with a broader perspective of the way in which it situates the Rabbis' discourse on sexuality, desire, and truth in the context of Mediterranean culture. That nevertheless should not blind us to differences in the ways in which that model is constructed.

The End of the Affair

What can be read in the *Symposium* and the *Phaedrus* as a representation of a mutuality of *eros* and *anteros*, as Halperin, Foucault, and Hadot read it, is explicitly deconstructed in the Talmudic narrative. The next moves in the narrative write the continuation and the end of the affair of the two Rabbis in a classical tragic ending that marks it both as a love story and as a doomed one, at one and the same time:

> Once they were disputing in the Study House: "the sword and the lance and the dagger, from whence can they become impure?"[36] Rabbi Yoḥanan said, "from the time they are forged in the fire." Resh Lakish said, "from the time they are polished in the water." Rabbi Yoḥanan said, "a brigand is an expert in brigandry" [i.e., sarcastically: You should know of what you speak; after all, weapons are your métier]. He [R.L.] said to him [R.Y.], "What have you

profited me. There they called me Rabbi and here they call me Rabbi!" [He (R.Y.) said, "I have indeed profited you, for I have brought you near under the wings of the *Shekhina*"].[37] He [R.Y.] became angry, and Resh Lakish became ill [owing to a curse put on him by R.Y.].

It is here that we remark most clearly the ambivalence built into this text. On the one hand, just as Rabbi Yohanan is to be apprehended as one of the great culture heroes of the Rabbis, one would expect that his inscription of the superiority of the love of Torah between men over the love of women would be the "winner" in any ideological contest within the text. But, on the other hand, it hardly seems reading anything into this text to see that that is hardly the case. Resh Lakish's outburst: "What have you profited me. There they called me Rabbi and here they call me Rabbi!" remains a very powerful indictment of the "pretensions" of the rabbinic sacred band. Resh Lakish is protesting that the male-male eros of the study house is precisely supposed to be nonhierarchical and nonviolent in its nature, but Rabbi Yohanan has just proven that it is neither. In the Talmud, there is no doubt that such insistences of male-male equality in the intellectual world are as false-appearing as they are in the world of heterosexual "love" or, for that matter, as far from mutuality and equality of desire or power as Pausanian pederasty.

Your promises of mutuality and reciprocity, says the bitter Resh Lakish, were entirely false. In truth, all you expected of me, brother Yohanan, was to be passive and receive your logos into my corpus. In his verbally violent and highly dismissive response to the disagreement on the part of his "friend/eromenos," Rabbi Yohanan indicates that nothing indeed has changed at all. Paradoxically, by saying that Resh Lakish is still a brigand, he is indicting his own practice with colleagues as no different from the practices of a band of brigands, precisely the charge that Resh Lakish brings against him. You are still a brigand means, in effect, I am still a brigand. The *bet hamidrash*, the space of the allegedly nonacquisitive true and mutual eros of men with men, is being set up as superior to the sexualized space of the family and that very set-up is being deconstructed as violent and hierarchical at one and the same time.

At the same time, however, that the eros of men with men is superior to the eros of the family, it remains the case that one distinct feature of the rabbinic ideology, which remains distinct whatever other similarities we may find with Christian and pagan Platonism, is the insistence on the necessity of marriage and procreation for everyone. Although one cannot offer any definitive explanation for this phenomenon, one way, at least, of thinking about it may be precisely in the total rejection of one aspect of Platonism, its repudiation of the life of the polis. For the Rabbis, from tannaitic times, the notion of an elite separating off physically from the main body of the Jewish people is anathema, and anathema as well the thought that as for procreation, we will leave that for the ignoramuses.[38] Rather than separating the population into two groups as some Jewish Platonists (notably Philo) and some Christians would do, the Rabbis seem rather to separate the spheres of a valorized homoerotic intellectual passion and a subordinated functional heterosexual world of getting and spending. Rabbi Yoḥanan would put it memorably: A millstone round his neck and he will learn Torah?!—but, nevertheless, he marries.

The Babylonian Rabbis (at any rate those who retold this story) do not seem to subscribe to the common Hellenistic notion (expressed in the *Symposium* by Aristophanes, by Zeno, by the Hellenistic novels) that "Eros is a god who contributes to the city's security"[39]—our story perceives a passion much more corrosive to the city than that—but neither will the narrative accept and revel in that corrosiveness (as Plato would have perhaps and surely some of the wilder of the "wild Platonists" of the Christian world, as well).[40] This bears out Satlow's observation of Babylonian rabbinic hostility to the Hellenistic ideology of *oikos* and *polis*, so prominent among the Palestinian rabbinic texts.

The Talmudic text seems much more self-critical than Plato's in its ascription of a utopian, decorporealized love between men, although it is, of course, very dangerous to underestimate Plato's self-knowingness. Although the "true" meaning of Rabbi Yoḥanan's invitation to Resh Lakish was that he join the homoerotic brotherhood of those who "learn" Torah together, there is a human woman involved, Rabbi Yoḥanan's sister according to the flesh, who has, moreover, become a mother in the meantime. Her place in the economy is elegantly delineated in the narrative:

> His sister [Rabbi Yoḥanan's sister; Resh Lakish's wife] came to him [Rabbi Yoḥanan] and cried before him. She said, "Look at me!" He did not pay attention to her. "Look at the orphans!" He said to her "'Leave your orphans, I will give life'" (Jeremiah 49:11). "For the sake of my widowhood!" He said, "'Place your widows' trust in me'" (loc. cit.).

It is hard for us to imagine a more devastatingly clear statement of Rabbi Yoḥanan's position here than the chilling "'Look at me!' He did not pay attention to her," nor a more devastatingly clear inculpation of that position. Strikingly—and this is what I most missed in my own former exculpation of this text—it is not entirely clear from the Talmudic text that it adopts the same position that we do instinctively, for when Rabbi Yoḥanan repents, it is of the failure of his love for Torah and the consequent failure of his love for Resh Lakish that he repents and not of the callous treatment of his sister:

> Resh Lakish died, and Rabbi Yoḥanan was greatly mournful over him. The Rabbis said, "What can we do to comfort him? Let us bring Rabbi El'azar the son of Padat whose traditions are brilliant, and put him before him [Rabbi

Yoḥanan]." They brought Rabbi El'azar the son of Padat and put him before him. Every point that he would make, he said, "there is a tradition which supports you." He [R.Y.] said, "Do I need this one?! The son of Lakish used to raise twenty-four objections to every point that I made, and I used to supply twenty-four refutations, until the matter became completely clear, and all you can say is that there is a tradition which supports me?! Don't I already know that I say good things?" He used to go and cry out at the gates, "Son of Lakish, where are you?" until he became mad. The Rabbis prayed for him and he died.

As we see from this quotation, it is not only Rabbi Yoḥanan who seemingly has no care—even in penitential retrospect—for his sister, the wife of Resh Lakish, or for his own nephews and nieces; the text shows no such concern either. It does not even bother to narrate their undoubtedly sad fate, let alone waste any energy on lamenting it. On the one hand, the text has raised that family to our consciousness; they cannot be simply ignored on the rabbinic reading of human life, but on the other hand, that raising to consciousness is almost immediately suppressed—but not, of course, totally, the net result being a dialectic or an oscillation between two positions. Finally, something very revealing is evinced when we go back and think a bit about the text with which I began. The Talmud compares the joy of learning Torah not with the joy of sex—with one's wife, with a woman—but the joy of sex with a beautiful female deer. Now, to be sure, this imaginaire is carefully kept clear of the bestial; it is the joy of the buck's love for his doe, not that of human bestiality, and yet, as just said, there is something very revealing here. The homoerotic passion generated by and for the female Torah, this divine intercourse\between men, between Rabbis, is so much sharper than any real corporeal intercourse with human wives that the Rabbis (or at least these texts) could imagine.[41]

The attraction of asceticism and even celibacy for the ancient Rabbis (and not only other ancient Jews, as had been pointed out in a pioneering essay by Steven Fraade) has been overlooked until very recently.[42] Recent scholars, however, have gone beyond Fraade in realizing how fraught the issue of celibacy was *within* the rabbinic community itself.[43] In contrast to my previous way of working, in which I saw absolute (or near-absolute) binary oppositions between Platonistic and rabbinic cosmologies and anthropologies, I see much more contiguity now at least in some rabbinic texts.

As with the question of martyrdom (which I have discussed in earlier work),[44] the Talmud simply will not settle down on one view or another with respect to the ratio between physical and spiritual eros (with women and men, respectively). I might suggest that what remains distinctive about Talmudic culture in the end may just be precisely this refusal to settle down on one view or another of such fraught matters as sex and death. Here, I have tried to expose the deeply unsettled (and unsettling) ambiguity of the rabbinic text on the question of homoerotic desexualized love and its relations to bodies, sex, and procreation. In the past, and especially in *Carnal Israel*, I tended to lift up only the positions that seemed most antithetical to "Christian" or "Hellenistic" ones. I now would see those very positions as always mixed and conditioned by the presence within the Talmud itself of positions much closer to those others in the contemporary Mediterranean world. On my current reading, the Talmudic narrative constructs and reveals an ideology of sexuality that is not nearly as different from that of the *Symposium* as I would have previously imagined. The same dual(istic) structure of corporeal versus noncorporeal passion (the same "instinct"[45]) is being advanced with the intensely homoerotic (but desexualized) male-male spiritual bonding over the seeking of wisdom (Sophia, Philosophia, Torah) clearly placed into a hierarchical circumstance in which it is read as far superior to the mere physical eros of sex with women and procreating children.[46]

The points of structural similarity between this rabbinic discourse and Platonic discourses on sexuality seem to me decisive. Although I have no theory with which to explain a historical connection between a story of Palestinian Rabbis inflected through a late ancient Babylonian Jewish redaction and the *Symposium* written in Greece eight hundred years earlier, these two texts do both seem to be enacting an epistemic shift with respect to their own forebears; for Plato, the pederastic eros of Athens; for the Talmud, the unqualifiedly positive orientation toward (hetero)sexuality characteristic of the Bible.[47] Although, to be sure, as I have tried to emphasize, the major difference is that the Talmudic text simply does not come down finally on one side or another, it is the very imagining of such a desexualized, but therefore sanctioned, space for an intense homoeroticism that is so strikingly new vis-à-vis earlier Judaisms and so strikingly close to the Platonic imagination adopted wholeheartedly (or nearly so) in late ancient Christianity.

In all of this, queerness itself is queered: pederastic homoeroticism may (not unlike gay marriage) inscribe a realm of male relationality that is superior to but still comparable with marital heteroeroticism, but Platonic eros (whether Greek, Christian, or rabbinic) sets itself against both pederasty and marriage in resistance to the conventions of the ancient city (and perhaps to sociopolitical "convention" per se) while disrupting the boy-versus-woman binary via the insertion of fictive female figures (Diotima, Torah/Wisdom) into the male-male erotic economy. This broader resistance is framed for Plato himself as the resistance of philosophy to rhetoric, for Christians as the resistance of the ascetic to the everyday, and for the Rabbis in an intricate and tense staging of the values of marriage and procreation (the values of the ancient city) in contradiction with the values of the spiritual *Männerbund* (Sacred Band) of the study of Torah.

CAN I REALLY COUNT ON YOU?

Laurence Paul Hemming

The purpose of this essay is very modest. Setting out from the way in which all contemporary accounts of sexed or gendered identity depend essentially on a twofold understanding of difference, a twofold understanding, moreover, that then structures the relationship between private sociality and public life or the polis as such, I ask, in accord with the spirit of this volume, whether in canon and tradition this twofold has always been present. Identifying one canonical text which has ordered sexual difference and gender identity quite differently (whilst at the same time taking into account and giving an explanation of the twofold) I indicate within the very limited space available that contemporary accounts need not be constrained by this binary, nor need they construct the relationship of domestic living to the political in the way that is now taken for granted, nor even do these accounts have to be restricted to sexual coupling itself. I wish, in other words, to indicate (and here I really can no more than indicate) a possible passageway to a more original ontological account of human sexual difference and domesticity, based on an appeal to a matter itself phenomenologically constitutive of the self as such.

The basis of much contemporary discourse on marriage and coupling is that it is for the sake of the preservation of the family as the most basic unit of society. The preservation of normal sexual relations is taken to have, not just a purpose in and of itself, and so to be its own good thing, but rather that its effect goes beyond its immediate goodness to extend to the stabilization of society as a whole. Here, therefore, is the moral drive for the preservation of normal, heterosexual, family life: without it, society as a whole is imperiled. The interpretation of society at issue here is essentially political: family life makes possible, stabilizes, and conditions for good purposes, the life of the polis. Marriage is a coupling of the two, the male and the female, as what is genuinely other to each other, in order to provide the most basic form of alterity on which an intersubjectivity can be resolved. One of the ways in which same-sex coupling has been questioned is on the basis of its inadequacy with respect to genuine alterity: it is morally flawed at an ontological level because it is not the coupling of the other with the other, but the coupling of the same with the selfsame: the argument runs that it is intrinsically turned in on itself.

The appeal to a sexed alterity, grounded in the natural difference between male and female, can seem to be very compelling, especially to anyone for whom there is no obvious reason to challenge it. It is only those who desire something which is not "normal" who seek to challenge the normal, preponderant construction of the body politic. While we may have compassion for those outside this normality, they must not be allowed to disrupt what is self-evidently natural. Recent religious accounts of sexual difference have sought refuge in accounts of this form: "The Church's teaching on marriage and on the complementarity of the sexes reiterates a truth that is evident to right reason and recognized as such by all the major cultures of the world."[1] These, however, have been theological accounts, grounding sexual difference not philosophically, but with reference to scripture or revelation, with all the attendant problems such accounts bring with them. John Paul II has argued that "in the 'unity of the two,' man and woman are called from the beginning not only to exist 'side by side' or 'together,' but *also to exist mutually 'one for the other.'*"[2] His argument arises strictly from an interpretation of the biblical account in Genesis.[3] Taken apart from scripture (and from its canonical place in Christian theology as an account whose primary meaning has been the inception, not of essentialized sexed identities, but of the cosmic narrative of salvation-history), the account relies strictly on a simple twofold: male and female. Moreover, this twofold is then grounded in a particular account of truth (it is visible and self-evident to "right reason") and politics (it promotes "the dignity of marriage, the foundation of the family, and the stability of society").[4]

In order to evade the inadequacies of these understandings and to attempt to provide a phenomenal basis for the appearance and manifestation of those sexed and gendered configurations which exceed the heterosexual, recent philosophical accounts of sexual difference have pursued explanations concentrating on social and metaphysical constructedness. In this the work of Judith Butler has been of particular importance, as she has seemed to provide a way out of the apparent impasse between constructionalism and essentialism. Nevertheless, in order to undertake this, she has (in an appeal informed by Foucault and Lacan, among others) explained sexual difference in terms of the distribution of power, so that all gendered identities are explained as deflections of, and appearing in virtue of, white male heterosexual identity, or what she has called the "heterosexual matrix." In raising the question of the very constructedness of the materiality of bodies by asking "whether a notion of matter or the materiality of bodies can serve as the uncontested ground of feminist practice,"[5] she has been led to transform her reading of the origins of the discussion of sexual difference in the West so that it is understood to arise from an intersubjectival and psychotherapeutic perspective. Interpreting these texts from the perspective of the heterosexual matrix, she asks "to what extent does the Platonic account of the phallogenesis of bodies prefigure the Freudian and Lacanian accounts which presume the phallus as the synecdochal token of sexed positionality?"[6] Having suggested that Lacan is not different from Plato in his origination, she transforms the whole discussion of the materiality in Lacanian terms: "for Lacan, the body, or rather morphology is an imaginary formation."[7]

The difficulty with Butler's account, quite apart from its metaphysical problems (which I do not propose to examine here), is that it further entrenches the whole discussion of sexual difference in the political sphere, since every deflection and representation of power is at the same time an extension of the effects of power. This is tantamount to saying that every appearance of an alternative to power is in virtue of the original that inaugurates and establishes power, or (for reasons that will become clear shortly) every appearance of the other (the second) to the origination of power is at the same time ineluctably bound to its original. Butler has circumvented the difficulties inherent in this account ingeniously: she demonstrates that the place of origination of power does not genuinely appear until its alternative makes its appearance. At one and the same time the existence of the second is the only thing that makes the first visible. She therefore argues that "the replication of heterosexual constructs in non-heterosexual frames brings into relief the utterly constructed status of the so-called heterosexual original. Thus gay is to straight *not* as copy is to original, but rather, as copy is to copy. The parodic repetition of 'the original' . . . reveals the original to be nothing other than a parody of the *idea* of the natural and original."[8]

Her choice of the word *matrix* is, however, neither accidental nor inappropriate.[9] The matrix she describes explains adequately the appearance of more occurrences of the other to the selfsame that legitimates it, whilst at the same time always ordering each other to the same as a formal binarism. Because the selfsame is also ordered to itself (as copy is to copy) *as* the only legitimated other to itself, its own self-relation is patterned in the same way as every alternative other also is to the selfsame. The metaphor of the matrix, therefore, explains a plurality of binaries to the ideal projection of the heterosexual, male, normality, since all alternates are ordered to it, and not in any sense to each other. All gender configurations are essentially binary in character because they are ordered, not to each other, but in appearing they make apparent (through their very difference from it and deflection of it) the normative, regulatory masculine heterosexual ideal (the "law of the father"); also, this binarism is itself bound to the public and the political.[10]

Alterity, with this gendered twist, is increasingly resolved by means of an appeal to intersubjectivity, and Butler (and others) have continued to discuss gender in terms of subjectivity and intersubjectivity. About the only serious philosophical critique of intersubjectivity is ushered in by

Martin Heidegger, in his implicit critique of Martin Buber. Heidegger criticizes intersubjectivity through his phenomenological description of *Mitsein* or *Miteinandersein*—"being with" or "being-with-another." It would be possible to assume that his critique and his description of *Mitsein* simply arise out of the phenomenological description of *Dasein*, but this would not be correct.[11] *Mitsein* translates a term to be found in Plato and in Greek thought—hardly surprising for one so steeped in Greek philology and philosophy as Martin Heidegger. That word is *synousia*—which can also be translated, for reasons that I will make clear, as "being-with" or "being-with-another."

I do not propose to reproduce Heidegger's critique of intersubjectivity here in detail, but to provide merely an outline in order to prepare for my next remarks. Although Heidegger understands *Mitsein* as inseparable from the sexed appearance of embodied humanity, nevertheless he argues that something already underlies and makes possible the appearance of sexed or gendered forms. He suggests that "*Dasein* is being-with with *Dasein*. This being-with with *X* does not come about on the basis of factically existing together, it is not clarified only on the basis of a supposedly more originally genus-like being of sexedly differentiated bodily essences, rather this genus-like striving-together and genus-like uniting metaphysically presupposes dispersal of *Dasein* as such, which means being-with in general."[12] *Dispersal* here is understood as the way in which *Dasein*, as not in itself any kind of "thing," is distributed all the way through individual existences. This underlying being-together, in making possible the appearance of gendered forms in "manifolding," concerns "the description of manifolding (not 'manifoldness') which lies precisely in every factically individuated existence as such."[13] Existence as already "the manifolding" underlies and makes possible the appearance of individuation and sexual difference, as such. On the same basis, Heidegger explains that "being-with-another thus cannot be clarified by the I-you relation and on its basis, but rather conversely: this I-you relation presupposes for its inner possibility that *Dasein* (not only the *Dasein* functioning as I but also as you) is defined as being-with-another; indeed even more than that: even the self-comprehension of an I and the concept of I-ness arise only on the basis of being-with-another, but not as I-you relation."[14]

What, then, is the significance for our question with regard to *Mitsein*, *synousia*? The word *synousia* appears in the speech of Aristophanes in Plato's *Symposium*, and it is fundamental for Plato in the working out of the meaning of *eros* in the text. I want therefore to undertake an interpretative reading of Aristophanes' speech, with a view to bringing to light an entirely different understanding of human multiplicity ("manifolding") that confirms the understanding outlined by Heidegger (although we are taking different steps to attain it to the ones he took) and that does not bind sexed identity to the health of the polis—indeed, which provides for the possibility of breaking the direct link between family or domestic social life and the life of the polis (exactly as it was for the Greeks). On this basis it is perhaps possible to indicate how political life and social life can be thought separately.

Here is a different understanding of the social. A *socius* (or *socia*) is one who belongs to a *societas*, and who can therefore never be thought of apart from the society of which he or she is already a member. But most societies of these kinds, having specific and identifiable *socii* or members, are essentially private, having no direct or immediate role in the body politic (although not without relevance for it). In this sense the social and the political can already be thought to be separate. If it were possible to understand that separation with respect to the character of sexual difference, it would, I hope, demonstrate how there is no straight line from the family to the political, or at least how it has not always been conceived in this way, a thought that receives a certain confirmation in the thought of Hannah Arendt.[15]

The speech of Aristophanes in Plato's *Symposium* is a remarkable text—cunning, knowingly adult, spoken by a man for mature male ears, somewhat ribald, allusive, crowded with innuendo. It is here that Plato chooses to place the myth of "the being (*physis*) proper to man and his occurrences."[16] The speech begins by naming an absence—the missing presence of the praise due to the *dynamis* of *Eros*, named here both as a god and in what he enacts. *Dynamis* does not name here power in the contemporary sense, but the inner force, the self-emerging meaning of what *eros* names. Considered under Plato's understanding of the essential connection of *dynamis* with *kinesis*, *dynamis* names what of *eros* *appears* in the realm of appearances. The *dynamis* of *eros* is therefore the life of the human being and what is brought to manifestation in that life. *Eros* as such, as a divinity, has no *kinesis* of his own; the force and capacity that he is must appear in some other way, in the realm of the things that are changeable (*pragmata*) and subject to movement (*kinesis*) and occurrence (*pathos*).

Here is the reason for the character of the speech—not that it is sniggering and adolescent, but on the contrary, that for *eros* and what it names to appear requires a withdrawing into a particular kind of company and a presupposed attainment of a certain maturity of outlook. If the *dynamis* of *eros* were genuinely and widely experienced (the word is *esthesai*, from *aisthesis*), it would be honored with temples and altars. As it is, none of these things is attained by the public understanding. Thus *eros* is characterized from the outset as something whose real force and capacity to be felt is hidden and difficult to see—despite everyone thinking they know what *eros* names, genuine experience of *eros* requires a way in, a passageway. *Eros* is here described as one most-loving toward humanity (*philanthropo-*

tatos). The comparison of *eros* itself being most affiliated to and loving for humanity is not accidental. The context is what it means to learn of the force (*dynamis*) of *eros*, in order that the one learning "may yourself become for others a teacher."[17] What is being said here, in the transition from *eros* to *philia* that is a self-becoming, whereby one exhibits in one's very self what one has learned and acquired, is that *eros* in its force has the capacity to fulfill itself, to saturate itself and so complete itself, for those who find a way in to what it names.

What is the passageway, the way in? What is at issue is the *physis* of humanity. We want to translate *physis* with *nature*, but this obscures its meaning. *Physis* really means the appearing-emerging of humanity in and for itself, its capacity to bring itself out into the open and be known. In this sense, *physis* has a fundamental connection with *phos*, light, and what comes into the light. For this reason, we should better translate *physis* as "being." At issue are the being and occurrences (*pathemata*) of humanity. In the first place, says Aristophanes, our being was other than it is now: the race of humanity was threefold, not two, as now, with a third kind of human comprised of equal shares of the other two. Thus, in addition to male and female there was a "man-woman" (*androgynos*), whose name survives although the thing itself has not. Here indeed, is the adult, knowing, step. To see the third requires an understanding of the "common" (*koinon*) to the two that are easily visible, but this in itself requires an understanding not common to all, but which has to be learned and acquired. To see the third, however, means to see all the occurrences (all the ways or modes of being) of the *single* being of the human.

Aristophanes breaks off from the description of the meaning of this being to undertake its description: the whirling, four-armed, four-legged original human being, comprised of doubled sexual parts, which walked on four legs, or if it ran, whirled in a circular motion, something akin to a kind of forward cartwheeling. There were three kinds of this being: one comprised of two male parts, another of two female, and a third made up of one male part and one female. The original human was therefore three kinds of doubles—born in its maleness of the sun, and in its female part, the earth, and in the third form comprised of both male and female, the moon. In other words, it has a reference to the up, down, and between of the structure of the cosmos.[18] Moreover its fastest motion and its shape, both circular (*peripheres*), also refer to what for the Greeks was the most perfect form of motion. In its running, the original humans moved analogously to the movement of the cosmos, and analogously to the ones that brought them into being—the gods themselves. The matters of these original creatures' thinking (*phronemata*) were of such magnitude as to aspire to once touch (*epecheiresan*) the things proper to divinity, and it is for this reason, and their corresponding rebelliousness, that Zeus decides to sunder each of the three kinds of human into two. The three were therefore split into their respective halves, with the result that we see only the binary of males and females, whereas in combination they made three kinds from the two. Nevertheless the three kinds persist, if not in their kinds, then in their *eros*—for there are men who seek men, and women who seek women, and men and women who seek their counterparted sex.

To return to Aristophanes' characterization of the *androgynos*, this being lives on in name only and having once been just one of the three kinds of human, now its name indicates a matter of reproach.[19] As things now stand, it denotes perhaps the effeminate man or the butch woman— the man who, it seems, desires to be penetrated by men, or conversely the sexually dominant lesbian. For the Greeks, a woman who assumes sexual dominance (especially in sexual coupling) is a shameful thing, a matter of reproach. Aristophanes, however, names this figure, not as what the *androgynos* is in himself or herself, but as what the *androgynos* points to and indicates or makes visible—if we will but see it—that opens up the possibility of seeing the originary human being in its fullness. The *androgynos* actually points to what it itself is not—to the original unity of the male and the female halves of the originary human being. Thus, the queer human *now* indicates that being who, having been sundered, would seek its sexual opposite. The queer, paradoxically, indicates in its sundered state the being it is not, the "normal" heterosexual *couple*. This is not a deflection of the male heterosexual, because in its sundered state it indicates the original twofolded male-female, *not* the single male or doubled male-male.

Thus the *androgynos*, precisely in being of one sex and seeking the same sex as itself, indicates this seeking in an *eros* that exhibits the characteristics of its sexual *counterpart*. In this way it makes visible the more originary being, *physis*, and manners of being, *pathemata*, of humanity. Although the term employed by Plato at points in the text, *arche*, indicates something prior and seems to relate to his use of the word *proton*, first or earliest, in fact what Plato indicates is something that is still immediately at work and underlying sexed identity as it is present now. *Arche* indicates the *yet-underlying* in the sense of the still-present, which as still-present will be brought to light through enquiring into *eros*. Plato gives this yet-underlying a specific interpretation within his own thinking, but if space permitted (which it does not) I would hope to make some further observations which, precisely by having demonstrated what Plato intends, will allow us to suggest a yet more originary understanding of what is at issue. We will have to rely on the possibilities alluded to by my reference to Heidegger to indicate that what Plato is attempting to indicate has yet to be fully philosophically explicated in a modern context.

The *androgynos*, in other words, actually indicates its relatedness to the normal and heterosexual *biologically* (in the modern sense, although Plato has no sense of the biological as we would understand it) rather than by an appeal to the constructedness of the sex/gender binary. Plato is, after all, writing before Butler, but the significance of this is that Plato is able to unmask the binary male/female as arising in consequence of, and standing beyond, a different *arche*, a different origination. He indicates the archaic third by exhibiting that one in whom the parts of the male/female are distributed equally throughout itself, whilst explaining how it can exhibit and point up through its *eros* the identity it actually is not. To repeat: it does not do this by deflecting the power of that identity, nor in any way reminiscent of the account Butler gives, but rather precisely by stabilizing the identity which it exhibits through its *eros*.

The problematic character of the *androgynos* is better explained by Zeus's threat to sunder the human physicality a second time, into quarters rather than halves, if the race of humanity maintains its rebelliousness. Although a humorous note in the text (suggesting that after such a sundering the human would be forced to move by hopping, rather than whirling or walking), the point of this further threat in the text has a twofold effect. First it indicates how it is possible for the *androgynos* to be indicated by what it itself is not, and second, to suggest that it would continue to be indicated even if the human were further divided. The *androgynos* therefore points to something which in a sense persists in every possible mode of being-human, first (in the original state) as something which is itself complete and fulfilled, and thereafter as something which through its *eros* is both awkward and disturbing, even embarrassing (hence the desire to reprove it), and at the same time something which will not absent itself.

The scene Aristophanes depicts after the original sundering is tragic— the sundered beings cling to their former halves, flinging their arms around them, and whenever they rediscover their original unity by finding that half from whom they were sundered, they perish from indolence. The word for indolence here is *argia*—literally a separation from work, indicating that the satisfaction of *eros*, the coming together of the sundered two, is the ceasing of a kind of work. Although the work in question is, in its sense, work related to keeping the body together, and so assumes a connection with attending to the work of getting food etc., there is a more underlying connection between *eros* and work (*ergon*). The fundamental work is really the work of recovering access to the *phronemata*, the things of thinking, to which the original human being had proper access prior to its being sundered. The speech began with an offer to explain the *dynamis* of *eros*: *dynamis* has a connection with *ergon*, work, in the sense that *dynamis* implies the self-working that becomes visible through *kinesis*, through movement. However, just as rest and the unmoved (*akineton*) has an essential connection with movement and is a form of movement, so what is without work (*argia*) has an essential connection with work and effort. Both *ergon* and *kinesis* have a connection with *dynamis*; however, the connection is not immediately obvious to see. This is because we now have an entirely voluntaristic understanding of work and effort. We now understand work and effort as a choice, a selection made as an alternative to indolence—in other words, we understand effort as something rooted in the will, the will of a subject. At the beginning, however, I noted that *dynamis* meant a self-emerging kind of force, not a force exerted on something (a Newtonian force) but an inner impulsion, something I cannot escape. Care should be exercised here, however, not to interpret *dynamis* in this context as something like a psychological drive or a compulsion. Rather, in just the same way that the real meaning of rest, as a kind of motion, is brought to light and exhibited by motion itself, so the real meaning of the indolence (*argia*) is brought to light and exhibited by that kind of work and effort toward which I am self-impelled. We discover, therefore, that the work *eros* points to is its fulfillment in *argia*, in a cessation from effort as the culmination, the highest point and rising-up of *eros*, to the genuine things of thinking. The effort and impulsion at issue indicates the connection not between *eros* and sensation, but between *eros* and a certain kind of thinking.

The *dynamis*, the force of *eros*, is therefore the opposite to the exerted force of Zeus, as that one who sunders the original human beings in two and so deprives them of their original circularity and completeness. In this sundered manner, the subsequent beings are themselves inscribed into *eros* itself, whilst deprived of the meaning of the impelled yearning of which they are now possessed: "Thus precisely originarily is *eros* of one for another implanted in the human being as something reaching for and combining to make one out of two and being healing for what is proper to humanity."[20] The sundering of the two is the deprivation from the human of its proper access and attainment to the *phronemata*, and at the same time its seeking for them: it is in this sense the need to work them out and regain access to them—it is *noein*, thinking, itself.

Therefore, *eros* is the way into the *phronesis* that makes the thoughts of men like to the thoughts of the gods. Here *phronesis* is to be taken in its meaning prior to the technical, moral sense given it by Aristotle. *Phronesis* is that kind of thinking in its relation to truth that is counterposed to *techne*, to productive thinking, the thinking that has as its objects effects in the world and that results in produced things: *phronesis* is the most deliberative thinking (akin in its meaning, albeit unthematically, to Aristotle's *sophia*, wisdom), the thinking that begins with sensation (*aisthesis*) but through a kind of working-out (the working-out of *noein*) produces the genuine things that arise from thinking, the *noemata*, or *phronemata*. The sundering of the human is at the same time a separation of the human from its capacity to have matters of concern (*phronemata*) that are like to those of the gods. Now to attain these again—that is, to engage in genuine highest thinking (what Aristotle will call *theorein*—contemplation, but the connection with divinity should not be overlooked)—will require finding not only a partner, but that matching half (*sumbolon*) that restores the original wholeness of the single creature.

Here is the basis for the passageway-in to the original life of humans—the passageway-in to the meaning of *eros* that Aristophanes seeks, and at the same time the reason why *Eros* himself is the one most loving towards men: *eros* itself heals the very separation from the capacity of the original humans to be analogous both to the cosmos as a whole and indeed to the gods themselves.

Here it becomes clear that thinking always presupposes the underlying being-together of being human. The *dynamis* of *eros*, as the drive and force to make into one the twofold, is at the same time based on something that cannot easily be seen and needs maturity and intelligence (*noein*) to be discovered. It is for this reason that the drive to make into one the twofold is not simply concerned with sexual coupling: "no-one, indeed, could suppose this being-with to be mere sexual coupling,"[21] rather the soul is striving for something it does not easily have the capacity to speak of. Sexual coupling is only the most obvious and immediate thing that exhibits the saturation of *eros* and brings it fully to light, whilst at the same time allowing ordinary everyday living to continue. As a kind of speaking-before-speaking, an exchange not based on a higher *logos* but that simply depends on the most direct physicality to satisfy itself, sexual coupling is the least of the manifestations of *eros*.

I have hesitated to translate *eros* itself, allowing us simply to take the name as it stands for the name of the god. Usually translated as desire, sometimes as love, often connected with explicitly sexual desire, in fact the myth recounted by Aristophanes allows us to see what *eros* is for itself: it is the passageway through to the genuine originary being of being-human in its connection with divinity. The ancients had no real word for sex: the things pertaining to sexual and romantic relations they named with regard to a goddess: the most specified form of which was the verb *aphrodisiazein*, in the active or passive depending on who was doing what to whom.[22] Sexual coupling is the most immediate and obvious form of something, which nevertheless from the outset is in part hidden and difficult to see. Sexual coupling, as the satiety (Plato speaks here of a *plesmone*) arising out of *eros*,[23] leads to a fulfilled *synousia*. This word means literally a "being-together-with," *Mitsein*. Because the becoming that is named is in the Greek text the optative part of the verb, it indicates both what is sought after and its achievement. The real purpose of *eros*, of which sexual coupling is only one way into, is the way *back* into a full being-together-with. This being-together is, however, the rediscovery of an original, and so proper being-together of the being of being-human, one that was already there *before* we encountered the most obvious binarism, the binary of men and women. *Eros* is therefore the basis for making visible and present what is in a sense already there, but difficult to see.

Sexual coupling, even insofar as it is present, is itself only partially able to be demonstrated (*delos*) and points to something further, something even less demonstrable, which can only be indicated by what Aristophanes speaks of as riddles and presages. *Eros* therefore is the original desire to make the two into one, but it is based itself, neither on the two nor on the one, but rather on the three that is the originary being (*physis*) of the human. For Plato, these numbers are not without significance. For the one, as the divine number, is also the number that is itself behind speech, but speaking, the same as for being, is itself always twofold, the "twofold in general." Here the twofold is found to be preceded by something else, namely the threefold, which is the originary being of the human. The threefold is not a simple three, however, for implied in it is a "more than three." If the original beings are male-male, male-female, female-female, there is implicit in this a fourth, female-male, which would be invisible in itself as it will always appear to be the same as the male-female; they will be indistinguishable. But formally, mathematically, these two must both be present: the three "hides" a fourth.[24] The one, two, three through which we have passed is really therefore the onefold, twofold, manifold, which corresponds to the single, dual, and plural forms of the Greek language as such.[25]

Why should any of this reference to the numerical be of importance? Except that, for Plato, number is that which is most ontologically basic, the underlying of all things, in a way that is later opposed by Aristotle. What Plato seeks to indicate in the underlying numerical reference of this myth told by Aristophanes is the way in which the twofold of male and female is distributed all the way through the threefold of the origin (*arche*) of human being as such: human being is essentially a "manifolding." All human coupling, insofar as it is mature and striving genuinely to reach the *phronemata*, the genuine things to be thought that are true and make us visible as like to the gods who begot us, is already distributed through the manifolding of human being as such. This manifolding is not twofold, but is the more-than-two that becomes precisely visible in the twofold itself; although it is not easy to see, it requires a working-out that passes beyond immediate experience but that is indicated by something which is for us an involuntary impulse, *eros*. At the same time, the originary twofold, precisely in its distribution or dispersal through the three as the many, makes possible the genuine, originary access to the divine one. It is for this reason that *eros* is the aspect of the divine that is most lovingly disposed to the human. *Eros* is *itself* the passageway by means of the two-fold from the manifold into the one.

If *eros* is the way into understanding the genuine relation of humanity as a manifolding to the things that are true and make us most like to the gods, what is the character of the manifold itself? Perhaps the most striking feature of original humanity in its threefold being is that it has two faces alike on every side, on a head "made round." The term Plato uses here is *kukloteres*.[26] The only other place where Plato employs this word is in the *Timaeus*, in particular in his description of the demiurge's manufacture of the living creature that is the Cosmos itself, with the four elements (the metaphysical "building blocks" of all things—earth, water, air, and fire) distributed all the way through it. The living creature is made in this way, *kukloteres*, because this very shape is "wholly the most perfect and most selfsame."[27] Most importantly of all, the faces of the original human being are not turned in towards each other, but outwards, facing opposite ways. The facing apart does not indicate speaking, but rather, both in their motion and what they reach for, the original humans are already capable of *phronein*, of deliberative thinking, the thinking that makes them reach up to be akin to the gods. The head of the original human is then itself entirely analogous to, and fashioned in the same way as, the whole of the cosmos itself. It is, literally, world-constituting for itself *as* itself. The two-facedness in the one head enables it to take in the whole of the cosmos at once. Being-together-with is at the same time being-with-the-all, however, this implies a facing-*outwards* that is able to take in all at once their belonging in the manifold.

Therefore *eros* turns out to be that seeking after a "one-with-whom" who can make present the original manifolding of the human being, and restore the genuine being-together-with that being human is. Although Plato does not say so, the means of exhibiting this *eros* is by means of a speaking, a conversing that was not required for the original humans. The turning inwards of the faces of humanity in order to speak is matched (and prior) to the turning-around of the sexual parts of the sundered humans that Zeus undertakes after he takes pity on the sundered beings as they travel around seeking out their original other halves, in order that they can once again mate and seek relief. This turning around of the "noble parts" takes place entirely separately from and subsequently to the work of Apollo on the sundered beings to turn around their faces and make up their bellies to enable them to function: in other words, specific attention is drawn to the disjunction in the actions taken. Although the myth should not be pressed too hard in its detail, as we can assume that the original being-together precluded speaking, so it precluded (because of the placing of the sexual parts) mating as well.[28] The turning of the heads takes place first in the text, the turning of the sexual parts comes a little later. However, what comes later is often first, often earlier in our appropriation of it—here again is an indication that sexual coupling is in itself only a passageway to something else, to logos, speaking as such.

There is much else that could be said philosophically here about the originary basis of *eros* and its connection with time and with Heidegger's understanding of care (*die Sorge*), but that is not what is at issue in this discussion. Does my reading of this philosophical text not rather suggest that there is more to be said of the meaning of the binary male/female than is current in much, especially religious, debate about the meaning and purpose of human coupling and combining, sexual or otherwise? The interpretation that John Paul II has given the early verses of Genesis has the effect of turning the male and female toward each other, locking them in an embrace that does not explain the essential connection with wider familiation—with children, but also with other forms of common (but not political) life, sexual or otherwise. In this, a merely binary interpretation seems less than wholly adequate to our instinctive understanding that the binary male/female is itself placed in the midst of something wider, which we struggle to bring to speech. Surely, however, the scriptural account of God in his creation of male and female tells against the wider context of the manifold and the plurality that I have claimed is, surely, only to be found in one place in the Western and Judeo-Christian canon. Except that the interpretation given by the Holy Father here is not the only interpretation that these verses have been given. Steven Greenberg has drawn my attention to the interpretation offered by at least some of the rabbis that is prescient for the whole of this discussion. Rabbi Yirmiyah bar Eleazar interprets the original Adam to have been androgynous, and further yet, Rabbi Shmuel bar Nachman suggests: "When the Holy One created the first Adam, he created it two faced and then (later) sawed it (in two) creating for it two backs, a back here and a back there. They asked him: but what of the verse 'and he took one of his ribs?' He answered them, (it really means that) 'he took one of the flanks' [the word is the same in Hebrew, *tzela*]. The word is also used to describe the flank or side of the tabernacle in Exodus 26."[29]

If the essential manifolding of human being is brought to light by the *androgynos*, is there perhaps more to be said of human coupling and combining than has so far been spoken?

CONTEMPLATING A JEWISH RITUAL OF SAME-SEX UNION

AN INQUIRY INTO THE MEANINGS OF MARRIAGE

Steven Greenberg

The debate in the United States on same-sex marriage has become a keenly contended social and political battle. The intensity of the conflict may be a bit puzzling. Why should the freedom of a minority to marry threaten marriage for the majority or the idea of marriage itself? How is it that the passions around this issue so often seem to surpass the issue's relative social importance? In part, the explanation lies in the significant transformations already under way in regard to both homosexuality and marriage. Until very recently, both marriage and homosexuality were governed by unquestioned cultural assumptions. Homosexuality was an abominable perversity and marriage a sought-after state of happiness, security, and continuity. Over the past thirty years, in Western societies both of these cultural foundations have been shaken. Homosexuality is no longer considered an unequivocal evil nor is marriage universally deemed an unequivocal good.

Much of the heat of the debate is a function of deeply held religious convictions. Many of the underlying categories of the controversy are theological and the questions they put to us are patently religious. Is nature—or, if you like, "the original intent of the Creator"—corrupted, expanded, or affirmed by homosexuality? Does the biblical creation story define marriage exclusively as the union of one man and one woman? What are the moral and religious meanings of gender? Of sexual pleasure? Is marriage a "natural" institution or is it a sociocultural one, open to change as society changes? Is the sanctification of homosexual partnership a victory for love, an overcoming of gender by justice, or a sign of the corruption and decadence of our time? Although the legal considerations of the civil code surely do not so specify, questions of same-sex marriage are bound up in terms of sacred text and liturgy, sin and sanctity, ritual and ethics, creation and redemption.

If we are to work through the question of same-sex marriage, we will have no recourse but to explore our religious traditions more deeply in order to understand how they have already conditioned our language, how they may be insidiously and inappropriately investing government in religious tests, and how they may still be able to inform, if not govern, the definition of marriage.

In service of this aim, the purpose of this essay is to explore the idea of same-sex marriage as a religious problem and, more specifically, as a halakhic problem. In traditional Jewish circles, religious problems are framed first and foremost as legal or halakhic problems, problems of praxis. For the sake of this inquiry, we will set aside the questions of the halakhic legitimacy of gay relationships and their formalization, and focus instead on what form such ceremonies ought to take. Should we employ the existing rituals of matrimony used for heterosexual couples, and if not, what other options are available? From the perspective of the Jewish law, what ought a same-sex wedding to look like?

On the surface, jumping over the question of the legitimacy of gay marriage may seem wildly presumptuous. The traditional Orthodox perspective, to date, is essentially univocal in its condemnation of same-sex sexual expression (if somewhat more vociferously for males than for females), and representative bodies have vehemently protested the adoption of same-sex marriage. There are even a few midrashic texts that explicitly decry same-sex marriage, the most famous being that of Rav Huna, the Babylonian rabbi who tells us that the generation of the flood was not obliterated from the world until they wrote nuptial songs for [unions between] males and [between humans and] animals. Beyond the midrashic material associating same-sex marriage with corruption and divine retribution, the rabbis explicitly prohibited such rites. In Deut. 18:3–4, the Torah prohibits copying the practices and customs of the Egyptian pagans. Which practices may not be copied? Those, say the rabbis, that were given legal force from the time of the fathers and their father's fathers. "What would they do? A man would marry a man, a woman a woman, a man would marry a woman and her daughter, and a woman would be married to two men" (Sifra 9:8). The contemporary Orthodox rabbi grounding himself in the halakhah would appear to be free from any duty to delve more deeply into the question. Two factors, however, suggest otherwise.

First, the Orthodox community has begun to actually meet its own gay members. For many, their first encounter with a gay Orthodox Jew was on a movie screen. Sandi Simcha DuBowski's documentary *Trembling before G—d* (released in October 2001) documented the challenges faced by gay Orthodox Jews. *Trembling* became a cultural phenomenon when hundreds of synagogues, Jewish community centers, religious school faculties, students, and professional and community organizations screened the film and held frank postscreening conversations involving the film maker, subjects of the film, and local rabbis. Although the changes are happening slowly, for many in the Orthodox community, homosexuality is no longer theoretical but quite up close and personal. The gay visibility that has so powerfully affected the larger culture is beginning to make inroads into the Orthodox community. Gay teens are coming out of the closet in high school, couples are divorcing due to the sexual orientation of a spouse, gay parents are seeking religious schools for their children, and gay people of all sorts are sharing their stories with their families, their friends, and their rabbis.

Second, Orthodox mental health professionals have become more confident in their rejection of the characterization of homosexuality as mental illness and are becoming increasingly unwilling to attempt "reparative therapy" with patients. As rabbis come to understand that gayness is not a curable disease but instead an unchangeable feature of a person's basic makeup, they slowly begin to reconsider both their rhetoric and their policies.

Although few if any traditional rabbis will be actively conducting same-sex ceremonies in the near future, they are being asked to weigh in on such events when they occur. Orthodox rabbis are being asked whether it is permissible for family members to attend the "wedding" of a daughter or brother. And once rabbis are in the loop, they begin to ask about the content of the ceremony, and in a number of cases they have quietly contributed to the planning of a "halakhically sensitive" commitment ritual.

My hope is that by exploring the details of praxis—in this case, those of the traditional Jewish wedding—and by considering their relevance (or lack thereof) to same-sex coupling, we may be able to tease out some interesting insights in regard to both homosexuality and marriage. At the very least, by beginning with the formal and liturgical questions involved in the creation of a same-sex wedding ritual, we will be able to clarify our terms, deepen our questions, and provide a much richer frame for the consideration of same-sex marriage.[1]

Deconstructing the Dish

The traditional Jewish wedding has a warm and venerable feel to it, and taking it apart in order to better understand it can be a bit demystifying. Many rabbis who conduct Jewish weddings and employ the traditional marital rituals have actively ignored their historical origins, consciously filling them with new meanings or slightly modifying them in order to make them consonant with contemporary experience. This ahistorical sleight-of-hand has helped to construct the Jewish wedding as a beautiful and unassailable black box.

Although the loss of naïveté required may be disenchanting to some, unpacking the structural and liturgical elements of these rituals will offer us an unusual opportunity to think about the possible meanings of marriage and to replace our shared confusion with a bit more understanding. In order to do this, we will first ground the conversation with a description of the structure of the traditional Jewish wedding ceremony and the basics of each ritual, and then we will return to each component and ask whether and how it might apply to same-sex couples.[2]

There are two rituals and one legal document that make up a Jewish wedding. They are the espousal ceremony called *erusin*, the nuptial celebration called *nisuin*, and the marriage contract called the *ketubah*. Formally speaking, *erusin* made a woman prohibited sexually to the world and *nisuin* permitted her to her husband. Once *erusin* was contracted, no other man could preempt the husband. Initially, *erusin* and *nisuin* were distinct rituals commonly separated by a full year, during which time families devoted themselves to preparing the dowry, the wedding banquet, and the couple's future home. Sexual relations were not permitted to the espoused couple until the completion of the *nisuin*.[3] The rabbis commonly referred to the *erusin* as *kiddushin*, meaning "sanctification," and the *nisuin* as *huppah*, meaning "canopy." In the twelfth century, the time lapse between the espousal and the nuptials was removed and these two rituals were fused together into a single matrimonial ceremony.

The *Erusin*

The *erusin* begins with two blessings: the first is the standard blessing recited upon wine and the second is the espousal blessing proper (*birkat erusin*).[4] "Blessed are you Lord, ruler of the universe, who has sanctified us by his commandments, and commanded us regarding forbidden connections and has forbidden us those who are merely espoused, but has permitted to us those lawfully married to us by *huppah* and *kiddushin*. Blessed are you, O Lord, who sanctifies his people Israel by means of *huppah* and *kiddushin*." This blessing is obviously said by or for the groom, the "us" being a collective reference to Israelite men. The blessing appears to have been instituted as a warning to couples who might otherwise have engaged in sexual relations during the original time lag between the two ceremonies.[5]

The *erusin* itself consists of an act by which the groom gives an object of value to his bride. Traditionally, he puts a ring (which he owns) on the right forefinger of the bride and recites the following statement: "Behold you are sanctified to me by this ring according to the laws of Moses and Israel." By accepting and so acquiring the ring, the bride gives to her groom exclusive access to her sexual body. She is now sexually off limits to all other men. Were the couple to recant at this point, a legal divorce

would be required. Fundamentally, the marriage is enacted by this transfer. The act must be initiated by the man and responded to freely by a
woman before witnesses. It is by definition a public affirmation that both
parties have knowingly and voluntarily entered into a marriage contract
with one another.

The legal means by which the espousal is contracted is acquisition. The
word used in Deut. 22:13 for taking a wife (*kihah*) is the same word used
in Gen. 23:13 for Abraham's "acquiring" the Cave of Machpelah. The
Mishna introduces the tractate of *Kiddushin* by telling us that "a woman
can be acquired (*kinyan*) by money, written document, or sexual intercourse."[6] Witnesses were required for all three methods. Because of the
immodesty of arranging for witnesses, sexual intercourse was essentially
eradicated by later authorities as a means of realizing a marriage contract.
The standard marriage ceremony was initiated by the transfer of an
object of value, typically a ring, from one party to another. The act is
unilateral and the man is the sole initiator of the transaction. Were a
woman to "take" a man by the same ritual formula (reciting the formula
of "Behold you are sanctified to me . . ." and the giving of a ring), the act
would have no halakhic meaning.[7] It is clear that he is buying and she is
selling—but exactly what is up for sale and what is meant by ownership in
this circumstance?

Because, formally speaking, ownership is about rights, one might say
that the husband acquires certain rights in relation to his wife's body.
Following the *erusin*, he "owns" an aspect of her body (of which he cannot
partake until after the *nisuin*). However, this is a very unusual sort of
ownership. When one owns an object, one has the right to do with it
whatever one wants, to restrict others from its use, to loan it to someone,
or to give it away.[8] This is not the case with a wife. A wife is not like a loaf
of bread that may be shared with others.[9] Moreover, the law does not
permit a husband to force his wife to engage in sexual intercourse. If she
refuses, he may try to seduce her, but he is not permitted to force her.
Moreover, whether he has desire or not, he is obligated to satisfy his wife's
sexual needs, at the very least once weekly. The ownership that *erusin* confers is neither absolute nor conventional.

Because the marital bond could not be understood as an ordinary form
of chattel ownership, the rabbis appear to have associated the woman's
change of status with another ritual metaphor, that of the sanctification
of property—*hekdesh*. Any person was free to make a pledge to give an
object or animal to the Temple by means of simple statement. Once ut-
tered, the object becomes *hekdesh*, the sanctified property of God, and
could not be used for any secular purpose. It is forbidden to the world and
permitted only to the custodians of the Temple. *Kiddushin*, like *hekdesh*,
is a method of transformation, a formula for the creation of something

holy. By an act of *kiddushin*, a woman's sexuality becomes *hekdesh*, sanctified and therefore off limits to all men other than her husband.

Nothing about the man's body is articulated by this traditional ritual. Her status changes, his does not. He is formally free to take other wives. Adultery is only the wife's sexual disloyalty. A married man may be branded a degenerate or a cad by the community, but his extramarital affairs with unmarried women are not formally considered adultery. Originally, polygamy was permitted to those men with the means to support and sexually satisfy more than one wife. Despite the formal permission, the norm throughout Jewish history was essentially monogamous, in part due to the pragmatic difficulties of sustaining multiple wives. For example, there is no evidence of a single rabbi in either the Jerusalem or the Babylonian Talmud having had more than one wife. Later in the twelfth century, under the influence of Christian custom and around the time that the ideals of romantic love were being popularized by troubadours in France, Jewish religious authorities began to strongly discourage and then finally to prohibit the practice of polygamy.[10]

Consequently, today, when a groom gives his bride a ring, he too is being formally limited to a single partner. So although the act is technically unilateral, the consequences are not. Still, the fundamental legal roots of *kiddushin*, even if they have been largely reduced to a metaphor, are deeply morally troublesome to the egalitarian sensibilities of many. And whether offensive or not, the unilateral nature of the ceremony is out of touch, not reflective of the actual social, economic, and emotional partnership that most contemporary couples wish to achieve."

The *Ketubah*

Following the *erusin* and before the *nisuin*, a marriage contract, called a *ketubah*, already drafted, signed, and witnessed, is given by the groom to the bride. The rabbis initiated the requirement of the *ketubah* in order to protect women from the unfettered male powers embedded in the inherited institution. Both prerogatives, that of marriage and that of divorce, were to be initiated by men. One needed a woman's consent to contract a marriage; but a divorce could be effected by a man even against a woman's will. Because few premodern women could earn a living wage, the sale of her pristine sexuality to a man who would support her for life was perhaps a woman's most fundamental power. Once her virginity was given away, a woman was particularly vulnerable to a husband's whims. Because a man was legally free to divorce his wife for any reason, a woman could easily find herself divorced, destitute, and practically without hope for remarriage. This problem so deeply concerned the rabbis that they created a disincentive for husbands to summarily divorce their wives by binding them to a contract to pay a sizable sum of money in just such a case.

The contract, called a *ketubah*, is not a marriage contract per se. It is an agreement that roughly delineates the duties of both parties in the marriage, marks the monies brought into the union by each side, and specifically obligates the husband to pay the wife prescribed sums of money in the event of divorce or of his decease. After the *ketubah* is read and handed over to the woman, the second portion of the wedding ceremony, the *nisuin*, begins.

The *Nisuin*

The *nisuin* is a public accompaniment of the couple to their shared domicile, an affirmation of the beginning of their intimate life together, and a celebration of their union with family and friends. The *nisuin* is marked by seven blessings that speak of the creation of human beings in God's image, Adam and Eve brought together in the Garden of Eden, and the future restoration of Zion in joy and delight. After the wedding blessings are recited, the groom breaks a glass to signify that the joy of the wedding does not completely erase the sadness of the destruction of Jerusalem and the Holy Temple, and with this gesture to the brokenness of life, the music, dancing, and celebration begin.

Following this ceremony, the couple is permitted and indeed enjoined to share sexual intimacy. Originally, the couple was accompanied to the groom's home or to a colorfully decorated tent symbolizing the groom's domicile, where the consummation of the marriage took place. Eventually, more delicate sensibilities determined that a symbolic nuptial chamber would be preferable and a canopy on four poles was substituted for the real thing. However, because there was still a need for a more private encounter (even if it did not include the first sexual intercourse), after the *nisuin* the couple is ushered into a private room where they can be alone together, unchaperoned, for the first time. It is a symbolic beginning of their now fully sanctioned sexual intimacy.

This is the essential format of the traditional Jewish wedding. Liberal rabbis have introduced egalitarian modifications of various sorts into the service, but despite these attempts, the fundamental legal structure of *kiddushin* has largely been retained. What elements of this service ought to be adopted by gay couples seeking a commitment ritual?

In order to create an appropriate gay wedding ceremony we will need to pay attention to the appropriateness of the various legal and liturgical elements but also to the implicit conceptual frames that give marriage substance. So, let us revisit the *erusin*, the *ketubah*, and the *nisuin* in order to imagine their relevance to gay coupling and commitment.

Erusin Revisited

The central legal engine of *erusin* is acquisition. Women are acquired by men through *kiddushin*, men are not acquired by women. Initially, the bride price was a serious sum of money, but eventually the real purchase became symbolic as the hefty sum was replaced with a token gift worth not less than the lowest coin of the realm. Still, the metaphoric frame of *erusin*, the idea of "buying" a wife, even if only a symbolic act, is surely disturbing for contemporary sensibilities, straight or gay. Liberal rabbis who use *kiddushin*, as well as some Modern Orthodox rabbis, make efforts to mask the origins of the rituals by adding elements to the ring ceremony.

Traditionally, the man places the ring on the woman's finger and says, "By this ring be thou sanctified unto me [i.e., You are exclusively mine] according to the laws of Moses and Israel." In order to create a greater sense of mutuality, Liberal rabbis innovated an exchange of rings. Non-Orthodox rabbis have made the mutuality total by having the woman use the same language that the man uses, "Be thou sanctified unto me . . ." For Orthodox rabbis, however, the double-ring ceremony is particularly problematic because if rings are exchanged in succession, then technically speaking no *kiddushin* has occurred. No transaction, no change of status, is effected because the parties have simply traded gifts, a ring for a ring. Some Modern Orthodox rabbis have tried to retain the one-sided halakhic act of acquisition while providing a sense of mutuality by adding a second ring ceremony later in the service, during which the bride gives the groom a ring and says a beautiful, if legally inconsequential, line from the Song of Songs such as "I am my beloved's and my beloved is mine" (6:3).

Jewish feminists have challenged not only the cosmetic adjustments of Modern Orthodox rabbis, but even the adjustments of Liberal rabbis, claiming that they do not address the fundamental problem of acquisition. According to Rachel Adler, the unilateral nature of the *kiddushin* is not the only problem. The problem of *kiddushin* rests as well in its fundamental legal ground as a purchase.[11] If Adler is right, then the double-ring ceremony, well-meaning as it may be, does not solve the problem. The adding of the bride's gift of a ring to the groom only responds to the dilemma of one commodification by adding another. In Adler's view, mutual dehumanization will not heal the ritual.

Adler's critique makes a good deal of sense, especially for gay and lesbian Jews. Even if heterosexuals might want to sustain the frameworks of *kiddushin*, why should gay couples do so? Because there is no venerable tradition of same-sex union upon which to build and no gender difference to enact ritually, however benignly, why would gay couples want to adopt *kiddushin*? Given that there are no traditions in regard to same-sex unions, why not be totally free to choose a mode of effecting and celebrating our unions that has no taint of inequality or commodification?

The question to ask at this point is why the sages of the Talmud employed the language of acquisition in the first place. Might the metaphor of ownership be more than a remnant of patriarchal domination? Despite the moral pitfalls of the language, it may be that marriage is bound up in ownership because, for all its uncomfortable associations, it still comes closest to what couples intend. The giving of oneself and especially one's sexual body to another in love is often articulated as a belonging. "You are mine" is what we mean when we give a ring. "I am yours" is what we mean when we let our partner place it on our finger.

Different couples imagine different sorts of relationships when they marry. They may or may not share their finances; they may or may not be able to live full-time in the same city; they may or may not have other families demanding of their time and money. But whatever couples may mean by their commitments in marriage, they are always committing to an exclusivity of a sort. Or to put it another way, although loving one person does not preclude loving another, in marriage we delineate a sort of access to our heart and to our body that cannot be shared with others outside the marital relationship.

Marrying is not like making a best friend or acquiring the perfect business partner or roommate. It is about a union that is unique and unlike all others. Although various cultures (and individuals) have marked the violation of exclusiveness at different points on a continuum from eye contact to sexual intercourse, the meaning of marriage is surely bound up in some mix of sexual and emotional exclusivity.

Marital ownership/exclusivity was once one-sided. Men "owned" women. What happens to the notion of ownership when it is mutually agreed on and mutually undertaken in love, when both "own" each other? Bilateral ownership may well transform the relationship from one of patriarchal possession and control into one of profound solidarity.

Monogamy in biblical tradition was primarily a limit in regard to female sexuality. If both parties are indeed "sanctified" to the other, then there would be no room for non-monogamous frames of marriage for either partner. Some members of the gay community have claimed that this restriction is a feature of heterosexual marriage that ought not to be carried into gay marriage. The structure of the *kiddushin*, as focused as it is on the giving over of one's sexual body exclusively to one and only one partner, would not tolerate such notions of open marriage.

Given this understanding of *kiddushin*, gay couples committing to an exclusive relationship may be inclined to appropriate the *kiddushin* ritual and give two separate gifts of a ring, each accompanied by the formal sanctification, "Behold, you are consecrated to me by this ring according to laws of Moses and Israel." Because at present there is no widely accepted Mosaic or rabbinic rule that could be said to ground this sort of "*kiddushin*" ritual for gay couples, it may be best to exclude the latter phrase. However, this excision leaves a significant vacancy in the ritual. The phrase "according to the laws of Moses and Israel" lets us know that the words spoken and the commitments undertaken have a social context and sanction in a particular community. Marriage as an institution has little meaning unless there is a communal administration of some sort within which it makes a difference. Unfortunately, we cannot already have what we are in the process of building. Because we are only now creating the norms and the community that will take same-sex marriage seriously, we cannot now have the authority we seek. In the meantime, couples belonging to religious communities that support same-sex marriage might add "according to the custom of . . ." and add whatever synagogue or communal or religious body is the acting authority.

Another possibility is to contextualize the commitment in a much more personal way by adding the phrase "before my family, my friends, and my God." The advantage is that this works without any real communal sanction and that it rings true to many people that what is most important to them is that their commitment be honored both by their close associates and by God. Its weakness is that it is so personal that it lacks any frame of convention. Were the couple to change their minds the next morning, they could, in fact, part without a trace, having nothing but their own feelings to which to be held accountable.

This is one of the most difficult aspects of social change. It demands the capacity to act before a stage has been built, to be without any context, indeed to do in order to weave the very context that will make being possible. Dramatic social change always includes a fantasy. It demands that one behave as if the redemption has already come. Gay couples are "marrying" in order to create the very possibility of same-sex marriage as a cultural and legal reality. As such, while there is no "administration" of gay marriage, no solid ground of social or legal responsibility to which to be held accountable, the oath taken before friends, family, and God may be the closest frame to duty that can be mustered.

In the absence of an administration that defines the terms of commitment formally undertaken at a wedding and enforces them, at the very least it would seem important to ensure that both parties actually understand what they can expect from one another, what they are committing to one another before God. In this circumstance, a more specific delineation of the contracted rights and duties to which both parties have agreed would seem to be an important part of the formal ritual. Were couples to entertain such a formulation, then there would be a need for a document drafted by both parties in advance that would address the details. Were such a document drafted, then each member of the couple in turn could place a ring on the partner's finger and say, "Behold, you are consecrated to me by this ring according to the promises I made to you."

Ketubah Revisited

The *ketubah* essentially accomplishes two tasks: it protects the woman from a man's power to summarily divorce his wife on a whim, and it sets out the obligations of each party. The standard *ketubah* requires the groom to promise one hundred silver pieces in the event of divorce or death. The bride is expected to bring from her family a dowry valued at one hundred silver pieces and the groom is to add to her dowry another one hundred silver pieces of his own. In total, every couple was expected to begin their lives together with two hundred silver pieces, and were he to divorce her, she would receive all three hundred silver pieces in the settlement. The protections of the *ketubah* were noble when they were enacted, but in practice contemporary U.S. divorce law exceeds these stipulations.

In addition to financial matters, duties and obligations of other sorts are recorded. He obligates himself to pay for her food and clothing and provide for her sexual needs, and she is expected to serve him and create a household according to "the custom of Jewish wives." The specific delineation of duties in the *ketubah* is highly gender role-determined and would not be typical or representative of the nature of marriage for many contemporary couples.

Historically, the *ketubah* was a template that was often modified to meet differing sorts of individual contractual interests. When the couples wished to stipulate duties and freedoms different from the norm, they were free, within certain limits, to change the language of the *ketubah*. A woman was free to ask that her *ketubah* specify that she would not do specific household chores and would instead contribute to the household income from her own resources, or she could ask for a stipulation that she be free to visit her family so many times a year and so on. These stipulations portray a male-dominant cultural norm in which a woman might easily be prevented from visiting her parents or siblings by her new husband and so might feel the need to make such interests explicit and contractually binding. Details of this sort, which helped to clarify the specifics of the particular relationship, were commonly worked out by families and by the couple in advance.

Heterosexual Orthodox couples desiring an egalitarian relationship still employ the standard *ketubah* in the interests of hallowing the rabbinic tradition. They adopt the form but not the social message. But it would make little sense for traditional gay and lesbian couples to follow suit.

Whether heterosexual couples find the patriarchal sex-role divisions problematic or not, gay couples simply do not have such gender distinctions to address, nor any long history of traditional ritual to honor. So if gay Jews choose not to use the *ketubah*, should another sort of document replace it? How should same-sex couples specify the duties and expectations of their relationships?

We could just dispense with the *ketubah* and its delineation of specifics altogether. It is common for marrying couples today to structure their own vows, which serves a similar purpose. Personal vows of love and commitment can be romantic and powerful, even if they are legally inconsequential. No one could take an ordinary wedding vow to court to prosecute for satisfaction of the terms, claiming the party of the first part did not fulfill "to have and to hold." Contemporary weddings are highly melodramatic affairs that speak grandiosely about romantic love, but whose formal commitments are vague—calling parties "to love, protect, and cherish" each other "till death do us part." The question that rarely gets answered at weddings is "What exactly are these two people committing to?"

Now, it may be that vagueness is an unavoidable element, or even a necessary feature of marital commitment. Marriage is the sort of commitment that grounds itself in persons rather than in a set of well-defined contracted duties, and for good reason. The full set of obligations that will ensue over a lifetime following the "I do" can never be anticipated, much less delineated. Love commits us to duties whose specifications we cannot know in advance. However true it is that a vow of love cannot be fully quantified into a set of actions, the modern penchant for sentiment over content may still be a disingenuous way to avoid the fact that duties contracted must be fulfilled no matter what one happens to be feeling. Feelings inaugurate our commitment to action; we do not commit to feel, we commit to do. If so, then what sort of marriage contract ought we to draw up? How do we formally articulate what we mean by marriage?

Of course, we may well need to invent totally new ways of contracting our love relationships. Rachel Adler has suggested the use of a legally binding relation described in the halakhah that is fully mutual and beyond gender, that of legal partnership.[12] Partners in an economic enterprise are *shutafim* in Hebrew. They are bound to each other in a mutual fashion and can obligate themselves in specific ways as determined by their agreement. Such a contract, a *shtar shutafut*, could replace the *ketubah*. It would mark the establishment of the partnership and stipulate the duties that both enjoined upon each other. Partnership was traditionally accomplished by each party putting assets into a bag and lifting it together, symbolizing the joining together of their individual properties into a single enterprise. This ritual might be added to the giving of rings as a formal way to mark the joining of two households into one and not the adoption of a woman into the household of a man. The text would stipulate the duties and obligations of each partner to the other that emerge from their shared love. Both would sign it along with witnesses. It would provide couples an opportunity to discuss in advance many sensitive concerns and allow them to construct a partnership to fit their unique circumstances. As well, the document ought to stipulate how the relationship may be terminated and under what conditions.

Shutafut is a model of formally and legally delineating what, in fact, a union demands of each partner. It marks a full disclosure of assets and sets up a clear set of commitments for two parties to join their resources together for the purpose of creating a shared home. Interestingly, the sages considered partnership to be more than the giving over of financial resources toward a shared endeavor. A medieval halakhic authority, Rabbi Abraham ben David Zimri (referred to as the Ra'avad), uses astonishing language to describe business partnership. Each party in a partnership, he suggests, becomes an *eved ivri*, a Jewish slave, to the other. Conceptually, Jewish slavery was a world apart from its harsh Roman counterpart or from the brutality of the European colonial slavery of Africans. For example, the halakhah obligated a master to give a slave food and lodging that was qualitatively similar to his or her own. Even so, the notion of partnership as slavery is surely jarring. However, here again, the mutuality of servitude transforms the very notion of slavery into something very different. Similar to the double-ring ceremony of *erusin*, the mutuality of slavery makes both parties slave and master, transforming a hierarchical relationship into a relationship with a profound union of rights and obligations. Each party enters into such a relationship knowing that he or she will serve and be served in love. Perhaps this is the deeper meaning of "I am my beloved's and my beloved is mine" (Song of Sol. 6:3).

It is customary in the establishment of a partnership (*shutafut*) that each party put something of value into a bag and then both lift the bag to inaugurate their joining together in a shared enterprise. This ritual marks the fact that the resources of two people are being pooled in the service of their new partnership. In order to situate this ritual in a more personal rather than merely businesslike context, it may be helpful to ask each partner to recite the line "I am my beloved's and my beloved is mine" from the Song of Sol. 6:3, which captures the ideas of partnership, mutual belonging, sexual exclusivity, and love, all in one.

The *erusin* is the decisive act of marriage. It is about the closing off of options. For some people, the choice of marriage is an act of determined ferociousness, a killing off of a myriad of potential lives in order to actually live one life. *Erusin* is the formal relinquishing of the infinite possibilities that loving one person uniquely demands. This sort of commitment entails a reckoning with mortality and a welcoming of finitude. Of course, a new—and in its own way infinite—territory is born by the decision to love one person. The joy of this new world is at the center of the *nisuin*.

Nisuin Revisited

Originally, the *nisuin* was the communal accompaniment of the bride to the home of the groom, the public recitation of the seven wedding blessings, the privacy of the couple (and originally the consummation), followed by the banquet. During the twelfth century, the canopy was instituted as a symbolic groom's domicile and in lieu of the couple's first consummation, the bride and groom are ushered into a private room in which they can share a few intimate moments behind a closed door before joining their guests at the banquet.

The *nisuin* is the joyous part of marriage. It is the ceremony that formally permits the bride and groom to be physically intimate with each other. If *erusin* is about sexual restriction, then *nisuin* is about sexual expression. The *erusin* moves from the public toward the private, while the *nisuin* moves from the private back to the public. The *erusin* is a segregation, the *nisuin* an inclusion, a weaving of the personal into the communal, by public acknowledgment and joyous celebration. This inauguration of the most intimate element of a couple's shared life is celebrated with family and friends amid dancing, music, and a lavish feast.

Last, the *nisuin* provides the cosmic frame for the whole affair. A wedding is about much more than the romantic joining of two lovers. It is about marking the love of two people as part of heaven's greater purposes. At the center of the *nisuin* is a story, a narrative that holds the power of what we are doing. If we are celebrating the love of two people, then a party will do. If we are tracing the lines in some grander plot in which the love of two is situated, then we have more solid ground for spiritual depth.

The master story of the traditional wedding is conveyed with the seven blessings chanted under the *huppah* before family and friends. They are arguably the most beautiful part of the service.

1. Blessed are You, Lord our God, Ruler of the universe, who created the fruit of the vine.

2. Blessed are You, Lord our God, Ruler of the universe, who created everything for your glory.

3. Blessed are You, Lord our God, Ruler of the universe, shaper of humanity.

4. Blessed are You, Lord our God, Ruler of the universe, who has shaped human beings in his image, an image patterned after his likeness, and established from within it a perpetuation of itself. Blessed are You, Lord, shaper of humanity.

5. May the barren one exult and be glad as her children are joyfully gathered to her. Blessed are You, Lord, who gladdens Israel with her children.

6. Grant great joy to these loving friends as You once gladdened Your creations in the Garden of Eden. Blessed are You, Lord, who gladdens the groom and bride.

7. Blessed are You, Lord our God, Ruler of the universe, who created joy and gladness, groom and bride, merriment, song, pleasure and delight, love and harmony, peace and companionship. Lord, our God, may there soon be heard in the cities of Judah and the streets of Jerusalem the voice of joy and the voice of gladness, the voice of the groom and the voice of the bride, the rapturous voices of grooms from their bridal chambers, and of young people feasting and singing. Blessed are You, Lord, who gladdens the groom together with the bride.

The first blessing over wine is the way the tradition inaugurates joyous celebrations. The second and third blessings introduce the theme of creation. The second blessing is surprisingly apt for a same-sex wedding. It affirms that everything, perhaps even same-sex love, was created for the glory of God. The third blessing honors the creation of the human being. This blessing surely could be contextualized to apply well enough to gay weddings. However, we will soon see that the themes of creation are particularly relevant to straight weddings.

The next four blessings open up increasingly larger circles of relationship, carrying the love of two into ever more expansive frames of reference. Blessing four is about planting within the human body the power to reproduce. One of the obvious ways that marriage expands the love of two is through family. The duty to reproduce is the first commandment of the Torah. It is considered an affirmation of God's creation to participate in the refurbishment of humanity.

Blessing five is both about children and about the redemptive renewal of Zion in the end of days, when our mother Sarah, the once barren one, will rejoice in the return of her children to the land of Israel. Especially for Jews, family is the foundation of the covenantal promise. God takes Abraham outside and says, "Look up to the heavens, and count the stars if you can . . . so shall be your children" (Gen. 15:5). The Jewish people is a chain of generations all bearing an ancient covenant with God begun with Abraham and Sarah. Jesus made disciples to carry his message; Abraham and Sarah made a baby.

Marriage extends the love of two outward, beyond the family to the community. The stability of community is aided by the fact that the disruptive power of sexual self-interest has been largely neutralized by marriage. Communities of singles are much more unstable, much more transient, and less prone to sinking roots in a particular place or building lasting institutions. Although this is surely a generalization to which there are exceptions, monogamous marriage is how sexuality can be given its due so that other socially constructive efforts can proceed more smoothly.

The focus of romantic love is narrow. In its most frantic tropes, romantic passion utterly abandons the world. *Nisuin* articulates the love of two not only as a turning inward, but also as a reaching outward toward others. It is a pious custom for brides and grooms to walk down the aisle toward the *huppah* reciting psalms and praying for the needs of others. The turning away from the self at this moment is deemed so powerful that heaven cannot help but answer these prayers.

The last two blessings draw an even wider circle beyond the Jewish people to include the world. Blessing six refers to the bride and groom as loving friends. It is a beautiful expression that suggests an emotional bond quite distinct from the patriarchal role divisions of the *ketubah*.[13] The blessing continues and reminds us that every groom and bride are Adam and Eve in Eden. They reframe every straight wedding as a return to Paradise. Were the world to end and leave only the bride and groom, humanity could begin again. The wedding ritual marks every straight wedding as a reenactment of the beginnings of humanity. Mystically, to witness a wedding is to see a glimpse of Eden, the very beginning when human loneliness was healed in the union of Adam and Eve.

Blessing seven is based on the prophecy of Jeremiah following the destruction of Judea in 586 BCE. Amid the ruins of the destroyed capital city, he promises that a day will come when there will again be singing and dancing in the streets of Jerusalem. He tells of wedding revelry and the sounds of children playing in the street. In Jeremiah's mythic frame, every straight wedding becomes a promise of a rebuilt Jerusalem, of a perfected world, more real and more attainable because it speaks not only of the lives present, but also of the generations to come that will be born out of this very moment. At every heterosexual wedding we are witnesses to the beginning and the end of time; we are carried back to Eden and forward to a Jerusalem rebuilt in joy and gladness, pleasure and delight, love and harmony, peace and companionship.

As beautiful and moving as these marital narratives are, they cannot be appropriated for a gay wedding because they do not constitute a gay story. The first few blessings might be salvaged, though by themselves they do not tell us what a gay wedding is, and the last four blessings do not seem right at all for same-sex weddings. Though gay couples are able to raise families, gay unions do not revisit Adam and Eve and the birth of life itself, nor do they promise the physical continuity toward the redeemed Jerusalem that Jeremiah envisioned. The linking of the generations past and future to a same-sex couple underneath the canopy is, at best, much less obvious. We must find more apt images and metaphors for gay love and commitment, not only for the love of truth, but for the realness and power of the moment that we are celebrating. The poignancy of the moment for straight couples works because the metaphors are experientially genuine, mythically alive, and emotionally compelling. To employ them when they are not cheapens what is actually true and wondrous about same-sex marriage.

In straight marriage, God is linking the generations, connecting us all to our ancestors and to our future progeny, to Eden and Jerusalem. What is God up to in gay marriage that could be honored and celebrated? In fact, the question may be asked even more boldly: What are homosexuals here for? What larger purpose do we suppose God may have in mind for gay people? Is there an inherited sacred narrative that may frame gay love as part of God's great plan? Of course, there is no ready-made biblical narrative. A historically reviled sexuality cannot easily find its holy way. However, there is a sliver of the creation story, an interpretive midrash of the rabbis, and a mystical ritual that may offer a possibility.

In the Beginning

The heterosexual focus of the creation story begins with Adam and Eve. Our starting point will be God and the origins, not of gender, but of partnership. Before creation, God alone fills existence. God's oneness is without division or separation. One is always all-powerful without needing any power-over to be so. One is stable and sure, unchanging and whole. The seed of creation is the idea of more than one. At the moment of creation, the magisterial oneness of God, according to Jewish mystics, concentrated itself to leave room for an-other. Creation begins with the possibility of two.

Two are a rickety thing, a temptation, a suspicious thing, an ecstatic, thrilling, dangerous thing. Two always have a history. The pain and pleasure of difference, the tragedy and glory of the lines that separate things, are the subtext of the first chapters of Genesis. Separation between things inaugurates creation. Light and dark, day and night, the waters below and above, the dry land and the seas are all separated. It is by these separations that creation unfolds. Much as the infant separates first physically and then psychically from its mother, little by little, the world comes to be by separations amid the chaos.

However, twos pose a problem. Separation is a birth pang that passes, but once there are two, how are they to relate? On the third day of creation, two great lights are created. The Hebrew word for lights (*meorot*) is missing a letter in the plural ending. The missing letter is not crucial for the meaning of the word, but the irregularity seems to suggest that something is wrong.

The sages explain that the pair of lights, the sun and the moon, was unstable in a way related to their being two. This twin creation became so highly problematic that God had to alter the original plan.

On the third day, we are told, God made the sun and the moon. "And God made the two great lights, the greater light to rule the day and the lesser light to rule the night, and the stars" (Gen. 1:16). Thus, after introducing the sun and the moon both as great, the text adds that, actually, one light was great and the other was lesser. The contradiction between the verses generated a legend that is recorded in the Talmud.

> "And God made the two great lights," but later it says: "the great light and the lesser light"! The moon said before the Holy One: Master of the world, is it possible for two kings to share (literally: to use) one crown? God said to her: Go and diminish yourself! She said before God: Because I asked a good question, I should diminish myself? God said: Go and rule both in day and in night. She said: What advantage is that? A candle in the daylight is useless. God said: Go and let Israel count their days and years by you. She said: They use the daylight [of the sun] to count seasonal cycles as well. . . . Seeing that she was not appeased, the Holy One said: Bring a (sacrificial) atonement for me that I diminished the moon! This is what R. Shimon ben Lakish said: What is different about the sacrifice (lit. ram) of the new moon that it is offered "for God" ["And one ram of the flock for a sin offering for God" (Num. 28:14) meaning for God's sin]? Said the Holy One: This ram shall be an atonement for me that I diminished the moon.[14]

The problem of two great rulers sharing a single crown is a problem that God does not anticipate. The problem is raised by the moon, and the Creator solves the problem with a fixed hierarchy. The moon complains that she got the raw end of the deal just for asking a tough question, one that ostensibly might have been thought out in advance by the Creator. Failing to appease her, God accepts the duty to offer a sin offering on the occasion of every new moon, a monthly atonement for the lesser status he forced on her.

The moon's diminishment is understood by the sages as a sin committed against the moon for which God asks to atone. The midrash is an invitation by the rabbis to project a world of restored harmony and equality. A liturgy of sanctifying the new moon was begun in Talmudic times and embellished by later mystical traditions. If God brings a sacrificial atonement for the diminishment of the moon, then there must be some desire on high to truly repent of the wrong done to her. The laws of repentance require it. We learn that there is no forgiveness for sins between parties until the offended party has been appeased. A sacrifice alone cannot right a wrong done. Implicit in the midrash of the first century is Rabbi Isaac Luria's prayer, *Kiddush Levanah,* for the moon's restoration.

Restoring the Moon: The Ritual of *Kiddush Levanah*

The monthly Jewish ritual of the sanctification of the new moon, *Kiddush Levanah*, is recited during the waxing phase of the lunar cycle.[15] Commonly, the prayer is said at the conclusion of the Sabbath falling during this period. On this Saturday evening following the end of the prayer service, the congregation files outdoors and, underneath a visible moon, chants *Kiddush Levanah*. The sources of the first paragraph are biblical and rabbinic, but the messianic prayer that follows is pure Jewish mysticism:

> They taught in the school of Rabbi Yishmael: Were Israel able to greet their Father in heaven only once a month, it would be enough. Abaye says: For this reason it should be said standing.[16] "Who is she, coming up from the desert, leaning on her lover?" (Song of Sol. 8:5)

> May it be your will, O Lord, my God and the God of my fathers to fill in the darkness of the moon that she not be diminished at all. And let the light of the moon be as the light of the sun, and as the light of the seven days of creation, just as she was before she was diminished, as it is said: "the two great lights." And may we be a fulfillment of the verse: "And they shall seek out the Lord their God and David their king." (Hosea 3:5) Amen.[17]

This tradition of the moon's diminution and its future restoration in the world to come is explicitly understood by Rashi, the most famous of medieval Jewish exegetes, as a veiled reference to women. He says that in the world to come, women will be renewed like the new moon.[18] This prayer, chanted before a waxing moon, imagines an increasing feminine light that will someday be restored to its full equality with the masculine light. If God atones for diminishing the moon and for the subjugation of Eve to Adam after the sin in the garden, then the way things are is not the way things ought to be or ultimately will be. The disharmonies that attended the banishment from Eden, the conflict between humans and the natural world, and the hierarchy of the sexes, these are just the beginning of a great drama, the last act of which will include God's joyous restoration of the moon.

Perhaps the place to end our same-sex marriage narrative is with the restoration of the moon and the healing of the hierarchy between men and women so apparent in the traditional wedding service. The ancient story of the moon's diminution and our monthly prayer for her renewal and restoration is already an established and venerable element of *Kiddush Levanah*, introduced into Jewish custom by mystics of the sixteenth century. It is a beautiful ritual, full of dramatic imagery and power of its own. Its relationship to gay marriage is twofold.

The moon is a veiled reference to the feminine in the world, or perhaps, as mystics might say, to the feminine face of God, the *Shekhinah*. Our prayer for its restoration is our hope that we have indeed learned how two can rule with one crown, the sharing of power without hierarchy. Perhaps this is what God ought to have said to the moon in the first place, unless of course, this is the sort of knowledge that can only be acquired over time, a great deal of time, and at great cost. Only the fullest of loves makes it possible for two to rule with one crown. In this midrash we are offered an image of a love beyond gender that embodies neither submission nor domination, but equality and partnership. Might it be that gay relationships are a harbinger of the moon's restoration, a forward guard to the coming redemption?

Remarkably, this text provides a narrative that also carries us back to both themes of creation and redemption. Although gay unions may not recapitulate creation and redemption in the same way that heterosexual unions do, it appears that the same two tropes are there after all. Straight unions are about the love of Adam and Eve that bears new life. Gay unions are about the flaws of the creation that we are called upon to fix. Gay couples, who by definition cannot employ the scaffold of patriarchy to work out their power arrangements, have little choice but to learn how to share a single crown. Whereas straight unions offer a promise of a future redemption in flesh and blood, gay unions help to pave the way for us to heal the very problem of difference, and in a gesture no less redemptive than the rebuilding of Jerusalem, to restore the moon to her former glory.

In practice, the ritual of *Kiddush Levanah* includes the giving and receiving of peace. Under the faintest sliver of the moon's white crescent, each of those assembled blesses the new moon and then turns to one another and says, "*shalom aleichem,*" peace be unto you, to which a reverse greeting is returned, "*aleichem shalom,*" unto you be peace. This greeting of peace is shared with three different people and often with a clasping of hands, so while one is seeking three different people to greet, one is being greeted by others. The effect is a moment of communal bonding that is overtly mutual and about the interplay between giving and receiving. What better way to articulate the communal effect of marriage than to spread out its hope of peace and love between two toward the whole community.

The mystical prayer for the restoration of the moon serves as a foil to the degradations of the biblical creation story that unconsciously inhabit the traditional wedding. Before the first couple leaves the garden, Eve's destiny is set in both desire and subjugation: "Your urge shall be for your husband and he shall rule over you" (Gen. 3:16b). For thousands of years, the ongoing punishment of Eve has become Adam's abiding interest prettified by gowns and flowers. *Kiddush Levanah* reveals the fractures of the story, grasps them as a challenge to God's goodness that will in time be fixed, and calls on us to insure that the love we honor at a wedding will be shared with the wisdom of heart by which two can rule with a single crown.

While there are surely other creative ways to conduct a Jewish same-sex wedding, this sort of religious inquiry has, I hope, demonstrated how a close reading of wedding traditions can help to clarify what we mean by love, sex, gender, sanctity, and most important, marriage. Ought marriage rituals to sustain or resist the traditional gender role division? How far ought contemporaries to take their commitment to gender equality? Does marriage by definition entail a commitment to monogamy or may couples opt out of monogamy? What, if anything, does marriage have to do with children? Are there specific duties that couples undertake to perform for one another and should they be explicit? Are there understood terms of release from the marital promises and should they be spelled out? What, if any, are the extended familial, communal, and religious responsibilities entailed by marriage? And last, in what ways might gay coupling differ in any of these matters?

By choosing the exclusive and monogamous structure of Jewish marriage (*kinyan*), creating new halakhic frameworks for enacting the formal relationship of couples (*shutafut*), and seeking a unique narrative to undergird and remythologize the ritual (*Kiddush Levanah*), I have not intended to resolve these questions, but rather to demonstrate how such a legal inquiry can be used to highlight what is at stake in the content of our wedding rituals, straight or gay. Whether the canopy and the rings are absolute necessities or not, a clearer understanding of what marriage means to us surely is.

ARGUING LITURGICAL GENEALOGIES, OR, THE GHOSTS OF WEDDINGS PAST

Mark D. Jordan

For Christian traditions, a wedding is always in part an acted prayer. The marriage that follows may be conceived as miraculous transformation or negotiated contract, as a concession to perishing flesh or a celebration of embodiment, as poison or libation for Eros. Indeed, the wedding itself may mark a dynastic alliance or regularize longstanding domestic arrangements. It may produce or repudiate civil effects, yield much or little to the expectations of nation, clan, or family. Still a wedding remains public prayer. However exactly it is conceived, the rite is an act on behalf of the church and before the church. It occurs within the larger cycle of a community's public celebration. It takes its place in a history of worship.

How are public prayers authorized? For many Christian churches, especially but not exclusively the "liturgical" ones, to have an approved place in the history of public worship is to enter a liturgical genealogy. The genealogy confers authenticity or legitimacy. It supplies precedents. A Christian wedding is counted authentic and legitimate—a *real* wedding—when it can cite appropriately a recognized tradition of previous weddings, leading back to some (apostolic) first. The genealogical appeal is not simple, of course, because the notion of "genealogy" is never more than an analogy. The analogy juxtaposes likenesses with differences. There are likenesses between traditional rites and families. For weddings, as for children, there is no exact reproduction, only variation and combination. The analogy also straddles differences. In ritual genealogies, parents do not beget children so much as they are begotten by them. A ritual is not procreated by a previous ritual so much as it claims to repeat—or reform—what has gone before.

When advocates for blessing of same-sex unions try to introduce new rites to public worship, they often justify them by tracing a new liturgical genealogy. They produce forgotten ancestors or recall lost lineages. Their opponents typically deny that the forgotten ancestors existed or that the lines belonged to the family. The opponents typically do not invite reflection on the logic of genealogical argument itself. Why should they, since that logic so evidently favors their wish to forbid the new rites? In liturgy, as in morals and scriptural exegesis, the most active opposition to same-sex love masks itself as a simple wish to conserve.

I do want to question the logic of liturgical genealogy—and not only because the claim to be conserving is untrue. Hunting for liturgical ancestors of same-sex rites has yielded startling historical discoveries, but they have hardly won over the opponents. The historical discoveries merely restage the controversy over authorization and legitimation that fuels the sex-controversies from the start. Before fighting again over whether churches should pray over same-sex unions, we would do better to interrogate the question itself. What kind of warrants can be provided for public prayers? How much do those warrants resemble a genealogy? And who gets to judge them? Stated so abstractly, the questions may seem both unanswerable and impertinent. Still, the consequences of ignoring them appear—quite concretely—as soon one tries to construct or rebut a probative genealogy without addressing them. Any hunt for precedents rests on assumptions that need careful questioning.

In what follows, I analyze genealogical justifications for same-sex rites in the so-called liturgical churches, that is, in Christian communities with standardized worship forms that claim some historical descent. The analysis applies much more obviously to Anglican, Eastern Orthodox, Roman Catholic, or Lutheran churches than to Baptist, Methodist, or Pentecostal ones. Yet the distinction between liturgical and nonliturgical is both historically changeable and conceptually misleading. In the years after Vatican II, for example, not a few Roman Catholic communities in the United States celebrated idiosyncratic eucharists that bore little relation to any approved Canon for the Mass. Then, again, it is not at all uncommon to hear American Baptists express their preference for a particular church by saying that it offers "a traditional Baptist service" or to hear Methodists describe at length the distinctive character of "Methodist liturgy." Absent a central liturgical agency, liturgical norms can be established and enforced by local custom or the politics of a particular movement. In short, the logic of liturgical genealogy may now cut across older denominational differences—as do so many other skirmishes in the great battle over same-sex love. Denominations often matter less than theo-political affiliations—another twist in the logic of liturgical controversy.

Influential genealogical arguments for Christian rites of same-sex blessing have so far taken two forms. The first form, the better known and more scandalous, argues that Christian churches long ago sanctioned rites that amounted to same-sex weddings. The second form, the more plausible, holds that Christian churches once offered other kinship rites to bind members of the same sex in affection, if not in copulation. The first argument seems to authorize a simple retrieval of those older rites into present circumstances. The second argument proposes that contemporary Christians remember the alternative kinship rites in order to correct their exaggerated concern with romance or sex. I refer to two arguments, but I am thinking of two books. Although neither book can be reduced just to the simplistic arguments made from them, each can suggest a form of argument. The first book is by John Boswell, the second by Alan Bray.

Premodern Unions

The most notorious argument on behalf of liturgical precedents for blessing same-sex unions is John Boswell's *Same-Sex Unions in Pre-Modern Europe*.[1] Its necessarily premature publication gives us fragments of three different monographs. The first paints with thick strokes a diorama of friendship and marriage in Greco-Latin antiquity and the early Christian church. The second fragment reinterprets a Byzantine and Slavic liturgical rite, called in Greek *adelphopoiesis*, which others had understood as a rite for establishing spiritual kinship. The third fragment surveys scattered mentions in medieval Byzantine, Slavic, and Latin sources of (what Boswell wants to recognize as) the rite.

Here I concentrate only on the second fragment, which is the cause and centerpiece of Boswell's project: the eastern Christian rite of sibling making. Boswell did not discover the rite. Indeed, he first read a version of it in a standard liturgical collection, Goar's often reprinted *Euchologion*, first published in 1647.[2] Boswell does raise three new questions about "the ceremony" (188). First, "does it solemnize a personal commitment as opposed to a religious, political, or family union?" Boswell replies at once, "The answer to this is unequivocally yes." Why? The ceremony "is unmistakably a voluntary, emotional union of two persons (always two: never more)." Boswell's next question is whether the ceremony celebrated "a relationship between two men or two women that was (or became) sexual?" Boswell answers: "Probably, sometimes, but this is obviously a difficult question to answer about the past, since participants cannot be interrogated" (189). Then he poses the third question, the most important: "Was [the ceremony] a marriage?" Boswell answers: "According to the modern conception—i.e., a permanent emotional union acknowledged in some way by the community—[*adelphopoiesis*] was unequivocally a marriage" (190).

Much energy has been spent rebutting Boswell's answers to the three questions. So, for example, there is evidence that *adelphopoiesis* was performed under conditions that we would not typically call "voluntary" and that it was embedded in ceremonies of group union. It did not preclude marriage to someone else. And so on. To answer that *adelphopoiesis* is "unequivocally" marriage also understates differences between features of the texts for the two rites. The rite of *adelphopoiesis* is not identical to eastern Christian rites of marriage. If it were the same, it would be redundant. In fact, the texts for the two rites do not much resemble each other. Boswell's best evidence for their resemblance depends on his reading through an ambiguous scribal mark in a single manuscript.[3] And so on. Still, in the end, it is less interesting to rebut Boswell's answers than to examine his questions. What kind of answers do the questions seek? Which answers will they admit?

Consider the first question. How are we to judge whether a ceremony solemnizes a personal commitment? By interpreting the letter of the liturgical texts? We would find it very difficult to translate terms such as *personal* and *commitment* into the language of the Byzantine rite. We have much less chance of connecting them with hypotheses about how the ceremony was "meant" to be used. Who is presumed to have the intention and how is its content specified? Official intentions about liturgical rites are typically established by reference to rubrics, to church law in its various forms (including local custom), and to pertinent church records. For dubious cases, there are formal or informal procedures of determination. Boswell is more interested in how the ceremony was used or viewed. Is his question then a statistical one about the opinions of some, many, most observers? There is no basis for a statistical answer. Or should we take it as a question about what participants "felt" in one or more particular cases? We have no first-person descriptions by officiants or participants in the rite. We do have long debates, for medieval Latin rites at least, about the extent and character of lay participation in liturgy.

Here it is worth remembering that some Christian churches, including the ones Boswell describes, have spent centuries elaborating legal models for intentions in weddings and other ritual acts. Church law specifies, for example, what minimum of intention must be present in the officiants or participants for a liturgical performance to be "valid." It further stipulates procedures for establishing such intention before or after the performance. In contemporary Roman Catholic procedure for annulling marriages, certain statements made publicly before a wedding can be used afterward to declare it invalid as a sacrament.[4] Again, according to current Roman Catholic procedure, a history of homosexual actions or declarations before a marriage can provide the basis for arguing that one or both participants in a marriage celebration were *incapable* of having the right intention to enter into it.[5] If there are questions to be asked about how a social historian establishes intentions, there are other questions, no less pertinent, about how liturgical intentions are established and adjudicated in church courts. Why should the ritual intentions reconstructed by a social historian be considered more real, in the past or the present, than the sacramental intentions proved in church proceedings? And even if some readers count them more "real," does that mean that they are likely to be more persuasive in church controversy over liturgical genealogies?

Take then the second question, about possible sexual relations between persons joined by the rite. Boswell regrets that they cannot be "interrogated." Even if they could be, we would need cunning to construe the honesty and completeness of their answers about sexual behavior. After all, a reader may entertain reasonable doubts about the reliability of contemporary sex surveys, as buddies may wonder about one another's recollections or representations of sexual conquests in conversation. Sexual banter has its forms and devices—including omission and exaggeration. Private avowals have forms and motives. Memoirs lie—most often to their authors. So even if we had loquacious reports by participants in historical Byzantine rites, we might worry a bit about their reliability. For the churches Boswell describes, such worries would be doubled or tripled by pessimism over self-knowledge in sin and the skepticism required for penitential practice. Skilled confessors expect that desire will deceive and that penitents will have trouble being entirely candid even when they want to be. Does a social historian enjoy explanatory privilege over therapists, confessors, and moral theologians when it comes to Christian sex? Is that because the social historian is more neutral, more expert, or simpler?

And so to the third question: Boswell admits that theologians would never have consented to view *adelphopoiesis* as marriage. Hence the eastern churches could never be said to have approved or blessed homosexual marriages "unequivocally," though this was the most sensational of the claims in journalistic announcements of Boswell's book.[6] In a crucial passage, Boswell allows himself to say only that *adelphopoiesis* "most likely signified a marriage in the eyes of most ordinary Christians" (191). But the "ordinary Christians" have just been described as constituting "a mostly illiterate . . . community" unconcerned with "theological or canonistic niceties" (191). How are we to understand, much less recover, the significations found by their eyes?

Christian theology has long disputed questions about the source or site of meaning in liturgy. It is striking that Boswell does not pose or pursue these questions within theology, whether historical or contemporary. Indeed, he deliberately sets theology aside in favor of the liturgical significations seen by "ordinary Christians." Boswell seeks the experience of the ordinary, which may be the majority or the average. That experience is presumed to be fundamentally similar to our own, where the "our" invokes a (hypothetical) current ordinariness. It corresponds to the "we" that holds "the modern conception [of marriage]—i.e., a permanent emotional union acknowledged in some way by the community." The most charitable reading of that perfectly general "conception" would take it as a piece of dialectic. It is as if Boswell were saying to himself, "Given what my typical reader is likely to think of 'marriage,' she or he would probably call the relationship created by certain performances of the rite of *adelpho-*

poiesis a 'marriage.'" Of course, the "modern conception" that Boswell has generalized is not specifically religious, much less Christian. The dialectical calculation poses problems not only of anachronism, but also of what happens when a post-Christian culture retrieves an old Christian rite. The calculation is also quite separate from Boswell's historical claim that some, many, or most "ordinary Christians" who observed the rite at some time past would have regarded it as a "marriage"—presumably according to their own notion of marriage and not according to the "modern conception." The dialectical calculation universalizes a dilute and secular "conception" of marriage. The historical claim requires us to imagine what a deeply religious, if also untutored Christian majority may have judged a "marriage" to be in medieval Byzantium or the Slavic kingdoms.

In stressing the difference between one model of social history and theology or canon law, my aim is not to replace Boswell's unequivocal answer about perceived ritual meanings with an equally unequivocal distinction between the secular and the religious or the Christian and the non-Christian. I do want to notice that Boswell's argument about a Christian liturgy is curiously unresponsive to the specificity of Christian liturgies or theological reflections on them. It is a troubling question for liturgists where the meaning of a rite is to be located, as it is always a question whether or how far the meaning can be specified and contained. Even on the textual level—before one gets to questions of performance or divine causality—the meaning of a liturgy cannot be reduced to any literal paraphrase. On a simple reading, Christian liturgy is a poetry of citation. Its poetic effects depend on the broader range of effects in canonical Christian scriptures. An ancient belief holds that the Christian bible speaks in all human genres, in every kind of voice. Scriptural texts present a singular polyphony: the reader finds the full range of styles on the literal line, with three or four or five lines of "spiritual" meaning underneath—or, rather, above. Liturgy relies on this polyphony to produce its own meanings. It produces them not as sealed artifacts, but as invocations or solicitations of divine action. It cites scriptural poetry in the service of eschatological gestures.[7] In many traditional views, the texts of Christian liturgy invoke notions of meaning and causality that suppose the nonlinear temporality of prophecy and typology, of emanation and return, of salvation history as a progress toward an already present eternity. In short, liturgical texts—not to say, liturgical events—claim to multiply the possibilities of human language as they bend time.

It is odd that an accomplished and erudite social historian should be so confident of extracting social *facts* about erotic relationships from liturgical texts. Of course, Boswell's ideal of social history was allied to powerful religious motivation that held less grand views about liturgical meanings, causes, and times. Certainly, Boswell intended for his last book to have liturgical consequences. (At one point he hoped that a publisher would produce both his scholarly book on unions and a liturgical edition of the recovered rite of *adelphopoiesis* for use by contemporary same-sex couples.)[8] Indeed, Boswell's arguments about the perceived meanings of liturgy may well imply a reformist theology of liturgy in which the people's practice of a rite determines its essential meaning—a meaning less eschatological than social. His refusal to engage liturgical questions explicitly would then seem part of a rhetorical strategy that deployed "neutral" social history as *praeparatio evangelica*—or, at least, a set of *praeambula fidei*. Social history would prepare for a demystified theology and a purified worship.

Much more might be said about this mix of disciplinary, religious, and rhetorical motives in Boswell's construction of *Same-Sex Unions*. Let me conclude by noting instead that an appeal to his position as a liturgical Christian writing for lesbian and gay believers ends up knotting the methodological questions more tightly. If we stress Boswell's religious purpose, then we construe his argument in this way: A sociohistorically demonstrable fact about the significance of a past liturgy is an immediately compelling liturgical precedent for modern believers. Such an argument gives liturgical antiquities something like legal force, if only the force of inciting permission. His book enacts a hope for church reform in the present by persuading queer Christians to retrieve (genealogically authorized) ritual meanings against official disapproval. Retrieval of a de facto liturgy of same-sex marriage becomes the best-plotted rebellion. Or so Boswell's book seems to suppose.

Premodern Friendships

The second form of genealogical argument about same-sex unions does not propose to retrieve a marriage-like liturgy. It urges contemporary Christians to recollect instead that same-sex couples once had well-established *alternatives* to marriage in Christian communities. Alan Bray's *The Friend* suggests this form of argument, though I repeat that my analysis will simplify Bray as much as it did Boswell.[9] *The Friend* tries to restore a lost notion of publicly celebrated Christian friendship through case studies of English friendships from the high Middle Ages into the nineteenth century. It reminds readers how Christian same-sex couples were either memorialized by church monuments or blessed with church rites. Bray's argument, disclosed fully only at the book's end, is that the lost notion of friendship may persuade contemporary Christians to see new possibilities for holy relationship.

The evidence for Bray's argument is complex. It cannot persuade when condensed. Bray's book reaches, with a remarkable span, from a monument in Constantinople of two crusaders kissing to the grave that John

Henry Newman emphatically willed to share with Ambrose St. John "on a hillside looking out cross Warwickshire" (288). The consideration of Newman ends with this lyrical paragraph, the last of the book's body:

> As in our own time the permafrost of modernity has at last begun to melt—and a more determinedly pluralistic world has bounded back into an often troubling life—the world we are seeing is not a strange new world, revealed as the glaciers draw back, but a strange *old* world: kinship, locality, embodiment, domesticity, affect. All of these things, but I would want to add that at times we are seeing them in something as actual—and as tangible—as the tomb of two friends buried in an English parish church. We did not see these tombs because they did not signify, but they are beginning to signify again. (306)

By emphasizing the contrast between the modern and the premodern, Bray means to forestall any appeal to a "modern conception" of either erotic relationship or friendship in interpreting the couples he considers. What the vowed friends had was precisely neither a contemporary homoerotic relationship nor a contemporary friendship. It was rather a vanished species of affect that was intrinsically public because caught up in a rich network of physical and social kinship, of "family" in a quite extended sense. The species permitted an ambiguous silence around the sexual, so that the language of passionate love could be deployed without automatically provoking suspicion of unnatural lechery. If suspicions were provoked in some highly visible or notoriously criminal cases, those cases can remind us how many others passed without social comment. After all, the monuments to friendship that concern Bray were placed prominently in spaces of Christian worship. Many of them remain there today. If we have overlooked them, the fault was in us, not in their perspicuous iconography. Leo Steinberg used the word *oblivion* to describe our contemporary blindness to the display of Jesus' genitals in familiar Renaissance paintings.[10] The word describes just as exactly our failure to see Bray's monuments even when we stand before them.

The public monuments had their parallel in public worship, in a liturgical or paraliturgical rite used to declare or swear friendship. Bray refers to variants of the rite in several different contexts. The ceremony often began with an exchange of rings, usually on the porch of the church, but it culminated inside, in an act of shared communion.[11] Both shared communion and the exchange of rings, we remember, were employed not only in weddings, but in a variety of ceremonies for establishing alliance, patronage, and other forms of fictive kinship (as we typically describe it). The phrase *fictive kinship* already misses the point—already succumbs to an impoverished modern notion of kinship. The forgotten ritual of Christian friendship was a way of uniting persons, families, and fortunes. It was sealed at the communion rail because that was the culmination of union, the perfect degree of kinship: incorporation into the one body of the one Lord.[12] Rites for swearing friendship ran parallel to traditional forms for celebrating Christian marriage, but they were not imitations of marriage. They were, alongside marriage, elements in a larger network that made and fostered many kinds of kinship.

In Bray's account, Christian faith held that the network linked earth to heaven. It was thus charged with creedal formulations and sacramental energies. It was subordinated to redemptive ends. Bray's book tries to maintain these same relations and subordinations even in its microhistories. One can see this already in the choice of funerary monuments as the linking device. One can feel it as well in the book's exhortations, which culminate in that last paragraph, but build throughout. Bray assembles an enormous collage of small bits of evidence for what friendship once signified in particular Christian communities, to particular pairs of friends who counted their friendship as part of their sanctification.

Bray could benefit on this point from the controversy surrounding Boswell's book. Bray and Boswell had been thinking about rites of sworn friendship at the same time, but their thoughts led them along diverging tracks. For Bray, the point was not just that Boswell made certain mistakes or missed certain texts (such as a Latin version of *adelphopoiesis*, the *Ordo ad fratres faciendum*).[13] Boswell's book served to confirm for Bray the deep difference between modern friendship and the older forms of alliance or association being celebrated by these rites and their English analogues. "While [Boswell] was engaged by the similarity that he believed he could detect between such a rite and modern marriage, I was struck by how different it was from modern friendship" (317).

In its emphasis on the details of the old friendships, in its exacting interpretation of funerary monuments and family relations, Alan Bray's book may strike some readers as a charming and impotent antiquarianism. They would be mistaken. Whatever there is of antiquarian curiosity or affection in *The Friend* is put in the service of theology—put in service not only elegantly, but quite traditionally. Bray wants to resituate ethical questions about sex within an ethics of friendship as "a larger frame of reference that lay *outside* the good of the individuals for whom friendship was made" (6). Bray's recovered ethics of friendship "overflow" the contemporary preoccupation with sex (7). "There is, of course, no return now to the friendship of traditional society, but the ethics of friendship have an archaeology . . . that can be recovered; and if this book in some measure helps to explain and find ways of transcending the ethical problems raised by friendship in a diverse world, it will have served its purpose" (8).

Bray's purpose assumes that genealogies can still persuade—that there is still force in an appeal to liturgical and ecclesial descent. He displays the old rites and monuments of church-blessed friendship because he believes that they will still command some respect or at least elicit a focused interest. Bray's effort to restore the broken genealogy of Christian friendship projects that genealogy into the future. When Bray imagines our reinhabiting the older forms of friendship, experimenting with them, giving them fresh content, using them to escape from the dark corridors in which the churches have tried to trap same-sex love—when he does this, he assumes that we will choose to make these experiments before trying others. He supposes that the forms have a claim on some believers because they come from an ecclesial genealogy. Is this supposition a theology? A believer's simple faith? An abiding confidence in the presence of the Holy Spirit? On any of these explanations, Bray's rhetorical strategy will only look more and more subtle. Indeed, his artful antiquarianism can seem a lure for those who would find direct theological claims or professions of faith unattractive. He would use antiquarian fascination in something like the way that Boswell may be using a blunt social history as propaedeutic to reformed religious practice.

Bray may also share with Boswell a churchly nostalgia (or eschatology)—a longing for a Christianity more like Eden (or the New Jerusalem). Nostalgia is the form of argument in Boswell's foundational book *Christianity, Social Tolerance, and Homosexuality*.[14] Nostalgia is more grandly and perhaps more desperately the form of argument in Boswell's book on unions. Before Boswell, nostalgia is the latent rhetorical motive in Derrick Sherwin Bailey's *Homosexuality and the Western Christian Tradition*.[15] Indeed, any effort to reinterpret one or another period of church history as favorable to same-sex desire—or at least as less violently opposed—may solicit nostalgia. In the same way that same-sex desires can be projected onto exotic foreigners, so too they can be cast back on remote ancestors. "Once upon a time, there was more ambiguity and more variety in blessing Christian relationships. Once upon a time, churches had other ways to talk about our loves—ways that did not search obsessively for genital contact or impure thoughts. Once upon a time . . ."

The nostalgia is potent, but does it make for convincing liturgical arguments? This question is more central for Bray's argument than some others that have been raised, including worries about his coyness regarding sex. I do worry about an elision of the sexual in *The Friend*, however much I know it to be deliberate. If Bray's strategy is to hold off on erotic matters, to leave them in surprising and constructive abeyance, he does risk acquiescing in the kind of silence that has constituted the history of so many churches around same-sex desire. But more important than this worry is the question about the argumentative assumption of Bray's liturgical nostalgia. The problem is not that nostalgia may divert liturgical genealogy into something other than neutral scholarship. Bray's scholarship puts him far beyond his critics. The trouble with nostalgia is that it can lead one to assume that liturgical genealogies are inherently convincing. The thrill of recovering the forgotten, the overlooked, or the repressed can produce its own concealment. It can hide the rhetorical challenge of showing why we should care about lost history. Indeed, it may be that the strongest nostalgia in Bray and Boswell both is the nostalgia for an epoch when historical discovery mattered to churchly debate. Why fret about a more exact history when the real fight is over the institutions that will determine what counts as church history—and who gets to be counted within it?

Hypothetical Genealogies

Two forms for arguing from liturgical precedents for same-sex unions play on what looks like nostalgia. We may well ask whether the slips in their forms of argument do not result from the very project of liturgical genealogy. Perhaps they do, but the slips become truly misleading not so much in Boswell or Bray as in attempts to appropriate them for the purposes of controversy.

One slip is the mistake of thinking that the genealogist's task is merely to find pertinent texts in eras past. The main task, in reality, is to sort out what can be meant by "pertinent." Controversialists often assume that old liturgical texts (or scriptural, legal, and moral texts) have something to say about exactly the sorts of same-sex relationships that contemporary Christians find before them. To locate genealogical precedents for blessing same-sex unions, then, they need only look back to earlier Christian marriage rites or to rites that run alongside them. The slip happens just here. It is the fantasy that contemporary Christians can readily identify which earlier rites might or might not be pertinent because there is some steady relation between rites and relations. The slip reduces lived ritual in both present and past. In the present, same-sex unions are blessed for disparate reasons—to inaugurate a new relationship or to celebrate the anniversary of an established one, to mark return to Christian practice or an epoch in its steady pursuit, to begin adult life or to prepare for the death of one or both partners. So a Christian reformer might look for liturgical antecedents to same-sex unions not only in wedding or friendship rites, but in confirmation, reconciliation, and extreme unction. Like contemporary heterosexual weddings, the blessing of same-sex unions is an umbrella that covers a number of different motives, motives that were often assigned to diverse rites in older churches.

Even if the reformer wishes to construct a genealogy for only one or two of those motives—the ones we imagine most closely analogous to traditional heterosexual marriage—she immediately risks a second slip. It is the slip of assuming that there is some rough agreement about what counts as the liturgical past. It is the convenient fantasy that the liturgical past is a stable whole. To clarify the second slip, I jump over the ambiguities of historical evidence to posit hypothetical discoveries. Imagine three historical finds in order to ask what sorts of liturgical arguments for blessing they might underwrite.

The first case: Imagine that there were convincing attestation of an early Christian rite that recognized or created an exclusive bond of same-sex affection, where "exclusive" meant that the partners could neither enter into another such bond nor be married in the church without renouncing their sworn affection. This is what some people think that the rite of *adelphopoiesis* did in practice and perhaps also what Bray hopes for in future experiments with vowed friendship. Would this sort of case be an adequate precedent for blessing same-sex unions in the present? Not without an explicit resolution of the sexual issue. Here I may disagree with Bray, who suggests that we would do better to exploit traditional silences in favor of a less individual conception of relation. Much contemporary discussion of relationships is indeed dominated by erotic obsessions whose proximate sources in late nineteenth-century clinics and courtrooms Foucault describes so vividly. Still our discussion is our discussion. Convincing genealogical evidence of an exclusive friendship liturgy that was ambiguous about erotic acts would not authorize blessing same-sex unions today that are presumed or proclaimed to be sexual. Its ambiguity would be trumped by explicit condemnations of same-sex desire elsewhere in the approved traditions. A strategic silence in the rite would be filled up with explicit prohibitions found elsewhere.

This is a difficulty for every Christian genealogy for blessing a contemporary lesbian or gay relationship. The diligent searcher can find rites with interesting ambiguities or rites that seem probably to have been used as cover for same-sex erotic activity (though the "probably" will be vexed), but finding them does not provide warrants for blessing all-too-eroticized relationships in our present. The explicitness of our hypersexed identities cannot fit within the ambiguities or enforced discretion of the attested rites. In order to invoke the genealogical warrant, you would need already to have established (healthy) Christian relationships built around ambiguities and enforced discretion. (Church history shows us many unhealthy relationships that hid inside ambiguity and discretion.) Rites for blessing ambiguous relations cannot be used to bless a relationship that has been deliberately, publicly, even painfully disambiguated. Reticent rites would work only for a future in which the genie of sexuality had been put back into an opaque bottle.

My second case: Imagine that someone discovered convincing evidence that an ancient Christian community had celebrated same-sex couples with an explicit grant of permission for appropriate sexual expression. Would this provide an adequate precedent for blessing same-sex unions in the present? No, because the community would immediately be dismissed as heretical—that is, as falling outside any possible genealogy. I am not merely predicting that some talking-head will have a ready reply for any eventuality. My point is that the limits of liturgical genealogy are drawn in most churches, even the most historically respectful, by law and official theology. Even liturgically based churches delimit liturgical genealogies with sharp lines, setting aside many second and third cousins, black sheep, and embarrassing bastards. If a scholar suddenly discovered a Christian community from the second century that blessed same-sex couplings, that community would be stricken from church history the next day.

My third case: Imagine simultaneous discoveries of widely scattered Christian communities that performed identical marriage rites for both other-sex and same-sex couples. Would this be, at last, an adequate precedent for blessing same-sex unions in the present? I am less sure about the answer to this hypothetical question. I can imagine that the discovery would persuade some Christians to support blessings now. For others, it would be evidence that all of those communities were heretical—or that the evidence, no matter how scientifically convincing, had been falsified (like dinosaur bones for "creationists"). For still others, the evidence might be dismissed on a plea of the development of doctrine. The more startling the hypothesized liturgical evidence, the more devices for managing it are already in place. The management of liturgical genealogies is, after all, a venerable task in churches.

We cannot easily imagine any historical discovery that would produce widespread conviction of the legitimacy of blessing same-sex unions. This conclusion can be a complaint about how little importance churchly debates give to historical evidence or a diagnosis of the role that present politics plays in the construction of any widely accepted account of the past. It can also be, more importantly, the discovery of limits intrinsic to the construction of any liturgical genealogy, including limits on the role of liturgy in arguments about legitimate sexual relations. After all, the discovery that early and widely scattered Christian communities had performed marriages for both other-sex and same-sex couples would significantly alter our standard histories of Christian marriage for *other*-sex couples. We have no early marriage rites from Christian churches in the West. We have no elaborate early theologies of marriage as a sacrament. What we can reconstruct is a slow, patchy development of various accommodations with various civil regimes for family.

Same-sex unions cannot be forced to produce either what cannot be given or what no other rite really has. The churches' present practice of Christian marriage between *other-sex* couples is not principally governed by an extended liturgical genealogy or by meticulous liturgical history. The staunchest advocates of "traditional" marriage in America typically defend a notion of marriage that is not more than decades old. The notion resulted from extraordinary reversals in American gender relations, family structures, and household economy during the last century and a half. These changes have been accompanied by changes in mainline church teachings on marriage preparation, family planning, and annulment or divorce. Similar changes, if less studied ones, have occurred in most Christian marriage liturgies, however traditional some of their pieces may sound. Taken as a whole, with their music, sermon, and nonrubrical additions or alterations, most contemporary marriage liturgies can be said to quote earlier rites without enacting them. They are as much innovations as the most spontaneous blessings for same-sex unions. If we begin with the assumption that same-sex unions must justify themselves by producing a detailed liturgical (or scriptural and moral) genealogy, we ignore the short and somewhat dubious genealogy behind our favorite white weddings. What is more important, we ignore how far it makes sense to conceive of liturgical texts as constituting a coherent, normative genealogy for any rite that confers ethical legitimacy on human relations.

Liturgical Ghosts

To presume that liturgical texts constitute a coherent, normative genealogy is to ignore the central dilemma of liturgical history: How do we understand continuity in dispersed performances? The dilemma appears at many points. It arises, for example, in regard to multiple performances of a single liturgical text. What unifies the various celebrations of this particular form of marriage? What variations are possible before it becomes another rite? The dilemma arises more grandly when it comes time to revise established texts or compose new ones. Must a liturgy always be composed out of earlier liturgies? If it were not, would we recognize it as a liturgy? Can there be completely new rites of Christian worship? The last century saw enormous liturgical revisions in most Christian denominations, often in contrary directions. From them we ought to remember at least the variety of relations liturgical experts can take to the liturgical past.

One relation reconstructs historical genealogy in order to confirm the continuity of sacramental doctrine—which is to say, of institutional legitimacy. Like the charts that show how this pope or patriarch traces succession back to the apostles, some liturgical genealogies are meant as demonstrations of orthodoxy. The demonstration must rewrite the surviving evidence. Traces of Christian worship from the first centuries are both fragmentary and ambiguous. They can be incorporated into an orthodox genealogy only by ingenious selection and interpolation. Selection insures that difficult texts will be excluded as impertinent (as belonging, e.g., to an *agape* rather than to a eucharist). Interpolation fills textual gaps with what they "must" have contained—"must" according to the needs of a later orthodoxy. Selection and interpolation can be done tacitly, subtly, or loudly and bluntly. Recent decisions by the Vatican agency for doctrine insist that research into the history of liturgy cannot contradict current teaching about sacraments.[16]

Another project of reconstruction has stressed the correction of prevailing orthodoxies. It has seen return or retrieval as the surest or most persuasive means of reform. Much of the Roman Catholic "liturgical movement" from the nineteenth century forward was animated by the passion of return to origins. The cry "*ad fontes!*" was not only a slogan for reforming theologians. There was an impulse to castigate, in the philological sense— to remove "accretions," "deviations," and even "impurities" in order to get back to an uncontaminated original in worship. This notion of retrieval owes something to a nineteenth-century philologist's critical edition (Lachmann) and a historian's interrogation of sources (von Ranke). Yet liturgical renewal owes just as much to the aesthetic project of modernism, both its formal experiments with language and its visual or musical severity. Not a few retrievals brought the archaic forward as an aesthetic "primitive"—like so many archeological figurines or tribal masks. Sometimes, curiously, retrieval operated in tandem with the impulse to make the liturgy more accessible to "the man of today," to use the favorite locution of Vatican II. Linking the two impulses was an ideal of simplicity, a simplicity that was at once the unadorned original and the democratic contemporary. Of course, reforming retrieval could go only so far in changing all-too-modern church structures or doctrines. Liturgical pieces could be taken from the early centuries or the eastern traditions, but they could only be quoted or sampled within an officially controlled frame that deracinated them.

These two relations to a liturgical past, the legitimating and the reforming, are more complicated than my brief contrast allows. Still, the contrast may allow me to suggest that the polemical moments of both relations tend to obscure three fundamental conditions of *liturgical* history, conditions that are particularly important for retrievals or reconstructions of marriage rites. The first condition is that any liturgical celebration will be a failed performance. The second is that rites will change as their subjects change. The third is that the status or category of "rite" or "ritual" will change most of all. Let me take them in order.

Quarrels over liturgical changes often seem to forget the conditions of any *performance*. Each performance, as Judith Butler ceaselessly reminds us, is both a citation and a variation. Any particular eucharist cites the liturgical norms of the particular community, but it also works variations on them. What is more important, any particular eucharist situates the liturgical norms—in the particular personnel and their performances, in musical and visual contexts, of course, but also in social and political circumstances.[17] These aspects of performance have been emphasized in applying the lessons of "ritual studies" to Christian liturgy. The emphasis draws attention away from aspects of liturgical thinking indigenous to Christian traditions. For many Christians, any liturgy must remain an incomplete register of traces of performed eschatological gestures. So, for example, believers will see a given Christian eucharist not only with its particular celebrants and setting, its repetitions and innovations, but also as a living citation of the Last Supper and as a living anticipation of heavenly communion. Those who do not believe should admit the citational aspirations even while they deny their truth. Remembering this much, both believers and unbelievers may be led to remember that a liturgy for blessing unions will attempt to accomplish something that eludes any description, much more any paraphrase. The words and actions of a liturgy of union are not supposed to be adequate figures for the recognition, consolation, or support they offer. Even if we had an ideal library of whole liturgical texts from the earliest Christian communities forward, we could consult them only as written records of multiply contextual performances that were never able to recall, exhibit, or complete their central preoccupations.

The second condition of liturgical history that is too easy to forget depends on the relation between a liturgy and the identities of its participants. The relation can be described by large theories about correlated changes in ritual and subjectivity. So, for example, Foucault's *Discipline and Punish* narrates a ritual genealogy in which the changing displays of punitive power both express and create that power's changing subjects. The gruesome judicial torture of Damiens the regicide gives way to the admonitory reminders of the utopian reformers.[18] So, too, one could write a ritual history of the churches' dealings with the subjects of same-sex desire. It would include disparate spectacles of public execution, homiletic denunciation, pastoral exhortation or correction, and then, in very recent years, grudging or enthusiastic acceptance. The different types of spectacles express and create different homoerotic subjects: the sodomite, of course, but also the pagan, the libertine, the invert, the homosexual, the homophile, and, in very recent years, the lesbian or gay.

Grand histories of the relation of rites to subjects should be told as reminders that liturgy asks the participants to perform certain identities after and outside any particular rites—in the church, the family, the world, but also in other rites. In a heterosexual church wedding, for example, the man and woman are invited into the elaborately defined (the overdetermined) roles of Christian Husband and Wife. Other rites have prepared them for these roles. They have been baptized, of course, and (in some traditions) confessed, brought to the eucharist table for the first time, and then confirmed. But the Christian Wife and Husband have often also been through rites of betrothal or engagement—and so they have already performed the transient roles of the about-to-be-wed couple. These roles have often been considered quite important as preparation for marriage.[19] In some churches at some times, the Christian Wife would go on to rites of "churching" after childbirth. She and her Husband could stand as godparents for the children of others or as important actors in the marriages of their own children. Each might stand, alone, as the principal mourner at the other's funeral. So the roles projected in a wedding liturgy have to be understood not only in relation to a grand narrative of the mutations of individual subjectivity, but as part of a cycle of liturgical or paraliturgical performances that extend or reinforce the identity.

For subjects with homoerotic desires, the cycle of public rites has until recently been largely punitive. There have long been private rites of avowal and consummation, often modeled on the standard (heterosexual) liturgies. Boswell and Bray both mention such rites. Boswell points to a passage in Montaigne. Two Portuguese "married, man to man, at Mass, using the same ceremonies that we do for our marriages, taking their communion together, reading the same wedding Gospel."[20] Bray points to Anne Lister's coded descriptions of private engagements and interprets them as an echo of much older liturgical forms.[21] Lister sealed her union with Ann Walker by taking communion together with her in the parish church on Easter Sunday. The history of American lesbian and gay communities could supply hundreds more examples of private rites between Christians performed in close or loose imitation of standard liturgies. We now have a growing library of published Christian rites for same-sex unions.[22] These are adaptations of cycles of Christian rites to subjects they were not meant to include—and that do not fit easily within them. But it may be more important to realize that in many contemporary settings these adaptations must fit in alongside cycles of other rites.

Lesbian and gay identities are adopted and enacted by Christians in a variety of rites outside the church: coming out, going into queer spaces for the first time, marching in a Pride parade. These rites cannot be dismissed as "merely" social or political. They are in fact liturgical inventions by emerging communities of Christians whose significant life-stages are excluded or repressed by the available liturgies. They can be as important for flourishing—indeed, for survival—as many recognized liturgies. Memorial services for lovers or friends lost to AIDS, for example, were not only liturgical improvisations in the face of the refusal of many churches to recognize the epidemic. They were also efforts to negotiate tensions between the rites of gay and Christian identities. The ceremonies that emerged after negotiation often seemed more vivid than many Christian liturgies—and not only for those who count themselves queer.[23]

Even if we did discover an intact Christian rite for blessing erotic unions between members of the same sex (as Boswell sometimes seemed to think he had), any retrieval of that rite would have to bring it into the prevailing relations between rites and subjects. If those subjects are also participants in the sort of lesbian and gay communities familiar from many large cities worldwide, they will participate as well in other cycles of rites connected to their queer identities. The retrieved rite of union would not only be conditioned by those "secular" rites, it would have to contend with them. The same point can be made without the impossible hypothesis of the perfect discovery. A liturgical project of retrieval must consider the changing relations of rite to subject. If the text or symbols of an identity-linked rite are reperformed for different subjects, they will produce different effects. The same will be true when the rites are performed for subjects who also participate in other, unanticipated rites for that same identity. Whenever the conditions of subjectivity change, so will the performance of rites that project or attach to subjects.

The third condition on any liturgical history follows. It can be suggested very briefly—though hardly exhausted. The categories we use to construct liturgical history have their own genealogies. The word *ritual*, for example, has gone through a marked change of meaning in the last two hundred years.[24] The change has shifted it in one direction from expert skill to symbolic expression, from a high technology to a fumbling pidgin. Similar genealogies could be constructed for *liturgy* or *rite* or *performance*. The shifts in our categories for liturgical history may make us wonder again, and for a third time, about the self-confident use of such histories to authorize or to resist liturgical retrievals and innovations. A marriage in a suburban American church cannot function *as a rite* in the same way that a marriage would have functioned in fourth-century Rome or in a thirteenth-century parish. It cannot because Christian rites must have a very different status in a pluralistic, democratic, and technocratic society than in those earlier ones. For the great majority of Americans, Christian liturgy is no longer the most potent *techne*.

The long history of Christian marriage is the slow effort to sacralize existing civil rites—followed, of course, by efforts to desacralize or resacralize them differently. The debate about blessing same-sex unions must raise fundamental questions about that history. Indeed, part of the importance of the debate is that it can raise these questions. Raising them will only complicate assertions made across the divide marked by the word *sacralize*. If Christian blessings on unions do nothing but acknowledge or accessorize civil unions, then Christian liturgy, with or without its history, is reduced to decoration or supplementary social control. If, on the contrary, Christian blessings of unions invoke a causality essentially different from the civil—if they do something more than ratify the local etiquette— then the history of Christian liturgy might indeed be essential to reform, so long as it is allowed to be what it is.

HOOKER AND THE NEW PURITANS

Kathryn Tanner

Because I believe that all the good theological and biblical arguments are on the progressive side, I admit to some discouragement at the seemingly intractable character of the debate over the morality or immorality of gay sex in the Christian churches, particularly in the Episcopal Church USA, of which I am a member. When it comes to gay sex, rational argument and the tools of persuasion have in my experience made little headway against ingrained commonplaces and what one might call the simple "ugh" factors of fear and disgust. I am increasingly convinced, however, that the issue of same-sex unions for the Anglican Communion can profitably be considered under the rubric of polity—that is, as an issue of church governance and proper liturgical forms.

As the flap over the consecration of Gene Robinson as bishop of New Hampshire underscores, the major worries of those unconvinced either that sexually active gay people should be church leaders, or that their relationships should have church sanction, are polity worries. The church has never done this before, and therefore should not do so now. For the case of same-sex unions, doing otherwise means changing the church's long-standing practice of marrying only men and women by extending marriage to gay people on the same conditions as straight couples, or it means legislating from whole cloth, without prior precedent, a new rite for blessing committed gay couples. Liturgy is at the heart of Anglican identity; the Episcopal Church USA doing one thing while the rest of the Communion does another therefore strikes at the heart of what holds Anglicans together. How can African or Asian primates look on when the Episcopal Church goes so woefully astray on liturgical fundamentals in conformity to Western mores? Altering the canons of church life is not appropriate when it contradicts the mandates of scripture; and that, opponents suggest, is what is happening now in the Episcopal Church. Both the ordination of sexually active gay people and rites giving church support to gay relationships ignore a contradiction with scripture that underlies them; scripture prohibits gay sex, and church canons cannot overrule scriptural law. Even when all the usual processes of decision making were strictly enforced—for example, a duly elected bishop was confirmed by both the House of Deputies and the House of Bishops at General Convention—those opposed to church decisions favoring gays have the right to contest them, for example, by withholding contributions or threatening secession or aligning themselves with a bishop in some other diocese or a primate in another province.

So we have here a number of very basic polity issues. The first concerns change in liturgical forms or in rules for church governance; the second, diversity in liturgical forms; the third, the role of scripture in regulations or rules for church life; and the fourth, the proper ways of contesting the decisions of the church when one disagrees with them. These are all questions of general principle and can therefore be treated, at least to some extent, without direct reference to the particular case, gay sex, over which there is so much heat but so little light!

The Anglican Communion is well positioned to take up such questions because the Church of England, from which it took its start, only came to some measure of self-definition over and against other Reformation churches in fights about these very same issues of general principle. Beginning with controversies between more conservative and so-called Puritan factions in the sixteenth century, the Church of England has a history of resisting reforms to its liturgy and structures of church governance that would bring it into greater conformity with Reformation movements on the continent. In these controversies over reform of polity, the Puritan faction made the question of scriptural mandates for church practice an inescapable consideration. Uniformity of practice within the Church of England, not just across post-Reformation churches, was also at issue because, for example, the powers that be in England were not above efforts to stamp out Puritan simplicity of rites when it seemed contemptuous of established practices, or Puritan questioning of episcopal authority when it appeared to them seditious. The question of when one could legitimately resist such legal mandates of conformity arose, naturally, in turn.

Richard Hooker is the usual authority that Anglicans turn to for help in answering such questions. He is undoubtedly among the most frequently cited figures in books about the Anglican tradition in general. To this day, fights over the character of Anglicanism are fought over how to read Hooker—for example, whether to read him as a Calvinist or not. As the author of the magisterial *Of the Laws of Ecclesiastical Polity*, he is in any case the best source for a sophisticated case in favor of the conformist strand of Anglicanism. One would, therefore, think that it might be hard to enlist him in an argument in favor of novel church rites for same-sex unions, but that is just what I will do.[1] The general principles upheld by those presently opposing liturgical reform are not Hooker's; they are, if anything, akin to the principles of Hooker's Puritan opponents. Hence the rather delicious (or salacious) double entendre of my title!

There was the temptation in sixteenth-century England to make a simple appeal to either church authority (John Whitgift) or long-standing tradition (Bishop Jewel) the pillar of the case against Puritan reforms: one must simply obey church mandates or follow the lead of established practice; the fact of church law or tradition is sufficient in and of itself to decide against further reform. Hooker, however, declined such strategies of authoritarian positivism—the underlying idea, that is, that what exists cannot be questioned—in favor of an appeal to Puritan conscience that would allow these critics of the Church of England to see the reasonableness of its laws and ceremonies.[2] It is appropriate to subject church rules and customs to evaluation and scrutiny, and to defend them from criticism by argument, because all good laws for human behavior go back to God's laws and God is a wise God who institutes rules for a reason, for the sake of an end. Proper regulations for human life can therefore be shown to be reasonable with reference to the point behind their institution; and "the nature of every law must be judged of by the end for which it was made, and by the aptness of things therein prescribed unto the same end" (3:10.1).[3] Indeed, God offers laws to humans in ways appropriate to their specific capacities: Humans, unlike the inanimate world that follows God's laws blindly, should, ideally, formulate and abide by laws because of their reasonableness, willingly because they see the sense of them. In accordance with this general sense of law, when possible revisions of church practice are floated (in an orderly fashion through the proper channels), Hooker recommends not the conversation-stopping appeal to what has always been done, typical nowadays of opponents of new rites for same-sex unions, but a trial, in which arguments for and against the reasonableness of church practice are heard.

There is no question that Hooker is very wary of change, especially when it is done precipitously and in a disorderly fashion, without any careful weighing of the possible benefits and costs. "Easiness to alter and change"—or, we might say, eagerness to innovate for innovation's sake—is for Hooker a great evil, leading to instability and confusion (4:14.2). No humanly instituted laws are perfect; one can always come up with some well-reasoned reservations about their adequacy. But if the simple possibility of improvement is turned into a sufficient cause for change, the same will hold for the new laws instituted on that basis, giving us no real reason to side with the latter over the former. Arguments for change must therefore be weighty, the damage without change serious, and the need urgent.

Reasonable courses of action for the sake of the ends God sets are, moreover, worked out publicly in the patient to-and-fro of human history, and therefore one should, indeed, give the benefit of the doubt to practices with a long pedigree. Long-standing practices have, just for that reason, the presumption of reasonableness. And so "that which the Church hath received and held so long for good, that which public approbation hath ratified, must carry the benefit of presumption with it to be accounted meet and convenient" (4:4.2). Because God's laws for human life are mediated through such historical processes, Hooker can even refer to "the general and perpetual voice of men" as "the sentence of God himself" (1:8.3). Humanly instituted laws can be the indirect means of God's own institution of law, especially where they have the universal consent of humankind. "The most certain token of evident goodness is, if the general persuasion of all men do account it" (ibid.).

Hooker nevertheless believes that long-standing customs can see the institution of error. Indeed, the greater the number of people who believe an error and the longer it has been propagated, the less likely people are to subject it to the appropriate questioning. "If two, or three, or four, agree all in the same tale, they judge it then to be out of controversy, and so are many times overtaken for want of due consideration" (1:4.8). "Lewd and wicked custom, beginning perhaps at the first amongst few, afterwards spreading into greater multitudes, and so continuing from time to time, may be of force even in plain things to smother the light of natural understanding; because men will not bend their wits to examine whether things wherewith they have been accustomed be good or evil" (1:8.11). Custom can therefore deaden people even to the existence of very good arguments against it. "Custom inuring the mind by long practice . . . prevaileth more than reasonable persuasion what way soever" (1:7.6).

Long-standing tradition is a sign of the goodness of a law but it is not what establishes it. Even the most ancient traditions can therefore be changed, when, for example, it becomes apparent that they no longer serve the general ends for which they were instituted or when the particular ends they serve have become obsolete. "When a thing doth cease to be available unto the end which gave it being, the continuance of it must then of necessity appear superfluous. And of this we cannot be ignorant, how sometimes that hath done great good, which afterwards, when time hath changed the ancient course of things, doth grow to be either hurtful, or not so greatly profitable and necessary" (3:10.1). Even episcopacy, which Hooker believes to be of apostolic institution, "could be taken away by universal consent upon urgent cause" (7:5.8).

Although the Puritans are the ones plumping for change and Hooker the one holding the line against them, it is the Puritans who have difficulty admitting the propriety of change in the organization and ceremonial life of the church over time. The Puritans indeed are hoping to reinstitute church practices that they believe to be old and original, simply *because* they are old and original. Although Hooker thinks episcopacy rather than the Puritan recommendation of presbyterian church governance is the more likely ancient tradition, he refuses to argue on the Puritans' mistaken general principle that would rule out changing forms of church life (3:10.8).

Even when they are of long-standing practice, the public institutions of church polity are just the sort of laws susceptible of change. The laws of nature, which are self-evident to human reason, are immutable; for example, it is self-evident, and therefore a rule for all times, that a society needs some rules or other to organize it. But the laws that specify how that natural law will be worked out for a particular society such as the church—a kind of positive law (i.e., "mixed" positive law), according to Hooker—are changeable, by virtue of the fact that there may be many different means to the same immutable end, many different ways of organizing public life for the sake of order and stability. The divine law—what reason could not deduce on its own and what is immediately given by God in scripture—specifies some required forms for public worship in Christian churches (e.g., the sacraments of baptism and eucharist, the need for public prayer and for the proclamation of the Gospel, etc.). But other organizational forms over and above those that God mandates as necessary for salvation, and the details of the exercise of those forms that God does mandate, are "merely" human positive laws, in the sense that they are left to the discretion of the church. Insofar as those rites and those details are not necessary means to the ends of the church—salvation—they are changeable when circumstances warrant.

Hooker does not talk very much about marriage in the *Laws* since, aside from such incidentals as the use of rings, it is not a matter that comes up a great deal in controversies with the Puritans. But marriage clearly falls on the side of changeable positive law in that it is not a sacrament in the strict sense for Hooker and is not, accordingly, a public rite necessary for salvation. It could not be the latter because no one would claim that everyone needs to be married in order to be saved (cf. 3:8.2). Hooker talks in Book Five about the ends of marriage in terms that are not specifically religious (procreation), and appropriately so, because the primary ends of marriage evidently concern, as Hooker would say, men qua men and not qua Christians. The religious rite is therefore lending its support to an important civil good that marriage furthers. But even if marriage as a public rite of the church were necessary for salvation—at least for those Christians engaging in sexual relations—what would need to be changed about the rite to cover same-sex unions (e.g., changes of pronoun, of scriptural texts perhaps) arguably involves incidentals and not substance (i.e., matters with a necessary connection to ends) and therefore falls under the rubric of changeable positive law as well. Presumably the religious end served by marriage is the communication of grace to Christian relationships—all public church rites have that sort of end for Hooker. But this is, as all ends are for Hooker, a general end that can (in principle) be served by any number of means; altering the rite to allow gay Christians to participate would clearly be one way to serve that end by bringing saving grace to this sector of the sexually active Christian membership.

Of course for Hooker one needs a very good reason to change even positive laws, especially when the practice being altered is of ancient provenance. Presumably the good reason in this case is the harm done to gay Christian relationships by withholding church rites from them. Hooker says that rites should not be changed simply because some small subset of the Christian population is harmed—for example, because a few members of the Church of England (the Puritans) might be scandalized by the retention of Roman rites. Rather than getting rid of such rites altogether, the harms to these sensitive souls can be mitigated by other means; these people can simply be educated about the proper way those rites are being employed in the Anglican Church. But the harm done in the case at issue for us is broader than that—harm is done to the general religious end of rites to bring the grace of Christ to committed relationships—and that harm cannot be remedied without some alteration or other of present rites (e.g., one alternative is a wholly new rite of blessing). Harm is done, moreover, to the whole body by the cramping of Christian charity and the promotion thereby of a mistakenly rigid understanding of the character of law.

Hooker, in Book Five of the *Laws*, consistently opposes himself to all rigid application of church law by Puritans so as to exclude exceptions and special cases. Infants should be baptized in consideration of their special status as children born within the church; private baptism is acceptable when the whole church cannot be assembled; lay people, even women, may baptize when circumstances prevent the usual administration of the rite by ordained men; and so on. To insist on laws without exceptions is to sin against the church's duty to extend the grace of God with all liberality to its membership, on the charitable assumption, which Hooker defends against the Puritans, that all are to be saved. It is to presume, erroneously, that God's working—the essential cause of grace's bestowal in the rite—can be hindered by irregular, indifferent incidentals of the rite itself. Summarizing these two points against Puritan rigidities in baptismal rites, Hooker expresses incredulity that thereby "the Church which is by office a mother unto such as crave at her hands the sacred mystery of their new birth, should repel them and see them die unsatisfied of these their ghostly desires, rather than give them their soul's right with omission of those things that serve but only for the more convenient and orderly administration thereof" (5:60.7). Insisting on laws without exceptions is in general to contravene the Anglican sensibility, as Bishop Paget so eloquently puts it in commenting on Book Five, of performing church rites "in the broad and generous judgment of a humble, hopeful mind, not cramped by narrow canons."[4] It is, finally, to misunderstand the character of general laws in which the ordinary course is ordinarily observed but not always (7:14.11). It is part of the very character of general laws that they be applied in equitable ways so as to take into account the special needs and mitigating force of particular circumstances (5:11.1–3).

Changing church canons to recognize same-sex unions does not, moreover, bring with it the strong inconveniences that only the weightiest of reasons for change could overcome. The least inconvenience is felt, Hooker says, in the case of laws for special occasions; when those occasions are no more, the laws themselves naturally lapse, without the need for further argument (4:14.1). Granted, this is not the sort of modification to marriage rites that recognition of same-sex unions brings with it. But that is at least in part because the change envisioned is even less radical in that it does not involve the actual abrogation of any rite. The Puritans were trying to rid the church of any and every practice that smacked of Catholicism; it was a radical winnowing down operation. In the present case, the requisite change may simply mean extending the usual rites of marriage to persons not previously eligible; arguably, this brings with it even less of an inconvenience than the lapse of a hitherto perhaps important but now out-of-date regulation. But neither do the changes required to recognize same-sex unions fit the case of greatest inconvenience, according to Hooker, where one denies the fitness from the very beginning of a long-standing law for an end whose importance is still felt. The abrogation of such laws scandalously calls into question confidence in lots of other laws. If even this law be wrong even though so many believed in it for so long, what else is safe? But again, no one in the present intra-Anglican controversy is arguing that marriages should not be performed anymore, or that marrying straight people now or in the past was wrong. The claim is not even being made that excluding gay people in the past from marriage rites was wrong, assuming that there were then no gay Christian couples clamoring as they are now for admission to the rite. There is change and then there is change; the exact sort—whether a rite is "altogether abrogated, or in part repealed, or augmented with further additions" (3:10.1)—makes a difference for the kind of justification required. The alterations of present church practice necessary to recognize same-sex unions are so minor, relatively speaking, that the recounting of harms given above is more than sufficient to justify them.

Such movements to extend marriage or augment it with a rite of blessing are unlikely to take place uniformly across the Anglican Communion. The U.S. and Canadian churches are perhaps the only churches in the Anglican Communion where such changes are a real possibility in the foreseeable future. But Hooker's general understandings of law and ecclesiastical polity give one no reason to be especially surprised or worried about this lack of uniformity across the Communion.

Changeable laws, because they are affected by circumstance, are unlikely in general to be universally applicable. The same laws are not found everywhere, but a great variety of them—and appropriately so. Changeable laws are positive laws and positive laws are framed to take into account the particulars of the times, places, and persons they regulate. "In laws, that which is natural bindeth universally, that which is positive not so" (1:10.7).

For example, a mixed positive law must take into account not just the law of nature that, say, every society needs a rule of life, but the particulars of time and place in order to specify that natural law appropriately for a particular group of people. "Some kind of regiment the Law of Nature doth require; yet the kinds thereof being many, Nature tieth not to any one, but leaveth the choice as a thing arbitrary" (1:10.5). What determines the choice is not natural law simply, but what seems "fit and convenient" to a particular time and place. A great variety of laws is also appropriate where positive laws have more particular ends (1:10.9). Hooker mentions the case of a law penalizing drunken misconduct more harshly than sober; such a law is certainly not appropriate everywhere, only (for example) in situations where a law mitigating the severity of punishment in the case of impaired judgment has led many people purposely to get drunk to avoid punishment. And so on for all the other types of positive law. Because they are always at least in part determined by particular circumstances, for positive laws "to be every where the same is impossible and against their nature" (ibid.). And therefore "to this appertain those known laws of making laws; as that law-makers must have an eye to the place where, and to the men amongst whom; that one kind of laws cannot serve for all kinds of regiment" (ibid.).

The specific rules that a church abides by for its public governance and right order are mixed positive laws like those of any other society, and therefore the same variety proper to societies is proper to churches: "he that affirmeth speech to be necessary among all men throughout the world, doth not thereby import that all men must necessarily speak one kind of language. Even so, the necessity of polity and regiment in all Churches may be held without holding any one certain form to be necessary in them all" (3:2.1). Divine law does specify some public forms of church life (e.g., baptism and eucharist, public prayer) as necessary for all churches, but what divine law does not specify, and the particular forms that the specified practices are to take (e.g., kneeling or standing for communion, wafers or bread, etc.), are again matters of circumstantially determined positive law, which appropriately varies from place to place. God has left such matters up to the determination of the churches, and each such church, as a self-legislating society in its own right, has jurisdiction to determine these matters in ways appropriate to its particular circumstances. "The Catholic Church is . . . divided into a number of distinct Societies, every which is termed a Church within itself" (3:1.14). Like any other "politic society," each of these churches—which Hooker basically identifies with national churches—has the proper power, within the limits that God's law and natural law allow, of making its own positive laws suitable for its particular circumstances. This was indeed the principle behind the Church of England's break with Rome to begin with—the desire for a church more in line with its own national character, requiring the direction therefore of national institutions rather than the Pope. It is again the principle that Hooker appeals to in supporting the Church of England's refusal to conform its governance and ceremonies to those of Geneva.

It is simply not appropriate to think, as the Puritans do, that God wants every religious society under the direction of divine law to have exactly the same polity. The Puritans were fond of using Israel as the model for this uniform polity because divine laws seemed so thorough and so precise in its case. But according to Hooker:

> the laws positive are not framed without regard had to the place and persons for the which they are made. If therefore Almighty God in framing their [Israel's] laws had an eye unto the nature of that people, and to the country where they were to dwell [Canaan]; if these peculiar and proper considerations were respected in the making of their laws, and must be also regarded in the positive laws of all other nations besides: then seeing that nations are not all alike, surely the giving of one kind of positive laws unto one only people, without any liberty to alter them, is but a slender proof, that therefore one kind should in like sort be given to serve everlastingly for all. (3:11.6)

Although the end to which God wishes to bring all religious societies may ultimately be one, God's wisdom shines through this respect for the particular situations of different societies, which makes the ways of his providence many (3:11.3).

Hooker clearly does not view this variety of polity among the churches as an unseemly accommodation to national political forms or social customs, as present-day critics of trends to recognize gay unions in the churches often allege. Such a charge would hardly make sense from the defender of an establishment church. But Hooker also repudiates the general principle underlying such accusations (4:6–7). Such a principle overgeneralizes in an unreasonable way scriptural mandates against the carrying over of Canaanite or Gentile practices into the life of God's people. The Puritans illegitimately universalize indefinite prohibitions: "be in nothing like the Canaanites" (or Gentiles) does not mean share absolutely nothing with them, but rather, do nothing they do that is idolatrous or against God's law (4:6.3). Because such general prohibitions do not rule out everything that others do—this would be an impossible recommendation in any case where God's people live intertwined with their non-Christian or non-Israelite neighbors—what they do not rule out, God's people are free to practice or not as circumstances warrant. The matters that fall under such a general prohibition are not, moreover, ruled out simply because others do them but because they are for some other reason wrong. Even if such matters were not the practices of Canaan or the Gentile world, they would therefore be prohibited in any case. Where more specific laws prohibit particular Canaanite or Gentile practices despite the fact that they are not against the law of nature or do not violate divine law, this is again not, as Hooker would say, simply for the purpose of "affection of dissimilitude with others" but for some more particular reason (4:7.3; 4:6.3). For example, although there is no reason in principle to avoid decking one's house with garlands as pagans do, it might be appropriate to prohibit the practice when Christians are tempted to do so simply as a way of avoiding persecution (4:7.3). It would of course be improper to imitate the ways of the wider world simply because they have become a model for you, but there is nothing wrong with taking over such ways by reason, and in the spirit of one's own religious commitments (4:7.1–2). Christians as a matter of fact have taken over lots of pagan practices—for example, Christmas trees, feast days, sitting after prayer. There is nothing wrong with this if such matters are otherwise indifferent or if Christians have remedied the faultiness of heathen use in the things they do that are similar (4:7.2, 5). Presumably marriage or blessing rites would be remedying deficiencies (e.g., resulting from the lack of grace) in the way committed partnerships among gay people are entered into in the wider society. Finally, as Hooker points out in the application of such considerations to the Roman Church, the parallel with paganism is faulty to begin with here because these are fights over proper practice with one's coreligionists. In the case of rites for same-sex unions, Christians are not borrowing such rites from another religion or even from an established civil practice, but rather are constructing specifically Christian rites in line with already established Christian practices for the recognition of committed partnerships. For all these reasons, blanket worries about accommodation to the wider culture are misplaced.

Differences in polity among Christian churches that reflect national differences in political forms or customs need not, moreover, have an adverse effect on the unity of the church. Hooker is, of course, writing before the development of a worldwide Anglican Communion; the church unity or communion he has in mind is that of the whole Christian world. But his general reasoning remains quite suggestive for the more circumscribed case of national differences within the Anglican Communion. According to Hooker, national differences of polity do not adversely affect church unity because church unity is more a matter of shared doctrine than shared discipline. On this difference between doctrine and discipline, Hooker writes: "to make new articles of faith and doctrine no man thinketh it lawful; new laws of government what commonwealth or church is there which maketh not either at one time or another?" "There is no reason in the world wherefore we should esteem it necessary always to do, as always to believe, the same things; seeing every man knoweth that the matter of faith is constant, the matter contrariwise of action daily changeable, especially the matter of action belonging unto church polity" (3:10.7). Therefore, "where the faith of the holy Church is one, a difference in customs of the Church doth no harm" (4:13.3). There are, he admits, some basic matters of discipline that must also be held in common: for example, the rites of baptism and eucharist. But where these fundamentals or essentials of belief and discipline are shared, differences on all other matters, and in the specific forms of the required elements of discipline, do not threaten church unity. The articles of the faith and the sacraments of the church are for all times and everywhere the way the church must tread, but that way remains despite variation in everything accessory to it: "to alter [those accessories] is no otherwise to change that way, than a path is changed by altering only the uppermost face thereof; which be it laid with gravel, or set with grass, or paved with stone, remaineth still the same path" (3:3.3).

Hooker admits that it is within the rights of the church universal to seek greater uniformity of practice. Presumably, more particular church bodies, such as the Anglican Communion, that span national differences could also appropriately seek greater uniformity, in order, for example, to establish more clearly the specific parameters of their particular communion as a visible society. Hooker argues, however, that great dangers attend how far and in what manner one seeks greater unity in discipline (4:13). "Neither deny we but that to the avoiding of dissension it availeth much that there be amongst them an unity as well in ceremonies as in doctrine. The only doubt is about the manner of their unity; how far churches are bound to be uniform in their ceremonies, and what way they ought to take for that purpose" (4:13.2). When, for example, the effort to establish unity of external forms goes too far, it is likely to produce a misplaced preoccupation with matters that are not all that important. "Yea sometimes it profiteth and is expedient that there be difference, lest men should think that religion is tied to outward ceremonies" (4:13.3). Requiring universal conformity on matters otherwise indifferent is also likely to create more dissension than it alleviates. "For if churches be urged by way of duty to take such ceremonies as they like not of, how can dissension be avoided?" (4:13.4). Without any established communion-wide judicial mechanism for deciding uniformity of polity, moreover, the mechanism for establishing greater unity is likely to be one in which each national church proposes its own ways for imitation by all the rest, leading to chaotically undecidable mutual recriminations. Hooker's citation of Augustine is apropos here: "if we will dispute, and condemn one sort by another's custom, it will be but matter of endless contention" (3:11.15). In the absence of such a communion-wide judicial mechanism, it is far better, then, to follow a law of "common indulgence," "as they cannot with modesty think themselves to have found out absolutely the best which the wit of men may devise, so liking their own somewhat better than other men's, even because they are their own, they must in equity allow us to be like unto them in this affection; which if they do, they ease us of that uncourteous burden, whereby we are charged either to condemn them or else to follow them" (4:13.10). If the whole church as a whole by agreed-on judicial authority ruled in favor of uniformity in things otherwise indifferent, then active dissent on the part of national churches would be improper. But absent that sort of mechanism, no national church has the authority to bind any other to its particular procedures and customs, no matter how numerous its members or ancient its practices (4:13.9). The present Anglican Communion has, in fact, no communion-wide institutions with legislative authority for the whole and therefore it must rest content "to admire the wisdom of God, which shineth in the beautiful variety of all things, but most in the manifold and yet harmonious dissimilitude of those ways, whereby his Church upon earth is guided from age to age, throughout all generations of men" (3:11.8).

No matter how apparently minor the alterations to church rites necessary for recognition of same-sex unions, such alterations would of course be improper if they violated divine law set forth in scripture. The church simply does not have the authority to legislate for itself in ways that contravene scripture. The Puritans argued that scripture gave exact positive directions for every aspect of church life, and Hooker contested that, but he never denied that the clear and manifest teachings of scripture overruled church legislation that ran contrary to them. As Hooker himself says, "laws human must be made . . . without contradiction unto any positive law in Scripture" (3:9.2), and that contradiction is all that opponents of rites for same-sex couples avow against them.

The Puritan sensibility of their complaint comes through nonetheless to the extent they deny the relevance of judging whether the apparent contradiction of scripture is real. If there were a scriptural law that said that gay relationships of any and every kind are always and everywhere to be condemned, or if scripture contained more particular laws or legal precedents for situations perfectly comparable to the present ones and there was no reason to think that these were temporary divine injunctions, then the contradiction would be plain and indisputable. But neither case holds. The first case manifestly fails to hold because none of the scriptural passages concerning homosexual acts exhibits a general legal formulation of the required sort. The second—on the word of the great majority of the most learned and sagacious judges whom Hooker says we should turn to for guidance on such difficult questions (2:7.6–8)—also fails to hold, if for no other reason than that the conditions to which particular scriptural law or precedents would pertain, then and now, are hardly comparable. "How [do the cases of scriptural condemnation of gay sex] relate, say, to the young man or woman, baptised, confirmed, communicant, converted and committed to personal faith in Christ and to holiness in life, perhaps longing to be ordained or commissioned to particular Christian ministry, who find themselves to be attracted strongly and only to those of the same sex, and in their own conscientious judgment unable to attain peace or stability until that fact is accepted positively?"[5] The clear suggestion is that such differences in application are serious.

One might try to argue that the often narrowly framed scriptural injunctions—for example, one must not lie with a man as with a woman in ancient Israel, the condemnation of a particular sexual act for a particular people a long time ago—are presuming a natural law prohibiting same-sex relations and therefore are more immutable and universal in formulation than they appear. Hooker indeed believes that scriptural laws often presume and re-publish laws of nature. But there are several problems with this. Natural laws, according to Hooker at least, are self-evident; and as the culture wars in the churches and the wider society make clear, these "laws" no longer appear self-evident to many morally conscientious and intellectually responsible people. Of course, natural laws should be self-evident and often are not because human reason is corrupted by sin; Hooker says, remember, that whole societies can go wrong about them and that is one reason that they need to be reaffirmed in scripture. But a serious problem for this line of argument is that, as the present controversies within the Anglican Communion make clear, many people in the churches also fail to see the self-evidence of condemnations of gay relationships; and their reason has presumably felt the influence of grace that Hooker thinks clears up the sinful impediments to reason's proper operations.

The bottom line here is the need to assess whether the scriptural passages referenced by opponents of rites for same-sex relationships are being extended further than scripture warrants. For example, how do we know, without some additional assessment, that these scriptural passages concerning homosexual acts are framing laws at all? Hooker remarks with reference to his Puritan opponents how common it is for those pleading "the law of God," "the word of the Lord,"

> to quote by-speeches in some historical narration or other and to urge them as if they were written in most exact form of law. What is to add to the word of God if this not be? When that which the word of God doth but deliver historically, we construe without any warrant as if it were legally meant, and so urge it further than we can prove that it was intended; do we not add to the laws of God, and

make them in number more than they are? It standeth us upon to be careful in this case. For the sentence of God is heavy against them that wittingly shall presume thus to use the Scripture. (3:5)

Even when scriptural passages are formulated as laws, it is a Puritan penchant, to which Hooker repeatedly returns in his arguments against them, to overgeneralize such laws—to make laws with indefinite extension into universal laws, to ignore the specific conditions under which a law is designed to apply, and the like—all for the sake of gaining greater certainty about specific forms of church polity on scriptural grounds than scripture as written reasonably allows. If these scriptural passages are indeed formulating laws, it is also necessary to assess the kind of law they are before assuming their validity for the present time and circumstances of the church. I have already suggested the implausibility of judging them now to be natural laws. The other alternative is that they are positive divine laws—that is, laws that are such only because God promulgates them. Nothing about such laws requires, however, that they always remain in force. A law is not immutable simply because God promulgates it but because of what it concerns. "Positive laws are either permanent or else changeable, according as the matter itself is concerning which they were first made. Whether God or man be the maker of them, alteration they so far forth admit, as the matter doth exact" (1:15.1). God made plenty of laws for Israel that are no longer judged pertinent to the church, and the same with laws made in the early church and promulgated in scripture— say, those of the Council of Jerusalem (Acts 15:29) that forbade Gentile Christians to eat "strangled" meat. A law's simply being in scripture therefore settles nothing, because much that scripture teaches about the proper forms of religious society "hath . . . become unrequisite, sometimes because we need not use it, sometimes also because we cannot" (3:11.16). "Neither God's being author of laws for government of his Church, nor his committing them unto Scripture, is any reason sufficient wherefore all churches should for ever be bound to keep them without change" (3:10.7). In some cases, "notwithstanding the authority of their Maker, the mutability of that end for which they are made doth also make them changeable" (3:10.2); in short, God had only a temporary cause for making them (1:15.3). In others, "laws, though both ordained of God himself, and the end for which they were ordained continuing, may notwithstanding cease, if by alterations of persons or times they be found insufficient to attain unto that end. In which respect why may we not presume that God doth even call for such change or alteration as the very condition of things themselves doth make necessary?" (3:10.4).

Ignoring the complexities that must beset any biblical case against present-day rites, opponents of rites for same-sex unions seem to fall into the sort of biblical positivism that Hooker objected to in Puritan scripturalism: scripture never says anything favorable about gay sex and that is that; there is no room for further argument. The issue here is not how these particular passages of scripture are best interpreted but the underlying general principles that govern the church's appeal to scripture as a guide for the particulars of Christian life. By suggesting, as they so often do, that those reading these scriptural passages differently are violating scripture's authority, the opponents of rites celebrating gay relationships seem to be excluding the relevance and propriety of difficult rational discriminations in figuring out what scripture is telling us. But according to Hooker, scripture itself requires us to use careful rational judgment if we are to follow its direction rightly: "Howbeit when Scripture doth yield us precedents, how far forth they are to be followed; when it giveth natural laws, what particular order is thereunto most agreeable; when positive, which way to make laws unrepugnant unto them; yea though all these should want, yet what kind of ordinances would be most for that good of the Church which is aimed at, all this must be by reason found out. And therefore, 'to refuse the conduct of the light of nature,' saith St. Augustine, 'is not folly alone but accompanied by "impiety'" (3:9.1). Scriptural direction is not offered to beasts for whom it would do no good, but to rational people to be interpreted and applied rationally (3:8.11). The light of scripture does not drown all other lights (2:4.7); in offering us one good—supernatural laws in scripture—God fully expects us to continue to use all the others that God delights in (2:4.5). It is therefore a Puritan error to think that people "cannot admire as they ought the power and authority of the word of God, if in things divine they should attribute any force to man's reason" (3:8.4). Human reason is simply one of the means—along with the gifts of grace that purify it—that God uses to convey divine positive law through scripture. The exercise of reason therefore does not take away from the authority of scripture, which remains a sufficient teacher of all things necessary for salvation. "Unto the word of God, being in respect of that end for which God ordained it perfect, exact, and absolute in itself, we do not hold reason as a supplement of any maim or defect therein, but as necessary instrument, without which we could not reap by the Scripture's perfection that fruit and benefit which it yieldeth" (3:8.10). Indeed, ignoring the place of rational assessment is one of the easiest ways of deflating scriptural authority. Should, for example, the new Puritans permit no assessment of whether the scriptural passages they cite so often mean in fact what they say they mean, their appeal to scripture threatens to become no more than a circular validation of their own prior judgments about gay relationships. If it is possible that the passages mean something else, we would, moreover, end up taking the condemnation of gay relationships on their authority rather than scripture's. "Even such as are readiest to cite for one thing five hundred sentences of holy Scripture; what warrant have they, that any one of them doth mean the thing for which it is alleged? Is not their surest ground most commonly, either some probable conjecture of their own, or the judgment of others taking those Scriptures as they do? Which, not withstanding to mean otherwise than they take them, it is not still altogether impossible. So that now and then they ground themselves on human authority, even when they most pretend divine" (2:7.9).

Even if, taking all the complexities into account, one could support a scripturally based mandate against any positive recognition of gay relationships in the present-day church, it is important to see that the case would amount at most to a probable conjecture. For all the vaunted talk of the word of God, the unavoidable complexities of the case mean that it really amounts to "that *some things* which they maintain, as far as *some men* can *probably conjecture*, do *seem* to have been out of scripture *not absurdly* gathered" (ibid.; emphasis in original). Such an argument is not strong enough to make abiding by such a scriptural mandate count among those things necessary for salvation. According to Hooker, what is necessary for salvation must always be "expressly contained" or "manifestly collected" out of scripture (3:2.2); one impugns the wisdom of God to think matters necessary for salvation would not be "plainly set down in scripture; so that he that heareth or readeth may without any difficulty understand" (Preface:3.2). Especially given the present level of disagreement among Christians about what the Bible says on these matters, it is wildly implausible to think scriptural laws against same-sex unions are of this type. In even the best-case scenario for the opponents of rites recognizing same-sex unions, scriptural laws concerning homosexuality simply cannot therefore be judged to be all that important. God surely cannot have expected or desired uniform judgment by all Christians everywhere in favor of such a law, as God does for matters necessary for salvation.

Probable conjectures from scripture, Hooker maintains, are also insufficient to justify individual dissent from church legislation that has taken place in good order and with due process. If, for example, the Episcopal Church USA at its General Convention in 2003 approved the consecration of a gay bishop or recognized, without condemnation, the decision of some of its bishops to allow rites for same-sex unions in their dioceses, a merely probable argument that these judgments violate scriptural law does not justify dissent on the part of individual persons under General Convention's jurisdiction. The Old and, now joining them, the New Puritans go wrong about this by holding up rights of private judgment in ways that sow confusion and disorder.

Hooker does suggest that legal authority, whether in church or state, must have the consent of the entire society behind it (1:10.4; 1:10.8). But he defines that consent very broadly. Even if one disagrees with a particular piece of legislation, one has consented to it insofar as one has consented to be governed by the decisions of the regular legislative bodies of the society of which one is a part. "A law is the deed of the whole body politic, whereof if ye judge yourselves to be any part, then is the law even your deed also" (Preface:5.2). Especially because the Episcopal Church USA is a voluntary society, one can surely be assumed to have given one's prior consent to the decisions reached by its established legislative bodies; it is therefore illegitimate to disobey those bodies when they have arrived at judgments conflicting with one's personal opinions. Because you have agreed to be governed by their decisions, "it is but justice to exact of you, and perverseness in you it should be to deny, thereunto your willing obedience" (Preface:6.5). Waiting to be personally convinced before obeying is perverse for the same reason (Preface:5.2).

Private persons who disagree with such decisions have, moreover, no "commission, whereby they are authorized to sit as judges, and we required to take their judgement for good in this case" (4:4.2); "private discretion which otherwise might guide us a contrary way, must here submit itself to be that way guided, which the public judgment of the Church hath thought better" (1:16.7). No one doubts that legislative bodies may make bad decisions, but they need to be repealed by the same public bodies that made them to begin with (Preface:5.2; Preface:6.3). "Laws that have been approved may be again repealed . . . by the authors thereof themselves. But this is when the whole doth deliberate what laws each part shall observe, and not when a part refuseth the laws which the whole hath orderly agreed upon" (Preface:5.2). Those who disagree with the decision, in short, have no proper authority to agitate through other than established channels for their reform—say, by calling their own conventions or carving out new jurisdictions under new leadership, as disgruntled conservative members of the Episcopal Church now seem to be doing; the decisions they object to would cease to be binding on all members only if the same legislative bodies that arrived at them in the first place took them back.

The only exception for private individuals to act on their conscience in disobedience of duly prescribed law is when a necessary argument, a demonstrative rather than merely probable case, exists that either natural law or the law of God, or some grave and imminent harm, enjoins against what has been legislated (Preface:6.6; 5:8.5). There are no demonstrative, invincible arguments of any of these sorts for the case at hand. Even were one to presume there were some, those who object would still have the burden of proof to convince others, rather than simply assume the undeniable probity of their own position: "where such singularity is, they whose hearts it possesseth ought to suspect it the more, inasmuch as it did come from God, and should of that cause prevail with others, the same God which revealeth it to them, would also give them power of confirming it to others, either with miraculous operation, or with strong and invincible remonstrance of sound Reason, such as whereby it might appear that God would indeed have all men's judgments give place unto it" (5:10.1). Unfortunately, the New—like the Old—Puritans are not inclined to accept that burden of proof: "let any man of contrary opinion open his mouth to persuade them, they close up their ears, his reasons they weigh not, all is answered with rehearsal of the words of John, 'We are of God; he that knoweth God heareth us': as for the rest, ye are of the world; for this world's pomp and vanity it is that ye speak, and the world, whose ye are, heareth you" (Preface:3.14). Indeed, it is the very unproven certainty with which they hold their own views to be the very word of God that inclines them to contest all due authority: "when the minds of men are once erroneously persuaded that it is the will of God to have those things done which they fancy, their opinions are as thorns in their sides, never suffering them to take rest till they have brought their speculations into practice" (Preface:8.12). Hooker is pessimistic about the outcome. Any other way but the general one he outlines of deference to the orderly mechanisms for decision making in the church breeds, he thinks, confusion and disturbance (1:16.6; 1:16.7): "except our own private and but probable resolutions be by the law of public determinations overruled, we take away all possibility of sociable life in the world" (1:16.6).

Hooker thought his own age was one "full of tongue but weak of brain" (1:8.2), in which "zeal hath drowned charity and skill meekness" (4:1.1). He says he was therefore tempted, with Gregory of Nazianzus, "to convey myself into some corner out of sight, where I may scape from this cloudy tempest of maliciousness, whereby all parts are entered into a deadly war amongst themselves, and that little remnant of love which was, is now consumed to nothing. The only godliness we glory in, is to find out somewhat whereby we may judge others to be ungodly. Each other's faults we observe as a matter of exprobration and not of grief" (Preface:9.3). I am tempted to end this essay with such a complex citational reiteration for added emphasis of the gloom—my citing Hooker citing Gregory—pessimistic souls all! But the continuing legacy of Hooker for the Anglican Communion gives me pause. It may yet be the case that "they who claim the general assent of the whole world unto that which they teach, and do not fear to give very hard and heavy sentence upon as many who refuse to embrace the same," will look back to consider whether "their first foundations and grounds be more than slender possibilities" (2:1.3).

AD IMAGINEM DEI

IS THERE A MORAL HERE?

Susan Frank Parsons

A persistent assumption in the Western tradition of thought is that human being is unique amongst beings, having a special capacity to relate to that which is beyond itself, a capacity that does not belong to other beings and that thereby sets human being apart as distinctive. From this assumption there has followed something further. That is, that in the course of any particular human life, this special nature of human being is to be both realized and protected, both made actual in the life of that individual and also guarded from any harm, from anything that would threaten the fundamental humanity that belongs with our being human at all. Here appears the moral. For it is the essence of the moral that it be the means by which authentic human being is achieved, and so in the Western tradition, moral knowledge and moral living are understood to be intrinsically related to the uniqueness of human being itself. It is not the intention of this essay to trace the diverse and often troubled course of this Western humanism. Rather here I seek to investigate one form that this way of thinking has taken in the current debate regarding the authorization of same-sex relationships and to indicate briefly another way of approach to these things.

It has been a feature of theological thinking within this tradition that human being is understood to be God's own special creation, God's good or even best idea. God has made human being originally in God's own image and so human beings in their special and unique nature are the image of God in this world. Therefore, conformity with this image, given and established in some ultimate sense at the creation of all things, has been taken to be the primary requirement of a fulfilled human life as well as the completion of God's good intentions for that life. This notion of the image of God, the *imago Dei*, has provided the ground, the fundamental premise on the basis of which moral decisions are to be made in the context of faith, and it is used as something of a test in the midst of new situations or dilemmas that arise. Thus it is asked: Does this action threaten our basic humanity and so imperil the *imago Dei* which is ours to be? In what sense may this decision complete or realize that image of God and so bring us into communion with God?

Such questions have played a major part in theological debates about sex and gender, and so it is unsurprising that they appear also in considerations of same-sex relations. For the moral and theological authority of these relations, it is argued, must be measured by their conformity with what this *imago Dei* is understood to be and must be judged for their potential damage to that image, discerned as to their possible dehumanizing effects that would prevent our most authentic fulfillment as human beings in obedience to God's purposes. This kind of argument has been developed and elaborated by Roman Catholic theologians to such an extent that its main outlines are now widely taken for granted as the debate about same-sex relations unfolds in the Catholic Church and elsewhere. A closer examination of this approach reveals the way in which heterosexuality has been written into this account of human being, and that in itself is interesting.

What comes to light in the course of such investigation, however, is an underlying question about what is going on in this theological anthropology. What is it doing? For these arguments constantly throw us back into a past that is said to be already laid down as foundational for human life, a past that is constructed or narrated from out of a contemporary situation and its needs, and that now demands our adherence and attention to its requirements upon our lives. If its primary intention has been to work out the way for human beings to draw near to God in their ways of deciding and acting, in conformity with the divine image and in obedience to God's will, it has now become almost exclusively a voice of power, of moral legitimacy and regulation that masks an emptiness lying within, and that may indeed prevent the very thing it most seeks to realize. Heterosexual relations are now required to be themselves the proof of what is believed, even when there is very little else to show for it, and so to be the witnesses brought forward and made to stand in evidence that these assumptions about human distinction are true.

Is this the only way to understand the being of being human in its relation to that which is beyond itself? Or might it be shown that what is beyond human being, to which human capacities most uniquely are related and towards which human being moves to its fulfillment, is the future? And further, that the moral needed here is one which will, in its own ways of knowing and deciding, in its *meth' hodos*, carry human being into the realization of this future, so that, in a real sense, it is a moral that accomplishes that of which it speaks, or does what it says? If this may be only briefly sketched here, it is nonetheless hoped that attention will be drawn to our modes of being with one another by which this future is made actual and to those bonds between human beings by which we accompany one another to our end in God. Such are also, of course, traditional ways of thinking that appear in discourses concerning sanctification and that are found among those who would learn from the saints. Attending to these once again may open another way to consider the matter of authorization for same-sex relations.

In a presentation to Canada's House of Commons Standing Committee on Justice and Human Rights, the Canadian Conference of Catholic Bishops has given one kind of answer to the central question which this essay investigates—*ad imaginem Dei*: is there a moral here? Responding by invitation to a government discussion paper on the legal recognition of same-sex unions, the Bishops urge the House to "do everything you can to preserve the definition of marriage."[1] Marriage, they argue, is facing many challenges in present-day society that threaten the "pivotal role" it has played throughout the centuries in providing stability for families that are built upon its foundation and for the wider society whose overall welfare it serves. Believing this institution to be one that has endured consistently for centuries, they set out its various dimensions—anthropological, personal, social, and religious—all of which lead to the same conclusion, they claim, that marriage is "distinct from all other forms of human relationships," a distinction that should be maintained for the good of all Canadians.

In the midst of their statement is a reference to the proclamation, found in the first pages of the Bible, of "the beauty of the relationship between a man and a woman, who are created in the image of God" and in whose continuing love and exercise of "the creative force that flows from this reality," namely, the capacity for procreation of children, "the couple becomes a sign of the very love of God." The image of God here serves as the central point from out of which the various dimensions of marriage radiate and derive their significance, and within which they fundamentally cohere, forming together that special definition of marriage which the Bishops hope will be saved. In saving the definition, so also will humanity be rescued from imminent peril and be brought to know the truth about themselves and how they are to live. Clearly, there is a moral here and marriage has a crucial role to play in its understanding and execution.

This is now a fairly standard line of moral argument within the Catholic Church, and so is not particularly remarkable in itself, since it seeks only to hold a line of defense against attacks rather than to engage in any deeper reflection on the substance of the issues at stake. Indeed, its assumptions about marriage are bolstered through a combination of statistical data collected in surveys and claims selected from among the social and human sciences that confirm the central argument and add force to its expressions of concern for the status and the future of this relationship. This assorted material is brought into focus and lifted onto a higher plane in speaking of the *imago Dei*, where the definitive nature of marriage is said to be established. For here, in its light, the explanation for the existence of marriage—its first cause, and the significance of its creation and preservation—its purpose, are ultimately grounded. Marriage can then be seen not only to be the pivotal realization of divine intention in human life, but also to have a special religious meaning as a sacrament, a sign of union, the solemnity of which the government is urged to respect as "an expression of faith."

The pattern for this episcopal presentation and the anxiety for human life it expresses have become especially prominent at least since the Second Vatican Council. Literature on the subject produced for the guidance of pastors and theologians, as well as for general encouragement of the faithful especially through this post-conciliar period, gives ample evidence of this way of understanding the moral life. Already noted during the Second Vatican Council was the precarious situation of man in the modern world, whose special dignity and value was under threat and whose capacity to witness to the existence and goodness of God was beset by various urgent crises. Seeking to proclaim "the noble calling of humanity and the existence within it of a divine seed," the *Pastoral Constitution on the Church in the World of Today* offered insight into the role that marriage and family life are to play in witnessing to this truth.[2] From its opening sentences, *Gaudium et spes* is marked by an awareness of the ambiguity that lies here, for the complexities of contemporary life are a sign of the success of human knowledge and skill even as they now overwhelm and threaten to deprive us of these very things. Awkwardly placed, as ones who seem now to be oppressed by fulfilled expectations, human beings "are questioning themselves" and are looking for that which will restore confidence in the meaning of human life.[3] The Council begins to take steps towards this restoration by speaking of *de homine ad imaginem Dei*, and so by affirming "the God-given character of the human person" and the values that proceed from this divine source.[4] For the Church is taught by the scriptures to understand "the true human condition" that springs from being created "with the capacity to know and love its creator,"[5] and to share "in the light of the divine mind." The Council takes this to mean that "human beings are correct in judging that by their intellect they are superior to the totality of things," and also that their understanding "is not bound simply by appearances but is capable of grasping intelligible reality with true certainty."[6] It is on the basis of such knowledge that the characteristics of a truly human life can be delineated and guidance through the outstanding causes for universal concern can be given.

One of these causes for concern is marriage and the family, with the community of which "the well-being of the person and of human and Christian society is intimately connected."[7] Thus it is said that God is "the author of marriage and its endowment with various values and purposes, all of which are of such vital importance for the continuance of the human race, the personal development and eternal destiny of the individual members of the family, and the dignity, stability, peace, and prosperity of the family itself and of human society as a whole."[8] Having sprung from this "divine fountain of love," it is "to be a reflection of his [Christ's] union with the church," made real in the meeting with God that takes place through this sacrament. "Genuine married love is taken up into the divine love and is directed and endowed by the redeeming power of Christ and the saving action of the church," so that husband and wife, parent and child, may "attain to their own perfection, their mutual sanctification, and their joint glorying in God."[9]

There is, then, in marriage a bringing together of divine and human in love that realizes and completes the creation. Ordinary human love is understood here to be something "willed by one person for another" that "embraces the good of the entire person," but this is elevated by God, it is healed, perfected, and raised so that it leads to the free and mutual self-giving that was originally intended by the Creator, permeating the whole of life as it is increased by its own generosity.[10] Such understanding of what lies at the origin of human being is to provide the basis for moral guidance concerning the indissolubility of the marriage bond, birth control, and relations between men and women, in order that the family can continue to "constitute the basis of society" and may serve in its own way the work of "redeeming the present time and distinguishing between eternal verities and their changeable expressions." Married couples, then, understood to be "made in the image of the living God and established with the true status of persons,"[11] have a most special role to play in this redemptive work.

What is noticeable within this material is the recurring insistence that the mode of gender identity and of sex in the marriage relationship be understood to be both exemplary of human distinctiveness as created by God and sacramental in communicating the gracious presence of God to and among human beings. The privilege accorded to this relationship is based on the presumption that there is a true image of human being which was in the mind and intention of God at creation, and that the correct understanding of God's good idea is the basis for theoretical and moral deliberation concerning the distinctive facets of human life and serves as the ideal to which any practical recommendations concerning life's dilemmas are to be referred. However, it is also the case that this privilege appears at a crucial period of reflection on the nature and meaning of human being, indeed on the future of humanity itself, not only within the Church, but within the wider culture, as it outlives the shocking evidence of its own inhumanity and the unsettling demise of philosophical and moral confidence in an ideological humanism. That the crisis of modernity should provide both the occasion for, and be especially exemplified in, these fervent appeals for the protection of marriage indicates that this privilege bears in its own way the cry for redemption that is heard in a troubled time.

The prolific writings of John Paul II give ample evidence that the crisis in these assumptions is at work even in his most serious efforts to address them with the gospel of life. For while there is no more ardent spokesman for this prevailing approach to marriage, the very difficulties of the fundamental theological anthropology on which it is grounded, and the untenable place that moral thought and action have come to occupy within it, nonetheless haunt his extensive reflections. This can be shown in particular within his catecheses on the creation of man and woman and on the sacramentality of marriage, given as weekly general audiences between 1979 and 1983. For here, three predominant currents of Western philosophical thought converge, lending their weight to the credibility of his case and providing a certain legitimacy to his moral persuasions.[12]

The first of these currents concerns the nature and role of metaphysical claims. The catechesis on creation takes as its starting point the saying of Jesus recorded in Matthew's Gospel, in which reference is made to what has been "from the beginning."[13] The Pope understands by this reference the "powerful metaphysical content" that lies concealed particularly within the later account of creation in Genesis 1.[14] It is this, he believes, to which Jesus draws the attention of his hearers. The content is there to be discerned within the text as something that can be known, found inside it and considered in itself, something that is laid down there or sedimented out of the events of creation and so available to any who seek to understand who and what they are, whenever or wherever they may ask. In this content is revealed the definition and the value of man, that is, the fundamental condition of our existence as the creature that is placed between heaven and earth and that alone bears the sign of the Creator in his body and in his knowledge of his own unlikeness to all other creatures. Such a unique condition is definitive of human being, for within its bounds can be discerned the ontological structure, the structure of being that is the being of one made in God's own image, who is valued as a good thing in God's sight, and is most specially favored with the gift of self-giving love manifested in God's own creative work. Thus "it can be said with certainty that the first chapter of Genesis has established an unassailable point of reference and a solid basis for a metaphysic and also for an anthropology and an ethic, according to which *ens et bonum convertuntur* (being and the good are convertible)."[15]

To enquire then about legitimacy, as the Pharisees had done, is to be directed to a fundamental truth that has been there from the beginning, to that which since the beginning of all things has been so. Thus Jesus, he says, "asked his questioners to go beyond . . . the boundary," *transcendere, met' ekeina*, in this case to go through the barrier that is the Fall, in order to see what is originally true of human being, which means that they are directed to stand at a place beyond historically and sinfully conditioned human being to find there the state of original and fundamental innocence in which all human existence is rooted. Such is an intellectual operation, which resolves then into right reason, *recta ratio*, whose responsibility it is to look after truth as correctness, for the Holy Father says, "The laws of knowing correspond to those of being."[16] This interpretation of the teaching of Jesus is indicative of an understanding of metaphysical claims as propositions concerning things that are unchanging, the correct grasp of which will guide human life safely into truth. Accordingly, Jesus' teaching is taken to be attentive to the requirement of being that one's moral decisions are to conform with this being itself. This is what the moral is.

If such a current of thought is broadly Platonic, having many resonances with the yoking together of the true and the good articulated in Books VI and VII of *The Republic*,[17] the second current is more recently Cartesian in its insistence upon subjectivity. Man's original condition as described in this catechesis is one of solitude, not caused by the lack of another human being, but a solitude that is "derived from man's very nature, that is, from his humanity."[18] This state of solitude is a fundamental *subiectum*, a *hypokeimenon*, that which is thrown under, and so is always already lying underneath. What is added to the account of human being by the earlier creation narrative of Genesis 2–3, the Pope suggests, is "the moment of choice and self determination, that is, of free will," by which man becomes "a person endowed with a subjectivity of his own."[19] Here an anthropological definition of man mirrors the theological one expressed in the *imago Dei*, and indicates the *proximate* and the *specific genus* of man as a "rational animal."[20] The experience of solitude yields to human consciousness a continually presenting awareness of his difference from God and from all else created by God, and therefore gives a personal knowledge of his utter dependence upon God's good will for his very being per se and for its significance. Solitude is here taken to be the presupposition of personal relationship, that out of which relationship is formed and to overcome which, relationships come into being at all. For we could not come into relationship with God unless we were made in the first place as ones set apart in his image, and we only come into relationships with other persons in reaching out across and thus overtaking the solitude that lies prior to them.

It is the nature of this solitude to bear the burden of what is missing and so to be melancholic, constantly in search of that which would come to meet it and touch its heart. Indeed, the catechesis suggests that such is the driving force of human will, of intentionality, which from the beginning searches for its own entity, its identity, its definition of itself. That everything encountered is inevitably instrumentalized to the will of this subject in its quest is unwittingly revealed both here and in the later cate-cheses on love. To come to know who one is as a human person is to experience, first, the "negative significance in this search," that is, the fact of not being able to identify oneself with any other being and thus of knowing what one is not. From this movement of separation into his own being alone, man is initially delineated as a person with a specific subjectiv-ity and is thus ready to stand alone as himself before God. Only then can he be "the subject of the covenant . . . constituted in the dimension of 'partner of the Absolute.'"[21] And only then can he know fully the meaning of his own body as the structure that "permits him to be the author of a truly human activity," and so as that which will express his person.[22] The substance of his solitude constitutes man "in a unique, exclusive, and un-repeatable relationship with God himself,"[23] and places him before an-other border that is to be crossed between himself and the woman made of his rib.

Which brings us to perhaps the most recent of the currents of thought that finds expression in these catecheses, that concerning the necessity for and the significance of relationship, of intersubjectivity, and of love by means of which the full realization of the *imago Dei* is carried out. The text of *Mulieris dignitatem* especially emphasizes the connection of person, communion, and gift which lies at the heart of the sacramental meaning of marriage. There it is explained that the image of God in man not only means that man and woman are each of them individually like God, "inso-far as he or she is a rational and free creature capable of knowing God and loving him." But there is a further meaning to this image that is disclosed especially in the creation of woman, namely, that dimension of "common humanity," of "interpersonal communion," into which both are called and without which they cannot exist.

For the meaning of Gen. 2:18 is said to be that "man cannot exist 'alone'; he can exist only as a 'unity of the two,' and therefore in relation to another human person."[24] To use the word *cannot* here, which is not in the biblical text, assumes the intrinsic connection of being and the good which lies at the foundation of the Holy Father's exegesis.[25] But this is now turned over to mean that what is not good cannot be. Thus, the ascendancy of the moral, of the ought-to-be, over being is accomplished. Indeed, this common humanity is something which is said to be, which is declared, but which has no other being than its being-posited as the necessary context for the realization of full personal subjectivity. The dif-ference between man and woman is required, then, to provide the space within which the personal gift of self from one to the other can be enacted. This mutual self-giving expresses the personal likeness of each to God by means of their difference from one another as masculine and feminine, and this is to be itself a sign of the living unity-in-communion of the triune God. For man and woman are called to live by love in this unity of two, and thereby "to mirror in the world the communion of love that is in God."[26]

What is interesting about this teaching as far as the argument of this essay is concerned is the way that the notion of communion has come to have a primarily moral interpretation. Love, being the personal willingness and capacity for self-giving that is lodged with the subject, is to accomplish and so witness to a correspondence between human and divine life. Such correspondence is understood to be analogical, which means both that it is indicative of the ontological difference between human and divine persons, but also that it provides a way of crossing over, of access, from one to the other. The moral expectation upon marriage lies precisely at this point. For marriage is to be "an effective sign of God's saving power" in this world, that is visibly demonstrated in the domination of concupiscence, which is self-control (self-mastery); in the spousal giving of conjugal rights to the body for sexual pleasure; and in participation in the mystery of creation through willingness to be progenitors.

In this way, marriage "signifies the ethical order," for it is given to historical man in this world "as a grace and at the same time as an ethos" which does not "pertain to the eschatological reality of the future world."[27] Rather the hope for the redemption of the body is brought into this world by the vocation of marriage, for it brings to mind our origin within this world and serves as a stable reminder of the mystery and thus the gracious gift of our creation. Thus it is said that "love is a power or a capacity of a moral nature, actively oriented toward the fullness of good," its role consisting in safeguarding the analogy, that is, the inseparable connection of the unitive and procreative meanings of the conjugal act, and its concern to protect the values of the *communio personarum* and of responsible parenthood.[28] Love's entire orientation to this world is lifted up by its obedient exercise of this power, becoming then a "higher power that confers adequate content and value to conjugal acts according to the truth of the two meanings."[29] In this way the sacrament of marital love is made to redeem the time of our sojourn in this world. The answer to the question posed in this essay is, thus, clearly again—yes. For "the foundation of the whole human 'ethos' is rooted in the image and likeness of God which the human being bears within himself from the beginning. Both the Old and New Testament will develop that 'ethos,' which reaches its apex in the commandment of love."[30]

In his book *After Aquinas*, Fr. Fergus Kerr reminds us that at least for St. Thomas "the little word '*ad*' is decisive in the explanation" of the image of God. For the text of scripture says, "*ad imaginem Dei*," *kat' eikona hemeteran kai kath' homoiosin*, to the image and likeness of God.

Kerr goes on, "There is indeed a likeness to God in a human being, not however a perfect but an imperfect likeness; hence the movement, the approach, indicated by '*ad*', the Latin preposition meaning 'towards'. A small bit of grammar carries a good deal of theology."[31] If the investigation undertaken so far has concentrated on one way in which this movement is understood and has exposed the logic of moral thinking that is required for its accomplishment, what remains is for us to consider the possibility that there is another way of understanding this movement, namely, in its temporality, and this means to understand the *ad* as a movement into the future, out towards that which is to come, into which we are beckoned by One who is before us.

For isn't the crisis in the assumptions that have so far carried us through the Western tradition of thought exactly the point at which we may become attentive to what has been lying hidden within it, which, now that we have come to a kind of end in the exhaustion of moral thinking by the posturing of power, we may hear and be attuned to? So that rather than construct some new alternative account of human being that might replace this worn-out and old-fashioned one, replacing it with something ever more inclusive or diversified or polyvocal or exotic and so joining the endless cycle of revaluing of values, we become aware as though for the first time that this grasp of the essence of human being is not ours to be had, that it is not an object of knowledge which might be detached from our living and so from our very selves. Every such construction is a temporal projection that seeks to secure our place within the flux of time on the solid ground it throws under us, so that we may take refuge in the shelter of its descriptions and live within its boundaries according to its law.

Already in the *Nicomachean Ethics*, Aristotle sets out the various ways of knowing upon which human endeavors depend, and finds them to be distinguished by their relation to time, to things changing.[32] Moral thought, as it has developed since then, has become locked into a successful collaboration of *episteme* and *techne*, between a way of knowing that finds the self-evident principles laid down as foundational for thinking, and a way of knowing that concerns itself with the crafting of things according to some idea of them. No more clear evidence of this partnership could be found than in contemporary arguments concerning sex and gender, and few more vehement demands for our submission to it than in the prevailing account of marriage in Christian ethics.

What is overlooked by this kind of effort is that distinctive way of knowing truth called *phronesis, prudentia*, which for Aristotle is especially the mode of knowledge that leads us in time, that shapes us as timely beings. It is *phronesis* that reaches out to the utmost, to the limit of the future, that lets itself be touched by what is there, and that receives what is of the future into its living. So that through *phronesis* we are informed by the future, by what is to become of us, developing those habits of behavior and our own quirky and lovable characters by which we are prepared for its coming. This way of knowing lives by anticipation and so by discernment of some end, some *telos*, that comes about as it is taken up, as it guides one by its promise into its completion. Such knowledge cannot be captured in any set of anthropological propositions, and is entirely lost when purportedly self-evident claims about the nature of human being are used as the basis for moral decisions. The resolution into mere *techne* inexorably follows.

To say that we are made *ad imaginem Dei*, which is nothing other than to say again the astonishing prologue to the *Secunda Pars* of Thomas Aquinas's *Summa*, is to speak of this future end *for* which we have been made.[33] It is to speak of our beginning, not as what *was*, but as what lies ahead into which we may let ourselves be taken as we are receptive to its promise. So the beginning means the future that begins in me, that is born in me as the why of my life, as the wherefore that I am to live towards. In thinking these words of scripture, we are taken to the limit of any human intellectual grasp of our raison d'être, to the threshold that cannot be crossed from this side, *to eschaton*, where we are brought into what is only made known to us and so accepted and learned through faith. Such words can be spoken in this boundary situation as they are given to be said, and so as they are understood to come from elsewhere, taken up by the one who listens and by the community that celebrates their reception. That they provide a continually inspiring articulation of the relationship of human and divine being is because they are not finished, because that of which they speak still awaits our coming and so calls to us to bring ourselves into their completion. So this is an address that comes from a future, from out of what is to be our end in God, and as such it puts in question who we now are and what we think we are doing and how we will ever find our way to what they portend. To reach out into what these words say is to risk our own self-understanding for what they might have to teach us, and so to be drawn into the very mystery they proclaim as it begins to take place in our souls.

The Christian understands these words as a summons into God's presence, as a call to become holy, to take up our place in God's own life. It is the vocation to sanctity that is universal; it is the common call upon all human beings and thus it is something that must be announced, proclaimed as in the words of Christ, "Repent for the kingdom is at hand" (Matt. 4:17). It is this vocation to which human life is finally ordered and into which every conversation, every friendship and union of persons, is to be drawn not on account of whatever happens between them, but on account of that into which they are called and so before which they are brought to stand together. This is what St. Paul says when he writes to the church in Corinth of partners sanctifying one another through faith, for one is drawn to look toward the future in God by the transparent witness of the other to its already being begun in the present, in faith, and so it begins too in their life with one another.[34] And this can only be what he means in that strange injunction for those who are married to live as though not married. His sense that the form of this world is passing away and his expectation of the imminent arrival of the kingdom are not some curiously primitive form of faith no longer quite plausible in a grown-up, sophisticated world.[35] These are entirely expressions of *phronesis* at work, carrying out the being-timely of human being toward its end in love.

Such are the lives of saints that we look to them for help here. A saintly life discloses to us the astonishing possibility of an intimacy-in-difference of divine and human being, giving us reason to hope that such also will be ours. Their tender awareness of the precariousness in which this likeness to God is held in frail earthen vessels, and their insistence that what is created is redeemed, are signs that it is the future which is "already"—not the past. Through them we may discern that what is made known *to* faith is true and it becomes true *in* faith, and that there is a necessary circularity in truth's rooting itself in the human soul. To pray with the communion of saints is to begin to know the compression of time into one's own being, as one's soul becomes the place wherein the future and the past are gathered together into the moment of truth's own demand for redemption now to be so. To follow them as they follow Christ is to be taught how an authorization works, and why an apology for truth in a troubled culture always lives from out of what is to come and so holds open the possibility for others to enter into and be directed by its way. A union of persons that is blessed is one that is led into this redemptive way by Christ himself, who calls us to be his disciples and, in walking along with him, to learn wherefore we have been made—*ad imaginem Dei.*

These concluding thoughts have been inspired by reading the *Dialogue* of St. Catherine of Siena, so she has the first word here.

> I will then, and I demand it from you through grace, that you have mercy on your people with the same uncreated love that moved you to create man to your image and likeness, when you said, "Let us make man to our image and likeness." And this you did, willing that we would share in all that you are, high eternal Trinity. . . . Who made you place man in this great dignity? With inestimable love you looked upon your creature within your very self, and you became enamored of her. So through love you have created her and have given her being, in order that she might taste and take pleasure in your eternal good.[36]

TRINITY, MARRIAGE, AND HOMOSEXUALITY

Eugene F. Rogers Jr.

In this essay I argue that Christian theologians would best understand marriage, including both same- and cross-sex marriage, as a form of sanctification that takes time both to expose faults for healing and to develop virtues for incorporation into the Trinitarian life. I do that by addressing a pair of objections. First I take up an objection from the Left that the New Testament devalues marriage, and that alternative patterns of friendship best represent its intent. Then I take up an objection from the Right that same-sex couples are unfit for sanctification. Both sides deny that same-sex marriages can sanctify: the Left because marriage cannot do the job, the Right because the job cannot be done.

I have defended marriage for same-sex couples against objections on the Right before.[1] To counter the claim that marriage would offer satisfaction of sexual urges to which a same-sex couple would not be morally entitled, I countered that Christian theologians understand marriage only shallowly as the making licit of sexual satisfaction. They would understand it better as a form of sanctification rather than satisfaction. Sanctification involves structure, specifically, a discipline or *ascesis* such as monks and committed couples undertake, in which God uses the perceptions of others one cannot easily escape to transform challenge into growth, into faith, hope, and charity.[2] No conservative has yet seriously argued that gay and lesbian Christians need sanctification any *less* than heterosexual ones. I rehearse that argument later. But I begin with the objection on the Left.

I

Among authors in the present volume, I encounter a different concern. Marriage has itself undergone critique as an exclusive, sexist and heterosexist, bourgeois, capitalist institution. Hopelessly co-opted by the powers that be, marriage can no longer carry forward Jesus' identification of friendship as the greatest value (John 15:13, 21:15), if it ever could. New Testament scholars find Jesus notably antifamily—he refuses to see his mother (Mark 3:31–35 and parallels), regards the family as a source of unbelief (Matt. 13:53–58) and strife (Matt. 10:21, 35), prefers the company of prostitutes and adulterers, and commends not only love of enemies

but hatred of families (Luke 14:26). Paul, too, describes marriage as reme-
dial or second best and manages to mention children hardly at all (1 Corinthians 7). The New Testament's critique of existing social structures
suggests, according to those scholars, that same-sex partnerships would
make better sense as liberating *alternatives* to bourgeois marriage.

Such a critique, although principled and accurate, can suffer from sociological naïveté. Arguments on the Right suggest that committed same-sex
couples should go away, because the partners look the same. Arguments
on the Left suggest that committed same-sex couples should go away,
because the commitment looks bourgeois. In each case, the aesthetic fin-
ishedness of the argument (in a phrase of Rowan Williams) strains against
observable features of socially constructed reality. Given that same-sex
couples are not going to go away, two questions press the theologian:
How is the Church or the Holy Spirit going to turn the phenomenon to
salvific purposes, that is, under what concrete liturgical form? And how is
the community going to regard the pairs so constructed?

Obviously, the Church or the Holy Spirit can construct human pairs in
many and various ways. I have no wish to deny the diversity of social forms
that have come and gone, under and without the name of *marriage*,
in the history of Christianity and other religions. I want to insist on
that variety.

Sometimes the critics of marriage sound as if only they know what marriage really is (a bourgeois power structure), curiously echoing conservatives, who also claim to know what marriage is (a lifelong public union of
one man and one woman for the procreation of children). The trouble is,
both sides make pseudo-historical arguments that smuggle in an essence.
Both sides essentialize something fairly recent and Victorian. (Upper-class
Victorian, I might specify; marriage forms varied by both class and place.)[3]
If the variety of social forms called "marriage" narrowed in the nineteenth
century, then twenty-first-century options seemed to narrow in turn. The
critics of same-sex marriage ask society either to reject or to repristinate
an upper-class Victorian form.

Furthermore, both sides reject same-sex marriage—whether because it
is same-sex or because it calls itself marriage—because they take offense at
what they see as a kind of parody. Rightists take offense because they see
same-sex couples aping, and thus mocking, conventional forms that
should, they think, lead to biological procreation. Leftists take offense
because they see same-sex couples co-opted by, and thus losing their capacity for improving, conventional forms that replicate oppressive power and
economic relations.

Queer theory seeks to trouble just that kind of binarism. Apply the
following remark of Judith Butler to marriage:

> To deconstruct the concept of matter or that of bodies [or marriage] is not to
> negate or refuse either term. To deconstruct these terms means, rather, to con-

tinue to use them, to repeat them, to repeat them subversively, and to displace them from contexts in which they have been deployed as instruments of oppressive power. Here it is of course necessary to state quite plainly that the options for theory are not exhausted by *presuming* materiality [or marriage], on the one hand, and *negating* it, on the other. It is my purpose to do precisely neither of these. . . . [My procedure] does not freeze, banish, render useless, or deplete of meaning the usage of the term; on the contrary, it provides the conditions to *mobilize* the signifier in the service of an alternative production.[4]

The present essay undertakes to mobilize the signifier *marriage* in the service of an alternative production. More theologically, the essay claims to acknowledge the work of the Holy Spirit in mobilizing signifiers for the production of grace. It is, after all, the Holy Spirit, in Christian discourse, who renews and diversifies, the Spirit who produces sanctification, human beings transformed by grace.

Butler has the advantage of being able to explain a bit of armchair observational sociology. Observers of culture or anyone with queer friends will notice that same-sex couples often want to mark their setting up of housekeeping and yet find themselves reluctant to use the words *marriage* or *wedding*. No matter how carefully the principals stick to the chosen lingo of *holy union, commitment ceremony,* or *celebration of partnership*, their guests, family, and friends tend to assimilate the ceremony to others they think it resembles, and call it a "marriage" or a "wedding." Especially afterward, they find it natural to say, "It sure was fun at your wedding." "It wasn't a wedding, it was a commitment ceremony." "Whatever, it sure was fun."

When two sexually linked people stand in front of a congregation, a minister, or a justice of the peace, exchange vows of mutual fidelity that they hope or intend to last for life, and go off (or return) to live together, then the performance looks like a wedding—and not at all for essentialist reasons, either; rather for Wittgensteinian ones, which comport rather well with Judith Butler.

Wittgenstein worried about conundrums of definitions, the puzzles of a philosophical essentialism anxious over black swans or white crows.[5] Before English speakers discovered Australia, philosophers worried, they had known what counted as a swan; its definition, its essence made it white. English speakers could talk about a black swan; but a black swan either named a pub or changed the subject; a black swan enjoyed the same status as a pink elephant, which belonged to an altered mental state, drunken or philosophical. In discovering Australia, English speakers also discovered birds sharing all the characteristics of European swans but color. Did that mean only that the definition needed revision in light of reality, or something deeper?

Wittgenstein thought talk of definitions and essences, including their ongoing revision in light of reality, gives an unsubtle and finally misleading account of how people talk and categorize and live. In language and in life, people recognize and categorize things much the way they identify a family resemblance. When people notice or try to notice that you look like your cousin, what they are looking for is hardly specific. You do not fail to resemble your cousin because your hair colors or complexions differ. You do not fail to resemble your cousin if your statures or body shapes differ. You do not fail to resemble your cousin if you are male and female, or straight and gay, or if you have different eye colors. You do not fail to resemble your cousin if you have different noses or ears, different cheek-bones or chins. The resemblance depends on no one criterion or short set of criteria. The resemblance can fail in an infinite number of particulars and still succeed. The resemblance is hardly about criteria at all. It is about a kind of ad hoc overlap that we call "family resemblance." Family resem-blance builds in a great deal of diversity—it has to. It builds in a great deal of parody—that is what makes your grandfather's lope so hilarious when it shows up in a sixteen-year-old of different temperament and body type. If the procedures of definition and essentialism work badly to describe how human beings recognize biological consanguinity—perhaps the best candidate among their social forms for essentialist treatment—why should those procedures work well for other social forms?

Just as we recognize (and create) similarities among biological families without using a criterion, so we recognize (and create) similarities among social structures without a criterion. We *already* do that with marriage. Consider what feature of the marriage ritual is "essential" in actual reli-gious ceremonies. For Catholics, it is essential that one not have been married before to someone still living. For Protestants not. And yet Cath-olics will not say that the Protestants are not married. For Catholics and Protestants alike, the essential moment of the sacrament is the exchange of vows. That moment *does not occur* in the Eastern Orthodox Order of Marriage, or of Crowning. Although an Orthodox couple expresses their intention to be married, they express that intention to the priest rather than to each other,[6] and the priest marries them, rather than their mar-rying each other, by announcing that they are crowned.[7] It is, in fact, usual to have friends hold the crowns until bestowed, and to say that the *friends* married (crowned) the couple. And yet readers unfamiliar with Orthodox weddings will ask, "What crowns?" Marriage crowns represent crowns of martyrdom, or *ascesis*,[8] with which they join the martyrdom of Christ by feeding each other the bread of his body dipped in the wine of his blood. In Judaism, what is essential is the *ketubah*, the marriage contract signed by witnesses—although many Jewish weddings take place without the parties knowing or much caring what the *ketubah* says, and with no intention of carrying out its more interesting conditions. And yet no Catholic or Protestant or Jew would say that any of those couples are not married. Not even to mention what makes a Muslim, Hindu, Zoroastrian, pagan, or civil marriage! And yet again, what could be *less* a marriage than one without an exchange of vows? What could be *less* a marriage than one without induction of the new body into the Eucharistic feast? What could be *less* a marriage than one without a *ketubah*? Well, somehow we do not have much trouble with those lacks of essentials. And if so, according to Wittgenstein, it is not because we are bad essentialists, it is because we are good at family resemblances. Proof of this "rule" is the status of common-law marriages: they obtain, after a number of years and a number of conditions of declaration or conduct varying from state to state, when a heterosexual couple simply lives together and gives out that they are married—without any ceremony at all. In Canada, where same-sex marriages are already legal, common-law marriages, according to the 2001 census, are even more common, at 14 percent, than in the United States.[9] If each author in the present volume wanted to call cross-sex marriages in his or her tradition "marriages," and same-sex marriages something else, the practices called marriages would exhibit more variety than the practices called something else.

Consider a modest proposal. If we are going to call same-sex marriages by a different name—perhaps to increase the variety of forms, to make room for diversity, to keep social forms from remaining monolithic, universalizing, and oppressive—then why not go on to adopt different titles before our names? Already Rightists are doing this by distinguishing "covenant marriages," in which the couples try to bind themselves so that the man is head of the woman and divorce is less easy. Then there is civil marriage. And remarriage. We would need a separate name for childless marriage. Or maybe two names, childfree marriage and postmenopause marriage. Then same-sex couples can have a union, or a variety of unions, each under their separate names. As in other societies, widows could mark their status by wearing black, and we could revive the old titles, not only Mr. and Mrs., Miss and Widow, but Master for the single man and Mx. for the divorced man, Md. for the widower, Ml. for the lesbian and Mg. for the gay man. Similar abbreviations identify the status and preferences of people in personal ads. Why not identify our names with them?

Even then, people will still refer afterward to the ceremony as the "wedding." And they will still regard the couple as married. And the *New York Times*, the *Washington Post*, and any number of hometown papers will still publish their pictures. And *Bride's* magazine, sexist, heterosexist, and deeply capitalist organ that it is, will still treat them all together. (As Judith Butler would point out, social pages in newspapers and the attempt to profit from love are not going to go away: our only choices are how to use and subvert them.) And little boys and their mothers will still have this conversation:

> WHEATON, Ill. — Mike and Sue Weinberg were out to dinner when their 6-year-old son, Jack, declared, "Mommy, I'm going to marry you." When Ms. Weinberg explained that she was already married, Jack persisted, "Then I'll marry Daddy."
> "You can't marry Daddy," Ms. Weinberg said patiently, "He's a boy."
> "But Mark and Kevin are boys," replied Jack, logic that his mother could not refute.
> Mark Demich and Kevin Hengst, the couple across the street, are not actually married.[10]

Members of same-sex couples will still try to get each other health insurance; they will still move in and own houses together; and they will still give each other durable powers of attorney for when they get sick. The courts will still need to divide their property when they break up, and their families will still recognize—or refuse to recognize—one of them as the chief mourner at funerals. It is in divorce court that the greatest body of same-sex marriage law has already been made, and it is in the refusal to recognize partners that families also recognize, despite themselves, the depth of the commitment they resist. The exception proves the rule, in the courts and even in Wheaton.

So if, in Butler's terms, one can only subvert or redeploy, but never freeze or banish a troublesome term, a Christian theologian will ask after the soteriological and Trinitarian principles for redeploying this one. Or if, in the terms of Michel de Certeau, marriage now has a margin policed by meanings generated at other sites, how can it become once again a site generating transgressive meanings of its own?[11]

II

The most important redeployment of the body in Christianity occurs when Jesus remarks, "This is my body, given for you." With that, he subverts and redeploys a structure of violent oppression—crucifixion—and turns it to a peaceful feast. He reverses the movement of the Fall, which began by counting divinity a thing to be grasped and ended by scorning the body, because the body gave Adam the lie, exposing him as a creature and not yet divine.[12] Adam enacts a pattern of seizure followed by scorn, the pattern not of the lover but of the rapist. Jesus re-befriends the body, and creates the bread of heaven, by counting divinity *not* a thing to be grasped. At the Last Supper, he performs a deathbed wedding: "You can't take my body," he says, "I'll give it to you."[13]

Jesus' eucharistic redeployment and subversion of structures of violence mobilize sexual and nuptial metaphors not only here. Syriac theology also tropes the Eucharist as deathbed wedding:

> The King's Son made a marriage feast in blood at Golgotha;
> there the daughter of the day was betrothed to him, to be his,
> and the royal ring was beaten out in the nails of his hands;
> with his holy blood was this betrothal made . . .
> he led her into the Garden—the bridal chamber he had prepared for her.[14]

> At what wedding feast apart from this did they break
> the body of the groom for the guests in place of other food?
> Wives are separated from their husbands by death,
> but this Bride is joined to her Beloved by death![15]

Bloodthirsty, yes. But no more bloodthirsty than the eucharistic meal. And not a model that joins the bride to her beloved in death by suttee, or by a man's violence against a woman, but by a man's refusal of violence, on behalf of a woman. No womanly self-sacrifice reigns here. But that is not the main point. Rather, Christianity constructs marriage here as a social form loaded with more meaning than it can bear, a tide of redemption and sacrifice.

A philosopher of religion, Jeffrey Stout, has explained more clearly than I how Christian theology accords social meaning to natural bodies:

> What is it, then, for a Christian to be sanctified? . . . [I]t is to be taken up by means of God's grace into the inner life of God, into the communion of Father, Son, and Holy Spirit with one another. When speaking of this, most of the Church's analogies have to do with bodies. God the Father, maker of heaven and earth, creates the bodies we have by nature, the natural bodies we are. But [God] also incorporates us into social bodies, which then transform what our natural bodies mean, by making them represent something socially.[16]

What does God or the Church cause bodies socially to mean? That, as Stout sees it, depends on the multiple levels of communities that incorporate those bodies. The ascetic commitment of monogamy or monasticism or both "incorporates a person into a series of communities: first, the community with one's marital partner [or fellow monastics]; second, the community of Christ's body, the Church; and third, the community of interpersonal love and joyous beholding that constitutes God's inner Trinitarian life."

Christianity, in several traditions, enacts a nuptial mystery. In the Bible, God espouses God's people, with an earthly fidelity and an eschatological fulfillment:

I will betroth you to me forever . . . I will betroth you to me in faithfulness; and you shall know [who I am].[17]

The kingdom of heaven may be compared to a king who gave a wedding feast for his son.[18]

"Why do [others] fast, but your disciples do not fast?" And Jesus said to them, "Can the wedding guests fast while the bridegroom is with them?"[19]

Then the kingdom of heaven shall be compared to ten maidens who took their lamps and went to meet the bridegroom.[20]

Hallelujah! For the Lord our God the Almighty reigns.
Let us rejoice and exult and give him the glory,
for the marriage of the Lamb has come,
and his Bride has made herself ready. . . .
Blessed are those who are invited to the marriage supper of the Lamb.[21]

Theologians deploy nuptial metaphors to suggest how God joins human beings into community with God by initiating them into that mystery. Among Catholics, Thomas Aquinas describes the incarnation as a *coniunctio*, or marriage, of God and the human being. Karl Barth, the twentieth century's greatest Protestant theologian, writes, "Because the election of God is real, there is such a thing as love and marriage,"[22] that is, he derives love and marriage as secondary, analogous forms of God's love for God's people. From the Syriac tradition, we have already seen the passionate poetry of Jacob of Serugh. The Russian theologian Paul Evdokimov devotes an entire book to interpreting Christianity by what you might call a "nuptial hermeneutics." He seeks to rescue marriage from the functionalisms of control of lust (Protestant) or procreation of children (Catholic), in order to save it for participation in the divine life, not by tantric satisfaction, but by ascetic self-denial for the sake of more desirable goods. Marriage and monasticism make for Evdokimov two forms of the same discipline, whereby Christians give themselves over to one or more others—either a spouse or a monastic community—from whom they cannot easily escape. Like all asceticism, that is a high-risk endeavor to make them better people.[23]

Sexuality, in short, is for *sanctification*, that is, for *God*. It is to be a means (but not only a means) by which God catches human beings up into the community of God's Spirit and the identity of God's child.[24] In that case, too, the "means" reduces to no mere functionalism, but itself already participates in the end: in community, in joy, in growth in virtue.[25] Monogamy and monasticism are just two ways of donating the body to represent in society, and to practice by asceticism, features of the triune life in which God initiates, responds to, and celebrates love, a wedding feast in which God invites human beings to take part. At a wedding, the partners represent the love of two, while the congregation participates in the rejoicing of a third, caught up into the office of the Spirit in the Trinitarian life. In a marital or monastic community, the parties commit themselves to practicing faith, hope, and charity in a form of life that will require plenty of exercise.

Human beings participate in those multiple communities—the Trinity, the Church, and the domestic church, or marriage bond—by giving their bodies over to the community as communicative signs. Many gay and lesbian people already practice donating the body to be publicly known. They call it coming out:

> The communicative acts of coming out certainly entail self-definition, but these acts of signification come through surrender to an interpretive community. Coming out is opening one's life to be told by others. This exposure is the source of dread and panic in coming out. It is also the outcome of a desire to be known, a desire for wholeness and a promise of unity of oneself and the world. Coming out articulates the sign-giving character of human, bodily life.

> For the church, a similar statement of identity and desire is at stake when the members of the body come out with their sexual commitments. Marriage and the celibate life write the body into the story of redemption. Both are communicative, sexual acts. They are means by which the story of redemption is written through human lives, as signs of God's reconciliation, a reconciliation of the body. Coming out is a wager, opening the body to a language of redemption, opening a way for the body's agency not only in the movement of desire but in the donation of one's agency as an interpretive sign.[26]

A nuptial hermeneutics, it goes almost without saying, requires embodiment. Embodiment, in turn, requires diversity. The Holy Spirit characteristically rests on bodies: the body of Christ in Jesus, the church, the sacraments, and the saints.[27] As the Spirit forms human bodies into the body of Christ, she gathers the diverse and diversifies the corporate, making members of one body. At creation, too, Christians see the Holy Spirit gathering and diversifying as she hovers over the waters. Suppose "be fruitful and multiply" belongs with "let the earth put forth vegetation" and "let the waters bring forth swarms" and "let the earth bring forth everything that creeps upon the ground" (Gen. 1:26, 1:11, 1:20, 1:24). In all those cases, the earth and the waters bring forth things different from themselves, not just more dirt and more water. In all those cases, they bring forth multiply different kinds of things. One might almost translate, "Be fruitful and diversify."[28] Indeed Christian thinkers had to fight *against* the notion that the diversity of creatures and persons resulted from the

Fall rather than from God. In Aquinas, a manifold of creatures fills the earth, so that God's creation will show no gaps:

> The distinction and multiplicity of things is from the intention of the first agent, who is God. For [God] brought things into being to communicate [God's] goodness to creatures, and to be represented by them. And since [God's] goodness could not be adequately represented by any creature alone, [God] produced creatures many and diverse, so that what was wanting to one in the representation of the divine goodness could be supplied by another. For the goodness which in God is simple and uniform is in creatures multiply and distributively.[29]

Maximus the Confessor makes the argument from Christology. Created distinction displays a good not only of creation, but a backward-effect of the incarnation. Human diversity especially shows how individual *logoi* participate in the *Logos*:

> If by reason and wisdom a person has come to understand that what exists was brought out of non-being into being by God, if he intelligently directs the soul's imagination to the infinite differences and variety of things as they exist by nature and turns his questing eye with understanding towards the intelligible model (*logos*) according to which things have been made, would he not know that the one Logos is many *logoi*? This is evident in the incomparable differences among created things. For each is unmistakably unique in itself and its identity remains distinct ["without confusion," using the Chalcedonian word *asung-chutos*] in relation to other things. He will also know that the many *logoi* are the one Logos to whom all things are related and who exists in himself without confusion, the essential and individually distinctive God, the Logos of God the Father.[30]

Creatures require the diversity that the Spirit rejoices to evoke. Multiplication lies always in God's hand, so that the multiplication of the loaves and the fishes, the fruit of the virgin's womb, the diversity of the natural world, and God's husbandry alongside (*para*) nature in grafting the wild olive onto the domestic does not overturn nature but parallels, diversifies, and celebrates it.[31] The Spirit's transformation of the elements of a sacrament just makes a special case of the Spirit's rule over all of God's creation.

But what *kind* of diversity or otherness does the Spirit evoke? Or what kind of *logoi* participate in the Logos? Serious majority opinion in earlier ages hardly regarded the sort of diversity represented by sexual minorities as the work of the Spirit or the *logoi* in the Logos. Yet it is not at all clear that such a determination follows. Conservatives will suppose that by referring to the diversity of creation I am begging the question. And yet, if the earth is to bring forth *not* according to its kind, more dirt, but creatures different from dirt and from each other, and if bodily differences among creatures are to manifest a plenum in which God leaves no niche unfilled, then the burden of proof lies on the other side, and weighs heavily, to show that one of God's existing things somehow cannot do its part in communicating and exhibiting God's goodness.

What controls such diversity? Conservatives and liberals would agree that the Holy Spirit would evoke only a holy diversity, ordered to the good, bringing forth the fruits of the Spirit, faith, hope, and charity. Because no human beings practice faith, hope, and charity on their own, but only in community, it is hard to argue for leaving lesbian and gay people out of social arrangements that alone train those virtues. In the words of Gregory of Nazianzus, from which Maximus develops his theory of *logoi* in the Logos, God intends individual human limitations for our good. So too then the limitations pointed out against same-sex couples, or for that matter against cross-sex couples: their "very *limitations* are a form of training" in sharing the good. The trick is to turn manifold created limits (as between those who can bear and those who can adopt children) toward the appreciation of *others*, so that the human being "in the future age when graced with divinization . . . will affectionately love and cleave to the *logoi*, . . . or rather, that one will love God's own self, in whom the *logoi* of beautiful things are securely grounded."[32] Differences are meant to make us yearn for and love one another as beautiful. "The life of the Christian community has as its rationale—if not invariably its practical reality—the task of teaching us to so order our relations that human beings may see themselves as desired, as the occasion of joy."[33]

Specifically, the Spirit illuminates the goods she sanctifies, so that human beings may come, over time, to recognize them. Properly formed members of the community can discern the Spirit at work, because they can recognize characters in stories by narration. What controls the diversity worked by the Spirit? Particular narratives with moral content enabling community members to recognize her at work.

In the signal narrative of blessing diversity, God promises Abraham that by him all the nations of the earth will become blessings to one another (Gen. 18:18). The promise to Abraham interprets "otherness" as primarily *moral*: in the sense that God makes the other the one that sanctifies, God identifies otherness as intended for blessing.[34] Under conditions of sin, otherness can lead to curse rather than blessing, to hostility rather than hospitality; certainly there has been enough cursing and hostility to go around in the sexuality debates. But God created otherness for blessing and hospitality. So the Eucharist turns the story of a violently hostile dealing of death into a hospitably blessing granting of life: "You can't take my body," Jesus says, "I give it to you."

In the best traditional Christian exegesis, human otherness reflects Trinitarian otherness. Human beings image God by loving one another (1 John 4:7–12). So interpreters as different as Augustine, Calvin, and the

Orthodox take the three visitors to Abraham in Genesis 18 as the persons of the Trinity. There the blessing of otherness fosters hospitality and thanksgiving, so that Christians see eucharistic overtones. The hospitality of Abraham, like the Eucharist, anticipates the eschatological feast, the wedding of the Lamb, where human beings take part in the Trinitarian life. Three persons in communion, one who blesses, one who receives blessing, and one who delights in their mutual blessing, the Trinity both grounds and draws in created distinctions.[35]

In concrete liturgical practices such as the Eucharist, human participation in the Trinitarian life does not bypass but involves the body. For large sectors of multiple Christian traditions, blessing does not float overhead but brings sanctification through particular practices of asceticism, a discipline or training through which lesser goods serve greater ones. This is not bizarre, antiquated Christian weirdness, but something in which American society already deeply if sometimes mistakenly invests: dieting and working out at the gym also discipline the body for spiritual benefits. Indeed, they do so for the greatest of these, love. Surely there are more effective disciplines than those.

Sanctification, to reflect Trinitarian holiness, must involve community. It does not happen alone. It involves commitments to a community from which one cannot easily escape, whether monastic, nuptial, or congregational. Even hermits and solitaries tend to follow the liturgy, the community's prayer. The solitude of the first hermit, Anthony the Great, brought him the gift of *sociality*, drawing people to him, because his "heart had achieved total transparency to others."[36] Symeon the Stylite retreated from society to the top of a pillar—which drew a church around him with him on his pillar at the crossing.[37]

But sanctification is a community matter also in traditions not thought of as particularly ascetic. So Karl Barth interprets the creation of the human being in the image of God as *Mitmenschlichkeit*, cohumanity.[38] The Catholic tradition after Aquinas tends to interpret sanctification with metaphors of Aristotelian friendship, in which the purpose of friends is to make one morally better.[39] In multiple Christian traditions, sanctification necessarily involves others.

Gay and lesbian people who commit themselves to a community—to those who have come out, to a church, or to one another in a domestic community—do so to seek greater goods, to embark on a discipline, to donate themselves to a greater social meaning. But under conditions of sin, a community from which one cannot easily escape—especially marriage and monasticism—is not likely to be straightforwardly improving. The community from which one cannot easily escape makes moral risk. It tends to expose the worst in people. The hope is that community exposes the worst in people so that it can be healed. So multiple Christian traditions portray Christ as a physician probing the wounds. Unlike modern medicine, however, the physician shares the patient's vulnerability; in ancient practice, the physician undresses to examine the patient; in this poem, the instruments of the examination and cure are those by which Christ himself suffered, as he explains to his mother at the foot of the cross:

"Be patient a little longer, Mother, and you will see
how, like a physician, I undress and reach the place where they lie
and I treat their wounds,
cutting with the lance their calluses and their scabs.
And I take [the] vinegar, I apply it as astringent to the wound,
when with the probe of the nails I have investigated the cut,
I shall plug it with the cloak.
And, with my cross as a splint,
I shall make use of it, Mother, so that you may chant with understanding,
'By suffering he has abolished suffering,
my Son and my God.'"[40]

For the risk to be worth it and to have the best chance of success, the community must have plenty of time and be made up of the right sort of people. A one-night stand may transform, but growth usually takes more than an instant.[41] The right sort of people will succeed in exposing and healing each other's flaws over time.

For gay and lesbian people, someone of the opposite sex is unlikely to represent the right sort of otherness for marriage, because only someone of the *ap*posite, not opposite, sex will get in deep enough to expose their vulnerabilities and inspire the trust that healing requires. The question is, what sort of created diversity will lead one to holiness? The answer will vary with creation itself. But certainly same-sex couples find in someone of the same sex the right spur to vulnerability and self-exposure. With someone of the same sex, they can undertake the long and difficult commitment over time and place to find themselves in the perceptions of another. A homosexual orientation, theologically understood, is this: "gay men and lesbians are persons who encounter the other (and thus discover themselves) in relation to persons of the same sex."[42]

That is no "merely psychological" difference, but also embodied difference, if only because sexual response is nothing if not bodily. (Difference cannot be reduced to male-female complementarity, because that would leave Jesus a deficient human being.) Some people, therefore, are called to same-sex partnerships for their own sanctification.

On this account, conservatives do not wish to deprive same-sex couples of satisfaction so much as to deprive them of sanctification. But that is contradictory, because so far as I know no conservative has ever seriously argued that same-sex couples need sanctification any less than cross-sex couples.[43] It is more than contradictory, it is evil to attempt to deprive people of the means of their own sanctification.

So far this account has centered on couples and communities and has made no sense of singleness. But

> In the New Testament, life outside of marriage has a privileged place. It is a special vocation and a sign of God's reign, a dedication of one's life to the kingdom (1 Cor. 7 is the standard text). . . . [R]emaining single, without taking vows, has become a vulnerable and misunderstood state. Singleness is informal—without ritual expression, without a coming out. As a result, singleness evokes suspicion as an uncommitted body, with no set pattern of constancy, with no clearly established communicative relationship of the body, and with no clear sign (sacrament) of embodied reconciliation. The problem is not with the single life *per se* . . . [but] a loss of depth [or diversity] in the church's language of family. If the biological, nuclear family were not dominant, then those who were not to enter marriages or formal vows still would not be considered "single."[44]

Modern categories define *singleness* in opposition to *marriedness*, in a drastic narrowing of family to nuclear biology. The term centers, despite itself, on couples. But biblical and traditional materials display no such category. They always show a person in relation to some other person or group. The trick is to regard people in terms of their commitments and pilgrimages. To what public commitments do they donate their bodies as signs? Whatever the answer to that question, it leads to no category of absence like "singleness." Jesus refrained from making public commitments of marriage or celibacy, retaining a *freedom* for the ultimate donation of his body in a sign of embodied reconciliation: "This is my body, given for you."[45]

NOTES

INTRODUCTION

1. This volume grows out of a roundtable organized within a much larger project on "Sex, Marriage, and Family in the Religions of the Book." The larger project was undertaken during 2001–2003 by the Center for the Interdisciplinary Study of Religion, under the direction of John Witte Jr., with support from The Pew Charitable Trusts through a grant to Emory University. The authors are grateful to all and each of these for their indispensable support and assistance.

CHAPTER ONE
"Surpassing the Love of Women"

I am grateful to Susan Ackerman, William Gilders, Tracy Lemos, Steven Weitzman, Marsha White, the participants in Brown University's Culture and Religion of the Ancient Mediterranean faculty seminar (January 2004), and the contributors to this volume for critical feedback on an earlier draft of this essay. Needless to say, any errors of fact or judgment remain my responsibility alone.

1. For the sexual interpretation among nonspecialists, see, e.g., Tom Horner, *Jonathan Loved David: Homosexuality in Biblical Times* (Philadelphia: Westminster, 1978), 26–39; Jody Hirsh, "In Search of Role Models," in *Twice Blessed: On Being Lesbian, Gay, and Jewish*, ed. Christie Balka and Andy Rose (Boston: Beacon, 1989), 84. For a nonsexual but homoerotic reading by a nonspecialist, see David F. Greenberg, *The Construction of Homosexuality* (Chicago: University of Chicago Press, 1988), 114. Greenberg speaks of "homophilic innuendos" throughout the passages in question and speculates that an explicit sexual relationship may have been present in the original text and deleted by editors. David Halperin understands the relationship to be erotic, though not sexual (*One Hundred Years of Homosexuality and Other Essays on Greek Love* [New York: Routledge, 1990], 11, 83). Among specialists, see especially the article by Silvia Schroer and Thomas Staubli, "Saul, David, und Jonatan—eine Dreiecksgeschichte? Ein Beitrag zum Thema 'Homosexualität im Ersten Testament,'" *Bibel und Kirche* 51 (1996):15–22, which argues that the relationship was homoerotic and "very probably" sexual as well ("eine homoerotische und sehr wahrscheinlich auch homosexuelle Beziehung," 15); David Gunn, *The Fate of King Saul* (Sheffield: Sheffield Academic Press, 1980), 93; and Erhard Gerstenberger, *Das dritte Buch Mose Leviticus* (Göttingen: Vandenhoeck & Ruprecht, 1993), 271. Martti Nissinen ("Die Liebe von David und Jonatan als Frage der modernen Exegese," *Biblica* 80 [1999]: 262) writes of the relationship as portrayed in the "History of David's Rise" as a friendship with some homoerotic coloring, though for him there is no evidence that it was explicitly sexual. Susan Ackerman argues for the presence of "eroticized

and perhaps sexualized language and imagery" in the narrative of David and Jonathan (*When Heroes Love: The Ambiguity of Eros in the Stories of Gilgamesh and David* [New York: Columbia University Press, 2005]).

2. See Frank Moore Cross's treatment, which emphasizes the kinship background of much of covenant discourse ("Kinship and Covenant in Ancient Israel," in *From Epic to Canon: History and Literature in Ancient Israel* [Baltimore: Johns Hopkins University Press, 1998], 11). For the covenant interpretation of the relationship between David and Jonathan, see Martin A. Cohen, "The Role of the Shilonite Priesthood in the United Monarchy of Ancient Israel," *Hebrew Union College Annual* 36 (1965): 83; Ernst Jenni, "*ahev* to love," in *Theological Lexicon of the Old Testament*, ed. Ernst Jenni and Claus Westermann, trans. Mark E. Biddle, 3 vols. (Peabody, MA: Hendrickson, 1997), 1:47, 48–49; Gerhard Wallis, "'*ahabh*," in *Theological Dictionary of the Old Testament*, ed. G. Johannes Botterweck and Helmer Ringgren, trans. John T. Willis, 11 vols. (Grand Rapids, MI: Eerdmans, 1974), 1:104–105, 109; Jerzy Wozniak, "Drei verschiedene literarische Beschreibungen des Bundes zwischen Jonathan und David," *Biblische Zeitschrift* 27 (1983): 213–218; P. Kyle McCarter Jr., *II Samuel* (Garden City, NY: Doubleday, 1984), 77; Cross, "Kinship and Covenant," 9–10; and Steven L. McKenzie, *King David: A Biography* (New York: Oxford University Press, 2000), 84. Markus Zehnder has published a detailed critique of Schroer and Staubli, "Saul, David, und Jonatan," in which he also interprets the love idiom in the Jonathan and David narratives as covenant discourse ("Exegetische Beobachtungen zu den David-Jonathan-Geschichten," *Biblica* 79 [1998]: 157–159, 165, 168–170, 174). For explicit denials of a homoerotic relationship, see, e.g., Cohen, "Role of the Shilonite," 83; Jenni, "*ahev* to love," 48; Zehnder, "Exegetische Beobachtungen," 153–179; Simon B. Parker, "The Hebrew Bible and Homosexuality," *Quarterly Review* 11 (1991):10–11; McKenzie, *King David*, 85, and Shimon Bar-Efrat in *The Jewish Study Bible*, ed. Adele Berlin and Marc Zvi Brettler (New York: Oxford University Press, 2004), 621. See also Michael L. Barré's review of Horner's book in *Catholic Biblical Quarterly* 41 (1979): 464: "As for David and Jonathan, the author shows no awareness that the language describing their relationship is largely drawn from treaty terminology." Martti Nissinen (*Homoeroticism in the Biblical World: A Historical Perspective* [Minneapolis: Fortress Press, 1998], 55–56) advocates the friendship interpretation, but without an explicit discussion of the covenant dimension evident in the texts. However, his recent article incorporates the covenant dimension (see "Liebe von David und Jonatan," 253).

3. See especially John A. Thompson ("The Significance of the Verb Love in the David-Jonathan Narratives in 1 Samuel," *Vetus Testamentum* 24 [1974]: 334–338), who analyzes the Jonathan/David materials in light of William L. Moran's observations with respect to covenant love ("The Ancient Near Eastern Background of the Love of God in Deuteronomy," *Catholic Biblical Quarterly* 25 [1963]: 77–87); Wozniak, "Drei verschiedene literarische Beschreibungen," 213–218; McCarter, *II Samuel*, 77; and Cross, "Kinship and Covenant," 9–10. See also Moran's comments on the love idiom in texts such as 1 Sam. 18:1–3, 16; 20:17 ("Ancient Near Eastern Background," 81, 82, n. 33).

4. On the use of the expression *to love x as oneself* in treaty settings, see Moran ("Ancient Near Eastern Background," 80), who cites a parallel in Esarhaddon of

Assyria's succession treaty. For the text, see Simo Parpola and Kazuko Watanabe, eds., *Neo-Assyrian Treaties and Loyalty Oaths* (Helsinki: Helsinki University Press, 1988), 6:266–268.

5. Cf. 1 Kings 9:13, 20:32–34, and the comments of Mordechai Cogan, *I Kings* (New York: Doubleday, 2000), 299, 468. There are also many examples of this usage in extrabiblical West Asian sources.

6. Though Wozniak ignores 2 Sam. 1:26, he finds in the narratives in 1 Samuel three different interpretations of the covenant between Jonathan and David. Whereas 1 Sam. 19:1–7 and 20:1–21:1 cast David as the subordinate partner and 1 Sam. 23:16–18 depicts Jonathan in the vassal role, 1 Sam. 17:12–18:4 suggests a treaty of equals ("Drei verschiedene literarische Beschreibungen," 217–218).

7. The classic treatment of covenant love is Moran's, and most of the following examples are taken from Moran's discussion ("Ancient Near Eastern Background").

8. On loving as establishing a covenant bond, see the comments of P. Kyle McCarter Jr., *I Samuel* (Garden City, NY: Doubleday, 1980), 282, on 1 Sam. 16:21, where Saul "loves" David and appoints him his weapon-bearer: "The king has given official recognition to the young man, has made a kind of legal commitment to him; that is, he has 'loved' him."

9. See William L. Moran, *The Amarna Letters* (Baltimore: Johns Hopkins University Press, 1992), 41, for the translation. The Akkadian text in transliteration may be found in Hans-Peter Adler, ed., *Das Akkadische des Königs Tusratta von Mitanni* (Kevelaer: Butzon & Bercker; Neukirchen-Vluyn: Neukirchener, 1976), 122.

10. See Moran, *Amarna Letters*, 43, for the translation; Adler, *Akkadische*, 128, for the transliteration of the Akkadian text.

11. See Moran, *Amarna Letters*, 125, for the translation; Jorgen A. Knudtzon, *Die el-Amarna-Tafeln*, Vorderasiatische Bibliothek 2.1 (Leipzig: Hinrichs, 1915), 326, for the text in transliteration.

12. See Moran, *Amarna Letters*, 200; Knudtzon, *el-Amarna-Tafeln*, 526.

13. See Gary Beckman, *Hittite Diplomatic Texts* (Atlanta: Scholars Press, 1996), 133, 135, for the translation. For the Akkadian text in transliteration, see Albertine Hagenbuchner, *Die Korrespondenz der Hethiter*, 2. Teil, Texte der Hethiter 16 (Heidelberg: Carl Winter, 1989), 281, 283, 284.

14. See Parpola and Watanabe, *Neo-Assyrian Treaties*, 6:207, 266–268; 9:18, 32.

15. Many scholars believe that the dirge is ancient, and a number think that it was composed by David himself. On the antiquity of the lament as indicated by its internal characteristics, see Frank Moore Cross and David Noel Freedman, *Studies in Ancient Yahwistic Poetry* (Missoula, MT: Scholars Press, 1975), 6, and Frank Moore Cross, *Canaanite Myth and Hebrew Epic* (Cambridge, MA: Harvard University Press, 1973), 122–123. Inclusion of the elegy in the apologetic "History of David's Rise" points to a tenth-century date of composition. (On the date of the "History of David's Rise," see McCarter, *I Samuel*, 27–30.) For an argument in support of the probability of Davidic authorship, see McCarter, *II Samuel*, 78–79. Points in favor of Davidic composition include the exact match of the dirge's content with the context in which it has been placed by the compiler, sug-

gesting that it was actually composed for the occasion of the deaths of Saul and Jonathan. Also, as McCarter points out, it would serve little or no purpose to compose such a dirge long after the deaths in question. Finally, there are the elegy's highly personal and boldly stated sentiments regarding Jonathan, which also do not suggest pseudonymous composition. Hans J. Stoebe has argued that vv. 25–27 of the dirge could well be an authentic Davidic composition, though he does not believe that the whole lament is (*Das zweite Buch Samuelis* [Gütersloh: Gütersloher Verlagshaus, 1994], 96). Text-critical aspects of this verse are ably dealt with by McCarter, *II Samuel*, 73.

16. On "the love of women" as sexual or sexual-emotional love, see the argument later in this essay.

17. See Moran, *Amarna Letters*, 41, for the translation; Adler, *Akkadische*, 122, for the Akkadian transliteration.

18. Moran, *Amarna Letters*, 43; Adler, *Akkadische*, 128.

19. Moran, *Amarna Letters*, 85; Adler, *Akkadische*, 208.

20. A similar pattern of comparison of members of the same class is found in 1 Kings 1:47, though it concerns the reputation of a king rather than his love in covenant. In this text, the servants of David bless David at the time of Solomon's accession as follows: "May God give Solomon a greater name than your name, and may he exalt his throne above your throne."

21. For another, more negative, view of Israel's youth, see, e.g., Ezek. 20:5–13; 23.

22. Moran, *Amarna Letters*, 71, Gernot Wilhelm's translation of the letter from the Hurrian. For the text in transliteration, see the references listed in Moran, *Amarna Letters*, 63.

23. Though the expression *the love of women* does not occur elsewhere in the Hebrew Bible, a number of texts suggest that it should have a significant sexual or sexual-emotional component. On this, see the discussion later in this essay. In any case, it is unlikely that *the love of women* is an expression for covenant love, given the usual sexual-emotional connotations of *love* when it is associated with women, and given that covenant partners are typically male and the discourse of covenant is cast in masculine terms (*brother, brotherhood, father/son*) in biblical texts antedating the sixth century BCE. Note, however, the later exceptions to this pattern with respect to marriage and personal relations (Mal. 2:14; Prov. 2:17; Ruth 3:10).

24. Because the word *nashim* can mean either "women" or "wives," contextual considerations must determine how it is to be translated.

25. My thanks to William Gilders, whose questions and suggestions have helped me to strengthen the argument at this juncture (oral communication).

26. Scholars who assume that *the love of women* refers to sexual love include Jenni, "*ahev* to love," 47; Halperin, *One Hundred Years*, 83; Parker, "Hebrew Bible," 11; and Cross, "Kinship and Covenant," 9. In contrast, Zehnder, following A. A. Anderson, suggests that the expression *the love of women* might refer to a mother's love for her children rather than to sexual love ("Exegetische Beobachtungen," 156). This seems highly unlikely, given that mothers per se are not mentioned, but rather women, and given the evidence for a sexual or sexual-emotional meaning of *love* in contexts where it is associated with the relations of men and women. On this, see Susan Ackerman, "The Personal Is Political: Covenantal and Affectionate

Love (AHEB, AHABA) in the Hebrew Bible," *Vetus Testamentum* 52 (2002): 440–441, and the discussion later in this essay. Also, the poet is comparing something he has experienced—Jonathan's love—to something else he has experienced—the love of a plurality of women, hardly a comparison suggestive of an individual mother's love for her child. David as both lover and beloved of a plurality of women occasions no surprise, given his portrayal in surviving narrative traditions (see, e.g., 1 Sam. 18:20, 28; 26:39–42, 43; 2 Sam. 3:2–5).

27. Ackerman ("The Personal Is Political," 452–453) understands only 1 Sam. 18:20, 28, to speak of a woman as the lover of a man, though I believe Prov. 5:19 is another example of this.

28. Note the explicit sexual dimension of the love of Jacob indicated by the verb *to come to* (*bo le-*).

29. On this hypothetical apologetic source document, see McCarter (*I Samuel*, 27–30), who, like previous commentators, compares the Hittite "Apology of Hattusili III."

30. Saul and Jonathan are presented as idealized warriors, the women of Israel as mourners who weep over their deaths.

31. Zehnder, "Exegetische Beobachtungen," 155–156. See, similarly, McKenzie, *King David*, 85; Parker, "Hebrew Bible," 11; and others.

32. McKenzie, *King David*, 85; cf. Zehnder, "Exegetische Beobachtungen," 173–175.

33. See especially Nissinen, "Liebe von David und Jonatan," 251–252, 260–261, 262, for a critique of such anachronistic practice among biblical scholars. The language of both Zehnder, and Schroer and Staubli, is similar to McKenzie's (e.g., "homosexuelle Beziehung"). A classic statement of the "constructionist" position is that of Halperin, *One Hundred Years*, 15–40, 154–168.

34. Saul M. Olyan, "'And with a Male You Shall Not Lie the Lying Down of a Woman': On the Meaning and Significance of Leviticus 18:22 and 20:13," *Journal of the History of Sexuality* 5 (1994): 179–206. The argument has been accepted by Nissinen ("Liebe von David und Jonatan," 258), among others (e.g., Bernadette J. Brooten, *Love between Women: Early Christian Responses to Female Homoeroticism* [Chicago: University of Chicago Press, 1996], 61; Jerome T. Walsh, "Leviticus 18:22 and 20:13: Who Is Doing What to Whom?" *Journal of Biblical Literature* 120 [2001]: 201, 204, 208). Though the date of the Holiness Source is debated, even advocates for an early date place the origin of H no earlier than the last half of the eighth century (e.g., Israel Knohl, *The Sanctuary of Silence: The Priestly Torah and the Holiness School* [Minneapolis: Fortress Press, 1995], 204–212; Jacob Milgrom, *Leviticus 1–16* [New York: Doubleday, 1991], 27); conventionally, it is dated much later.

35. Though the law of Lev. 20:13, like other laws in Lev. 20, betrays signs of redactional expansion (see Olyan, "And with a Male," 186–188), there is no evidence to suggest that a proto-form of it was or even might have been in existence in the tenth century, very likely the time of the composition of the Lament.

36. See, e.g., James C. Vanderkam, "Davidic Complicity in the Deaths of Abner and Eshbaal: A Historical and Redactional Study," *Journal of Biblical Literature* 99 (1980): 521–539; McCarter, *I Samuel*, 28–30; and Steven Weitzman, "David's

Lament and the Poetics of Grief in 2 Samuel," *Jewish Quarterly Review* 85 (1995): 354–355.

37. On this, see my full argument in *Biblical Mourning: Ritual and Social Dimensions* (Oxford: Oxford University Press, 2004), 53–54.

38. The same literary technique is repeated in 2 Sam. 3:31–37 with Abner's death. There, David orders public mourning for Abner and composes a dirge for him. His actions lead the people to believe that he is innocent of Abner's death. For the lament's function in the larger literary context of 2 Samuel as a whole, see the perceptive observations of Weitzman, "David's Lament," 354–359.

39. Olyan, "And with a Male."

40. E.g., to the unions identified by John Boswell in *Same-Sex Unions in Premodern Europe* (New York: Villard, 1994), if they were indeed what Boswell claimed.

CHAPTER TWO
Family Idolatry and the Christian Case against Marriage

1. Rodney Clapp notes that the church may be called "the last great stronghold of family idolatry" (*Families at the Crossroads: Beyond Traditional and Modern Options* [Downers Grove, IL: Intervarsity, 1993], 12). See also Janet Fishburn, *Confronting the Idolatry of Family: A New Vision for the Household of God* (Nashville: Abingdon, 1991), especially 107. The idolatry of the family can be seen by a careful analysis of one study that argues that "the healthy family as we know it today would not exist but for the profound influence of religion, especially Christianity, through the ages" (Anthony J. Guerra, *Family Matters: The Role of Christianity in the Formation of the Western Family* [St. Paul: Paragon House, 2002]). Guerra states that the most important factor promoting the "healthy family" is religion (xxi–xxiii). He also insists that no one religion "has a monopoly" on the value he attributes to religion in general in promoting and protecting "family values" (xii–xiii). Because there is no belief or doctrine that all "religions" hold in common (not even monotheism or the belief in "God" at all), the only thing that all "religions" must hold in common (in Guerra's construction) is the promotion of the family. But that is what Guerra is highlighting as the fundamental value of Christianity. Unwittingly perhaps, Guerra has substituted "family values" for all other doctrines, beliefs, and practices as *the* central aspect of Christianity of any importance. The theological word for that is *idolatry*. (Incidentally, the "healthy family" for Guerra is the modern, nuclear family, consisting of a heterosexual couple, only once married, and their immediate children; see pp. xii–xiii, xiv, xvi, xvii.)

2. See Kathy Rudy, *Sex and the Church: Gender, Homosexuality, and the Transformation of Christian Ethics* (Boston: Beacon, 1997), 119.

3. On the novelty and aberration of the 1950s ideal family when compared to most of human history and most cultures, see Stephanie Coontz, *The Way We Never Were: American Families and the Nostalgia Trap* (New York: Basic Books, 1992), 25–29.

4. Byron R. McCane, "'Let the Dead Bury Their Own Dead': Secondary Burial and Matt. 8:21–22," *Harvard Theological Review* 83 (1990): 31–43.

5. T. W. Manson, *The Sayings of Jesus* (Grand Rapids, MI: Eerdmans, 1957), 131; François Bovon, *L'Évangile selon Saint Luc (9,51–14,35)* (Geneva: Labor et Fides, 1996), 471.

6. "Q," from the German word *Quelle*, which means "source," is the designation given to a hypothetical document many scholars *believe* was used by both Matthew and Luke in the writing of their own Gospels. If they both used it, it obviously would represent a source earlier than their own texts.

7. Elizabeth A. Clark, *Reading Renunciation: Asceticism and Scripture in Early Christianity* (Princeton, NJ: Princeton University Press, 1999), 242–250.

8. John Chrysostom, *On Virginity*, 14.6.

9. Or that of Thomas in the precise sense. Thomas has a man excuse himself in order to arrange the wedding of someone else (Gospel of Thomas 64).

10. François Bovon, *Luke: A Commentary on the Gospel of Luke 1:1–9:50* (Minneapolis: Fortress Press, 2002), 1.114.

11. I take it that Barnabas is not married because no wife or family is ever mentioned for him, he travels around with Paul, likewise unmarried, without a family, and he is mentioned in this capacity by Paul in 1 Cor. 9:6. Though the precise verse in which Barnabas is mentioned refers to working for a living rather than living off contributions from the churches, the context also includes "traveling around with a sister-wife" as Peter and other apostles had done. I take it that Paul then includes Barnabas with himself as someone who has not taken advantage of that "right."

12. Commentators generally note that Barnabas serves as a positive example and Ananias and Sapphira as negative examples of the communalism expected of early Christians in Acts. See, e.g., C. K. Barrett, *A Critical and Exegetical Commentary on the Acts of the Apostles* (Edinburgh: T. & T. Clark, 1994), 2.257–271; Joseph A. Fitzmyer, *The Acts of the Apostles* (New York: Doubleday, 1964), 315.

13. They are not "normal" for several reasons. They have no children, nor a "stable" household, but rather are themselves fairly itinerant; Prisca (or Priscilla, as in Acts) is often mentioned first, implying higher status for her, at least for the author, than her husband; their "household" is permeable enough to include Paul in it at times. Paul moves in with them, works with them, and relocates with them. Their relationship, in any case, cannot be made into a "nuclear family," and neither does it look like the traditional extended family of antiquity.

14. For the activities of Satan in Luke-Acts, see Susan R. Garrett, *The Demise of the Devil: Magic and the Demonic in Luke's Writings* (Minneapolis: Fortress Press, 1989).

15. The "togetherness" of Ananias and Sapphira "violated the togetherness of the Christian community" (Ben Witherington III, *The Acts of the Apostles: A Socio-Rhetorical Commentary* [Grand Rapids, MI: Eerdmans, 1998], 218). Ananias and Sapphira represent a "counter-community . . . over against the spirit-community that shares its possessions" (Luke Timothy Johnson, *The Acts of the Apostles*, Sacra Pagina Series, vol. 5 [Collegeville, MN: Liturgical Press, 1992], 87; see also 89).

16. For most people in the Greco-Roman world, separation meant divorce, even legally. According to Roman family law, which may not have even applied to non-Roman Christians and Jews, divorce was effected simply by one of the partners "willing" to be no longer married. Abandonment was almost always sufficient for

divorce. Moreover, without marriage laws to regulate the daily lives of most inhabitants of the Greco-Roman world, "divorce" most normally would have been effected simply by "separation."

17. I take the language of "relativization" mainly from Stephen C. Barton, *Discipleship and Family Ties in Mark and Matthew* (New York: Cambridge University Press, 1994), *passim*. Though Barton is dealing with Mark and Matthew rather than Luke, I believe he, even for those contexts, is too eager to downplay any possible "antifamilial" message in the texts. Referring to Mark 10:1–31, for instance, he claims, "Nevertheless, it should be pointed out that this material reflects no animosity to family and household *per se*, something we had cause to observe in relation to earlier pericopae, as well. Instead, their significance is made relative to cross-bearing discipleship for the sake of Jesus and the gospel" (107; see also 122). It is hard to evaluate such a claim, which is repeated several times in one form or another in Barton's study, because Barton never really explains what "animosity" means or what "*per se*" covers. Certainly it would be stretching the evidence to say that it shows that Jesus had some personal, psychological hatred ("animosity") to the family *in the abstract* ("*per se*"). But it is just as unlikely that the texts make *only* the point—similar to modern Christian piety—that Jesus and the gospel are to demand "relatively" more loyalty than one's household. Rather, the statements clearly teach the replacement of the traditional household by the eschatological community of God initiated by Jesus. There is nothing "psychological" or "abstract" going on here; it is rather a radical challenge of the "normal family" by the kingdom of God.

18. Tina Pippin, *Death and Desire: The Rhetoric of Gender in the Apocalypse of John* (Louisville, KY: Westminster/John Knox Press, 1992), 57–86.

19. References to pollution: 14:1–5; filth or dirt: 22:11; "abomination" (*bdelygma = bdelysso*, meaning "rot" or "stink"): 21:8, 27; see also 7:14; 16:13; 17:4; 18:2; 19:2. One can also discern the obsession by noting the many references to fire and sulphur, i.e., "purifying" substances.

20. See Dale B. Martin, *The Corinthian Body* (New Haven, CT: Yale University Press, 1999); and Martin, "Paul without Passion: On Paul's Rejection of Desire in Sex and Marriage," in *Constructing Early Christian Families: Family as Social Reality and Metaphor*, ed. Halvor Moxnes (London: Routledge, 1997), 201–215.

21. I have elsewhere shown that modern attempts to read Paul as a "gender egalitarian" do not stand up to scrutiny, though such claims do continue to be made, presumably by those wishing to "save" Paul from his fairly obvious, and natural for his time, hierarchical view of gender. See, e.g., Martin, *Corinthian Body*, 230–233; contrast James D. G. Dunn, "The Household Rules in the New Testament," in *The Family in Theological Perspective*, ed. Stephen C. Barton (Edinburgh: T. & T. Clark, 1996), 55.

22. See R. P. Reardon, *Collected Ancient Greek Novels* (Berkeley and Los Angeles: University of California Press, 1989); and Judith Perkins, *The Suffering Self: Pain and Representation in the Early Christian Era* (London: Routledge, 1995), 44–76.

23. See Andrew S. Jacobs, "A Family Affair: Marriage, Class, and Ethics in the Apocryphal Acts of the Apostles," *Journal of Early Christian Studies* 7 (1999): 105–138.

24. J.N.D. Kelly, *Jerome: His Life, Writings, and Controversies* (New York: Harper and Row, 1975), 102.

25. David Hunter provides a collection of early church writings on marriage: David G. Hunter, ed., *Marriage in the Early Church* (Minneapolis: Fortress Press, 1992). It is telling that although Hunter clearly attempted to balance the "negative" views with the few available "positive" views of marriage, the book is rather thin. There just are not enough "positive" views in early Christianity to balance out the "negative" ones.

26. For brief introductions to the controversy, see Kelly, *Jerome*, 181–182; and Peter Brown, *The Body and Society: Men, Women and Sexual Renunciation in Early Christianity* (London: Faber and Faber, 1989), 359–362. For the original texts: Jovinian, *Iovinianus: Die Fragmente seiner Schriften, die Quellen zu seiner Geschichte, sein Leben und seine Lehre*, ed. Wilhelm Haller (Leipzig: J. C. Hinrichs, 1897). The best and most up-to-date research on the Jovinian controversy is contained in articles by David G. Hunter; see especially "Resistance to the Virginal Ideal in Late-Fourth-Century Rome: The Case of Jovinian," *Theological Studies* 48 (1987): 45–64; "Helvidius, Jovinian, and the Virginity of Mary in Late Fourth-Century Rome," *Journal of Early Christian Studies* 1 (1993): 47–71; and "Rereading the Jovinianist Controversy: Asceticism and Clerical Authority in Late Ancient Christianity," *Journal of Medieval and Early Modern Studies* 33 (2003): 453–470, reprinted in *The Cultural Turn in Late Ancient Studies: Gender, Asceticism, and Historiography*, ed. Dale B. Martin and Patricia Cox Miller (Durham, NC: Duke University Press, 2005). John Gavin Nolan's earlier study (see *Jerome and Jovinian* [Washington, DC: Catholic University of America Press, 1956], an abstract of his Catholic University dissertation) is too biased in favor of Jerome and against Jovinian to be reliable. Nolan often takes Jerome's obvious exaggeration and misrepresentation at face value—with regard, for instance, to Jovinian's alleged lack of education.

27. These translations are from Hunter, "Rereading the Jovinianist Controversy," 453; for the Latin, see Siricius, *Epistolae*, 7.4–6 (*Corpus Scriptorum Ecclesiasticorum Latinorum* 82/3:301).

28. Hunter, "Rereading the Jovinianist Controversy," 453.

29. Hunter, "Resistance to the Virginal Ideal."

30. Jerome, *Against Jovinian*, 1.7, 2.35, and 1.33, respectively.

31. Jerome, *Against Jovinian* 1.40; trans. W. H. Fremantle, with G. Lewis and W. G. Martley, *The Principal Works of St. Jerome*, Nicene and Post-Nicene Fathers, 2nd ser., vol. 6 (Grand Rapids, MI: Eerdmans, 1979).

32. See, e.g., Augustine, *The Good of Marriage*, chapter 6. For the English of this as well as other excerpts from Augustine's relevant writings, and including an excellent introduction, see Elizabeth A. Clark, *St. Augustine on Marriage and Sexuality* (Washington, DC: Catholic University of America Press, 1996). See also Elizabeth A. Clark, "'Adam's Only Companion': Augustine and the Early Christian Debate on Marriage," *Recherches Augustiniennes* 21 (1986): 139–162; and Philip Lyndon Reynolds, *Marriage in the Western Church: The Christianization of Marriage during the Patristic and Early Medieval Periods* (Leiden: Brill, 1994), 259.

33. Augustine, *Good of Marriage*, chapter 9; translated in Clark, *St. Augustine on Marriage and Sexuality*, 51.

34. Edmund Leites, *The Puritan Conscience and Modern Sexuality* (New Haven, CT: Yale University Press, 1986), 80–83.

35. Lawrence Stone, *The Family, Sex and Marriage in England, 1500–1800* (London: Weidenfeld and Nicolson, 1977), 135.

36. Christopher Hill, *Society and Puritanism in Pre-Revolutionary England* (New York: Schocken Books, 1964), 453.

37. Guerra, *Family Matters*, 30.

38. Stone, *Family, Sex and Marriage*, 136.

39. See Stone, *Family, Sex and Marriage*, 141.

40. William Perkins, *Works* (Cambridge: Cantrell Legge, 1618), 3.671. Perkins goes on to say that had the Fall not occurred, the single life should have no place in the world at all, but because of the exigencies of existence after the Fall, *some* people, no doubt only a few, may do better to remain single *if* they "have the gift of continence."

41. Edmund S. Morgan, "The Puritans and Sex," in *The American Family in Social-Historical Perspective*, 2nd ed., ed. Michael Gordon (New York: St. Martin's Press, 1978), especially 364, 371.

42. Thomas Taylor, *Works* (London: Printed by T.R. & E.M. for J. Bartlet the elder and J. Bartlet the younger, 1653), 190.

43. William Gouge, *Of Domesticall Duties: Eight Treatises* (London: John Haviland, 1622), 18.

44. Levin L. Schücking, *The Puritan Family: A Social Study from the Literary Sources*, 2nd ed. (New York: Schocken Books, 1969), 65–66.

45. Edmund S. Morgan, *The Puritan Family: Essays on Religion and Domestic Relations in Seventeenth-Century New England* (Boston: Boston Public Library, 1944), 85.

46. Morgan, *Puritan Family*, 86–89; Guerra, *Family Matters*, 43.

47. Morgan, *Puritan Family*, 9–14; Schücking, *Puritan Family*, 67; Hill, *Society and Puritanism*, 458–462.

48. For other Christian ethical critiques of the Puritan family model, see Lisa Sowle Cahill, *Family: A Christian Social Perspective* (Minneapolis: Fortress Press, 2000), 51.

49. Much of my point here is dependent on Michael Warner, *The Trouble with Normal: Sex, Politics, and the Ethics of Queer Life* (New York: Free Press, 1999).

50. The focus on the family is ultimately *antisocial*. It is politically quietistic, opposed to social reform, and "tolerant of economic injustice." The "private family" is therefore socially *irresponsible*. See Coontz, *The Way We Never Were*, 97–98. Or as Jessie Bernard has put it, "Marriage is a cheap way for society at large to take care of a lot of difficult people. We force individuals—a wife or a husband—to take care of them on a one-to-one basis" (*The Future of Marriage* [New Haven, CT: Yale University Press, 1982], 161; quoted and affirmed by Brian W. Grant, *The Social Structure of Christian Families: A Historical Perspective* [St. Louis: Chalice Press, 2000], 147).

51. Even an author intent on affirming the normativity of marriage for Christians (though she does suggest that it should now be balanced with "a favourable account of celibacy") admits that "the 'Christian family' makes plenty of people feel

excluded, not strengthened" (Helen Oppenheimer, *Marriage* [London: Mowbray, 1990], 87, 110).

CHAPTER THREE
Marriage and Friendship in the Christian New Testament

1. For an historical review of the many forms marriage as an institution has taken over the past two millennia, see John Witte Jr., *From Sacrament to Contract: Marriage, Religion, and Law in the Western Tradition* (Louisville, KY: Westminster/ John Knox Press, 1997).

2. H. S. Benjamins suggests Eph. 5:22ff, Titus 1:6, and 1 Tim. 2:11–15 as examples of New Testament texts in which "marriage is valued positively." See H. S. Benjamins, "Keeping Marriage out of Paradise: The Creation of Man and Woman in Patristic Literature," in *The Creation of Man and Woman: Interpretations of the Biblical Narratives in Jewish and Christian Traditions,* ed. Gerard P. Luttikhuizen (Leiden: Brill, 2000), 94. Since Eph. 5:22ff and 1 Tim. 2:11–15 both concern the subordination of women to men within the marital union and, in Timothy's case, the larger church as well, from a modern perspective on marriage neither reference seems to indicate a particularly positive view of marriage. Titus 1:6 is simply a stipulation that a bishop or elder be the husband of only one wife, suggesting perhaps more about the continued presence of polygamy within Christian communities than about the positive value of marriage. The only New Testament text I can find that values marriage positively without any apparent qualifications is Heb. 13:4, "Let marriage be held in honor among all, and let the marriage bed be undefiled; for God will judge the immoral and the adulterous." See note 16 in this essay for a discussion of the verse.

3. Those who wish to argue that the presence of these codifications of marital order in and of itself substantiates the status and positive regard the New Testament holds for marriage are also required to argue that same positive regard is held for slavery, because the passages regulating household order include not only husbands and wives, parents and children, but also masters and slaves. If the mere existence of the household codes endorses marriage, it also endorses slavery. That dual endorsement would seem to me to undercut in a serious way the moral standing of the views on marriage in these texts.

4. Partly, I believe, because of the dearth of positive images of marriage in the New Testament, many theologians, pastors, and liturgists use the story of Jesus' turning the water into wine at a marriage feast in Cana in John 2:1–11 as the clear proof of Jesus' personal approval and valuing of marriage. Although a marriage feast is the setting of this first "sign" Jesus accomplishes in the Gospel of John, the marriage itself is not the focus of the miracle but instead the lack of wine for the party. If every setting of a sign or miracle in John indicates Jesus' personal approval of the event, then John also has Jesus promote group bathing (John 5:2–9), conversations with government officials (John 4:46–54), sitting on grassy hillsides (John 6:3–14), and visiting graveyards (John 11:17–44). The fact that no one uses the settings of these other miracles in John as an indication of Jesus'

personal values underscores the inappropriateness of using the Cana wedding feast setting in that way.

5. For a somewhat different reading of Mark's position, see Dale B. Martin's essay in this volume.

6. For thorough discussions of this issue, see J.T.A.G.M. van Ruiten, "The Creation of Man and Woman in Early Jewish Literature," in *Creation of Man and Woman*, 34–62; and Benjamins, "Keeping Marriage out of Paradise," 93–106. See also Gary Anderson ("The Garden of Eden and Sexuality in Early Judaism," in *People of the Body: Jews and Judaism from an Embodied Perspective*, ed. Howard Eilberg-Schwartz [Albany: State University of New York Press, 1992], 47–68), who argues that the Rabbis did see marriage in the Garden whereas the Church Fathers did not.

7. Philo, *De Opificio Mundi*, 151–152. See also the discussion in Thomas H. Tobin, S.J., *The Creation of Man: Philo and the History of Interpretation*, Catholic Biblical Quarterly Monograph Series 14 (Washington, DC: Catholic Biblical Association of America, 1983); and Annewies van den Hoek, "Endowed with Reason or Glued to the Senses: Philo's Thoughts on Adam and Eve," in *Creation of Man and Woman*, 63–75.

8. See Mathew Kuefler, *The Manly Eunuch: Masculinity, Gender Ambiguity, and Christian Ideology in Late Antiquity* (Chicago: University of Chicago Press, 2001), 255–273.

9. For a fuller discussion of this Aggadic tradition of creation of male and female, which also appears in Leviticus Rabbah 14:I, see Jacob Neusner, *Judaism's Story of Creation: Scripture, Halakhah, Aggadah* (Leiden: Brill, 2000), 219–264; and Kristen Kvam, Linda Schearing, and Valarie Ziegler, eds., *Eve and Adam: Jewish, Christian, and Muslim Readings on Genesis and Gender* (Bloomington: Indiana University Press, 1999), 69–85.

10. Philo, *De Opificio Mundi*, 152. Some early Christians, as the Coptic Gospel of Thomas indicates in its exegesis of Genesis 1, also understood original human creation as being undivided and singular, which then quickly devolves into a duality that mars the true undivided image of God. Returning to that undivided, singular state becomes the purpose of Jesus and the goal of Christian life. For this analysis, see Elaine Pagels, "Exegesis of Genesis 1 in the Gospels of Thomas and John," *Journal of Biblical Literature* 118, no. 3 (1999): 477–496.

11. Plato, *Symposium*, 191–192. Consider also Laurence Paul Hemming's essay in this volume.

12. Early Christian and Jewish exegetes recognized the presence of two somewhat conflicting creation stories in Genesis 1–3, and resolving this exegetical problem encouraged many of them toward creativity and theological expansion.

13. *Complementarity* has become the preferred term for the created relationship of male and female in the writing of some recent conservative commentators. See, e.g., Robert Gagnon, *The Bible and Homosexual Practice: Texts and Hermeneutics* (Nashville: Abingdon, 2001). What exactly *complementarity* might mean for that relationship is rarely touched on or explained. In my opinion, the reason it is not explained is that *complementarity*—beyond a sort of low-level assumed genital anatomical "fit"—almost certainly requires defining the broader female role in the "complement" as the more traditional passive and subordinate position to the

male's dominant, purposeful, and decision-making role. Being clear and open about the meaning of *complementarity* would almost surely lose popularity for the term and the idea behind it.

14. Demosthenes, *Against Neaera*, 122.

15. For more discussion on the fictive nature of New Testament family, see the essays in Halvor Moxnes, ed., *Constructing Early Christian Families: Family as Social Reality and Metaphor* (London: Routledge, 1997).

16. The one seemingly positive reference to marriage in the New Testament in Heb. 13:4 may also be related to this view of marriage as a curb on sexual passion. The verse appears within a series of imperatives on proper behavior at the end of this rather late letter, a series that provides little help in interpreting this verse's import. Although the second part of verse 4 is clearly concerned with the purity of marriage and the rejection of sexual acts that might break marriage vows, especially prostitution and adultery, both associated with sexual passion, the command to honor marriage in the first part is more ambiguous. Does the author of Hebrews demand that marriage be honored because the tendency in early Christian communities is to avoid marriage, and the author of Hebrews, like Paul, thinks that marriage can be usefully employed to control passion? Or is the author simply using a general rhetorical convention in speaking about marriage that has nothing to do with particular issues in the Christian community?

17. David Konstan, *Friendship in the Classical World* (Cambridge: Cambridge University Press, 1997), 1.

18. For studies on the importance of friendship in antiquity and in the New Testament, see John T. Fitzgerald, ed., *Greco-Roman Perspectives on Friendship*, Society of Biblical Literature Resources for Biblical Studies 34 (Atlanta: Scholars Press, 1997); and John T. Fitzgerald, ed., *Friendship, Flattery, and Frankness of Speech: Studies on Friendship in the New Testament World* (Leiden: Brill, 1996).

19. For a full discussion of Ben Sira's views on friendship, see Jeremy Corley, *Ben Sira's Teaching on Friendship*, Brown Judaic Studies 316 (Providence: Brown Judaic Studies, 2002).

20. The idea of friendship with God was fairly common in antiquity. See David Winston, ed., *The Wisdom of Solomon*, Anchor Bible 43 (Garden City, NY: Doubleday, 1980), 188–189.

21. Gregory E. Sterling, "The Bond of Humanity: Friendship in Philo of Alexandria," in *Greco-Roman Perspectives on Friendship* (Atlanta: Scholars Press, 1997), 203–223.

22. Philo, *De Specialibus Legibus*, I:52.

23. Whereas Aristotle's classic understanding of friendship delineated three forms of friendship—the altruistic, the utilitarian, and the pleasurable—Ben Sira, Philo, and the New Testament authors clearly seem to value the altruistic as the only true meaning of friendship.

24. Jean Bethke Elshtain, "Happily Ever After? Sex, Marriage, and Family in National and Global Profile" (speech given at the conference "Sex, Marriage, and Family and the Religions of the Book," Emory University, Atlanta, March 27, 2003).

25. See, e.g., Thomas E. Schmidt, *Straight and Narrow? Compassion and Clarity in the Homosexuality Debate* (Downers Grove, IL: InterVarsity Press, 1995), 45;

or John Stott, *Our Social and Sexual Revolution: Major Issues for a New Century,* 3rd ed. (Grand Rapids, MI: Baker Books, 1999), 200.

CHAPTER FOUR
Why Is Rabbi Yoḥanan a Woman?

This essay is part of a much larger project to reevaluate the place of rhetoric in ancient and late ancient culture. One enormous piece of this has to do with the role of Plato in those cultures. In this essay I take up a question having to do with Athenian norms, Plato, and Rabbinic Judaism. I wish to thank Mark Jordan for inviting me to the conference in which this essay (in very, very inchoate form) was first discussed and for the attendant stimulation to keep going. Cynthia Baker, Jonathan Boyarin, Virginia Burrus, G.R.F. Ferrari, Willis Johnson, and Dina Stein have been encouraging and critical presences in the production of the essay from very early in its life. I would like also to acknowledge here the steady scholarly comradeship of a young colleague, Ishay Rosen-zvi, who has been gently but firmly pushing me for several years now to reconsider some positions of *Carnal Israel.* He also read a draft of this essay and made some great critical suggestions.

1. In both rabbinic and Christian writing, this chapter is understood as the contrast between true religious wisdom, "wife of one's youth," and heresy. I shall be expanding on this point in another context, *Deo volente.*
2. See the near-classic Claudia V. Camp, *Wisdom and the Feminine in the Book of Proverbs,* Bible and Literature Series (Decatur, GA: Almond Press, 1985); and Michael V. Fox, *Proverbs 1–9: A New Translation with Introduction and Commentary* (New York: Doubleday, 2000), 331–359.
3. Eve Kosofsky Sedgwick, *Between Men: English Literature and Male Homosocial Desire* (New York: Columbia University Press, 1985).
4. Michael L. Satlow, *Jewish Marriage in Antiquity* (Princeton, NJ: Princeton University Press, 2001), 13–14; and Musonius Rufus, for whom see page cited in next note.
5. Satlow, *Jewish Marriage,* 33.
6. Daniel Boyarin, "Literary Fat Rabbis: On the Historical Origins of the Grotesque Body," *Journal of the History of Sexuality* 1, no. 4 (April 1991): 551–584; Daniel Boyarin, "Homotopia: The Feminized Jewish Man and the Lives of Women in Late Antiquity," *Differences* 7, no. 2 (Summer 1995): 41–71; Daniel Boyarin, *Unheroic Conduct: The Rise of Heterosexuality and the Invention of the Jewish Man,* Contraversions: Studies in Jewish Literature, Culture, and Society (Berkeley and Los Angeles: University of California Press, 1997), 127–150.
7. See the remarks of David Cohen, *Law, Sexuality, and Society: The Enforcement of Morals in Classical Athens* (Cambridge: Cambridge University Press, 1991), 174. On this point, I could not agree more with Cohen: "A culture is not a homogeneous unity; there was no one 'Athenian attitude' towards homoeroticism" (*Law, Sexuality, and Society,* 201).
8. My colleague Ronald Hendel has emphasized this point, which will be taken up, *Deo volente,* further when I attempt to consider the relations between Hellenic Sophism and Near Eastern (and Egyptian) Wisdom.

9. Not least by me in the past. This essay is highly revisionist with respect to both *Carnal Israel: Reading Sex in Talmudic Culture*, The New Historicism: Studies in Cultural Poetics, vol. 25 (Berkeley and Los Angeles: University of California Press, 1993), and *Unheroic Conduct*. See the important critique of my earlier work in Ishay Rosen-zvi, "The Evil Instinct, Sexuality, and Forbidden Cohabitations: A Chapter in Talmudic Anthropology" (in Hebrew), *Theory and Criticism: An Israeli Journal*, no. 14 (Summer 1999): 55–84, in which Rosen-zvi writes: "This article tried to evaluate anew the concept of the 'evil instinct' in rabbinic discourse on sexuality. It seems that a full evaluation of the 'instinct' requires a new investigation of that which has been grasped in contemporary research as the great gap between the Rabbis and early Christianity with respect to sexuality. . . . Indeed, with all that has to do with sexual practice (marriage, procreation, marital relations, divorce), there is no doubt that there are crucial differences, but with respect to the metaphysical foundation which generates the discourse and gives it meaning, it may be that the difference is not so great." I follow here in the wake of my youngers and betters.

10. David M. Halperin, "Why Is Diotima a Woman?" in *One Hundred Years of Homosexuality and Other Essays on Greek Love* (New York: Routledge, 1990), 113–151 and 190–211, is, of course, a notable exception to this generalization. I shall be building on this landmark essay immediately below.

11. After doing so much work in the 1980s to disrupt this hyphenated term, I find myself coming back to it as a convenient moniker for the cultural complex formed by what might be called Jewish Hellenisms, including the various "Judaisms" of the first centuries BC and AC, Rabbinic Judaism, and late ancient Christianity. There is no attempt to indicate that these are ipso facto the same or necessarily similar to each other, but, on the other hand—and this is both retained and amplified from earlier work—neither is to be considered self-identical, and the ways that each is riven sometimes connect interestingly and importantly with the ways that the "other" is riven, such that fault lines occur that split both so-called Rabbinic Judaism and so-called Christianity in the *same* way and not necessarily between them. See Daniel Boyarin, *Border Lines: The Partition of Judeo-Christianity*, Divinations: Rereading Late Ancient Religions (Philadelphia: University of Pennsylvania Press, 2004). For a much fuller version of my analysis of the *Symposium*, see my essay "What Do We Talk about When We Talk about (Platonic) Love: The *Symposium* and Christian Eros," forthcoming in *Toward a Theology of Eros*, ed. Virginia Burrus and Catherine Keller (New York: Fordham University Press).

12. Halperin, "Why Is Diotima a Woman?" 124.

13. Cf. Martha Nussbaum's version of Halperin's point: "Here, then, Socrates too, takes a mistress: a priestess instead of a courtesan, a woman who prefers the intercourse of the pure mind to the pleasures of the body, who honors (or is honored by) the divine rather than the merely human." Martha Craven Nussbaum, *The Fragility of Goodness: Luck and Ethics in Greek Tragedy and Philosophy* (Cambridge: Cambridge University Press, 1986), 177. While still emphasizing Aspasia as *hetaira*, Nussbaum does hint at the point that I would make: Diotima is the woman—philosopher—who "prefers the intercourse of the pure mind." From Diotima to Hypatia is not, I think, such an enormous epistemic leap. And let us not forget the strong ancient traditions that there were (a few) women in the Academy. See Konrad Gaiser, *Philodems Academica: Die Berichte über Platon und die Alte Akademie in zwei herkulanensischen Papyri* (Stuttgart-Bad Canstatt: Frommann-

Holzboog, 1988), 154, cited in Pierre Hadot, *What Is Ancient Philosophy?* (Cambridge, MA: Harvard University Press, 2002), 61.

14. Halperin, "Why Is Diotima a Woman?" 124.

15. Ibid., 129.

16. My colleague, G.R.F. Ferrari has pointed out to me that only recently he has come to realize that this is not a necessary conclusion; neither the text explicitly, nor Greek custom, would demand that a priestess be celibate. However, the very fact that it is only recently that such an assiduous reader of Plato has sensed this suggests to me that it is, indeed, deeply encoded within the text that she is, in fact, a virginal or celibate woman (if not qua priestess, then qua philosopher). Whether or not Lady Diotima had children, the tradition could hardly be faulted, I think, for assuming that it is implied in the text that she had none.

17. Which in the end, is quite different from Halperin's in *its* end. For Halperin, Diotima turns out to be "not so much a woman as a 'woman,' a necessary female absence" ("Why Is Diotima a Woman?" 149). For me, Diotima is exactly a woman but a woman who represents the absence of another woman, not for specific political reasons having to do with gender, but for reasons having to do with the reproduction of the democratic polis as opposed to the philosophical academy.

18. See the briefest of hint in this direction in Nicole Loraux, *The Invention of Athens: The Funeral Oration in the Classical City* (Cambridge, MA: Harvard University Press, 1986), 323.

19. Plato, *Gorgias: A Revised Text*, ed. and trans. E. R. Dodds (1959; reprint, Oxford: Clarendon Press, 2002), 23–24; Dennis Proctor, *The Experience of Thucydides* (Warminster, Wilts, England: Aris & Phillips, 1980), 6; Loraux, *Invention of Athens*, 311–327; M. Pohlenz, *Aus Platos Werdezeit* (Berlin: Weidmann, 1913), 264–292; A. E. Taylor, *Plato, the Man and His Work* (London: Methuen, 1960), 42.

20. Plato, *Euthyphro, Apology, Crito, Meno, Gorgias, Menexenus*, trans. Reginald E. Allen, The Dialogues of Plato (New Haven, CT: Yale University Press, 1984), 329.

21. Reginald E. Allen, "Comment, Menexenus," in ibid., 320.

22. Halperin, "Why Is Diotima a Woman?" 138–139.

23. Plato, *The Republic*, ed. G.R.F. Ferrari, trans. Tom Griffith, Cambridge Texts in the History of Political Thought (Cambridge: Cambridge University Press, 2000), 200–201.

24. Andrea Wilson Nightingale, *Genres in Dialogue: Plato and the Construct of Philosophy* (Cambridge: Cambridge University Press, 1995), 43.

25. It is only recently that the enormous gap between Pausanian erotic theory in the *Symposium* and that of Diotima/Socrates/Plato has come clearly into focus. Not long ago, it was easy to find statements of the following sort in the literature: "in the *Symposium* Plato feels no necessity to make Socrates or Diotima speak about it [heavenly eros], but entrusts to Pausanias the task of explaining the difference between what he calls 'vulgar (πάνδημος) Eros' and 'heavenly (οὐράνιος) Eros.'" Anders Nygren, *Agape and Eros*, trans. Philip S. Watson (New York: Harper and Row, 1969), 51. This leads, of course, to a total and totally misleading conflation

of the view of Pausanias (the Athenian demotic view of love) and that of Plato. For this argument at length, see Boyarin, "What Do We Talk About."

26. Plato's moves here have to be correlated with other, even slightly earlier, movements within Athenian thought. Plato's own vision of *philosophia*, of course, owes much to Parmenides, but also, as Froma Zeitlin has argued, much as well to Aeschylus. The very foundations of philosophy as a specifically European practice, according to her, are grounded in "bring[ing] together phallos and head . . . for the ending of the [*Oresteia*] is also concerned with a shift in modes and behavior, as it charts a progression from darkness to light, from obscurity to clarity. Representation of symbolic signs perceived as a form of female activity gives way to the triumph of the male *Logos*. Representation and lyric incantation yield to dialectic and speech, and magic to science. Even more, this 'turning away from the mother to the father,' as Freud observed, 'signifies victory of intellectuality over the senses'" (Froma Zeitlin, "The Dynamics of Misogyny: Myth and Mythmaking in Aeschylus's *Oresteia*," in *Playing the Other; Gender and Society in Classical Greek Literature*, Women in Culture and Society [Chicago: University of Chicago Press, 1996], 211). Zeitlin proceeds to provide an extensive list of the ontological oppositions grounded in the primary opposition of male as Apollo and female as Erinyes that grow from this "turning" or "victory" (Zeitlin, "Dynamics of Misogyny," 112) and that are characteristic of Greek philosophy from some pre-Socratics to Plato and Aristotle. These relations will be further worked out, *Deo volente*, in the longer version of this study.

27. Pierre Hadot writes:

> Socrates' task—entrusted to him, says the *Apology*, by the Delphic oracle (in other words, the god Apollo)—was therefore to make other people recognize their lack of knowledge and of wisdom. In order to accomplish this mission, Socrates himself adopted the attitude of someone who knew nothing—an attitude of naiveté. This is the well-known Socratic irony: the feigned ignorance and candid air with which, for instance, he asked questions in order to find out whether someone was wiser than he. . . .
>
> According to Cicero, "Socrates used to denigrate himself, and conceded more than was necessary to the interlocutors he wanted to refute. Thus, *thinking one thing and saying another*, he took pleasure in that dissimulation which the Greeks call 'irony.'" (Hadot, *What Is Ancient Philosophy?* 26–27, emphasis added)

And yet again, "Socratic irony consists in pretending that one wants to learn something from one's interlocutor, in order to bring him to the point of discovering that he knows nothing of the area in which he claims to be wise" (Hadot, *What Is Ancient Philosophy?* 26–27). The question, of course, is how does this sit with the vaunted "say what you mean" principle that Nehamas makes the hallmark of Socratean sincerity versus his Sophistic opponents (Alexander Nehamas, "Eristic, Antilogic, Sophistic, Dialectic," *History of Philosophy Quarterly* 7 [1986]: 3–16)? It would seem that the principle of sincerity applies only to the opponents, whereas Socrates is permitted to utilize rhetoric, mirabile dictu, to convince of his point, once again completely disrupting any notion of mutuality in the "conversation." I wonder if Hadot himself is aware of the irony in his own phrasing: "the mutual accord which Socrates *demands* from his interlocutor at each stage of the discussion" (Hadot, *What Is Ancient Philosophy?* 26–27, emphasis added). Or yet again: "A true dialogue is possible only if the interlocutors *want* to dialogue. Thanks to this agreement between the interlocutors, which is renewed at each stage of the discussion, neither one of the interlocutors imposes his truth upon the other" (Hadot, *What Is Ancient Philosophy?* 63). I may be forgiven for wondering whether "Protagoras" or "Gorgias" or "Meno" would agree to this description. (See, too, Daniel Boyarin, "Thucydides, Rhetoric, and the Democratic Party; or, Thucydides Contra Plato," paper presented at University of British Columbia, 2004.) Lest I seem even more arrogant than I think I truly am, let me say that Hadot's account of Socrates is a compelling and attractive one. As with other pro-Socratic commentators, Hadot gives us, undoubtedly, the Socrates that Plato wants us to buy, but this ignores the fact that to do so, we have to accept not only the idealized picture of Socrates, but even more dangerously, the slanders of his interlocutors. At the very least the difference between Hadot's (to my mind idealized) picture and more suspicious ones seems to demonstrate the perspicuity of another insight of Hadot's, namely, the fact that there are so many different Socrateses owing to the complexity of the Platonic portrait to which must be added the other portraits as well, especially Xenophon's. Hadot points out that such seemingly incompatible schools as the Cynics and the Epicureans all trace their ancestry to Socrates. See especially the beautiful—if to me, not entirely convincing—reading of Eros in the *Symposium* as Socrates in Hadot, *What Is Ancient Philosophy?* 42–50.

28. See Eugene Rogers's essay in this volume and Rogers, *Sexuality and the Christian Body: Their Way into the Triune God*, Challenges in Contemporary Theology (Oxford: Blackwell, 1999).

29. Michel Foucault, *The Use of Pleasure*, vol. 2 of *The History of Sexuality*, trans. Robert Hurley (New York: Vintage, 1986), 240.

30. Cf. K. J. Dover, *Greek Homosexuality*, updated and with a new postscript (Cambridge, MA: Harvard University Press, 1989), 164–165.

31. David M. Halperin, "Platonic *Eros* and What Men Call Love," *Ancient Philosophy* 5 (1985): 161–204, is, in itself, a profound interpretation of the *Symposium*, to my mind the most compelling I have seen yet. It underplays, on my reading, the sharpness of the value-distinction that Plato makes here and elsewhere between two kinds of lovers, who are different ab ovo, as it were. See especially Halperin, "Platonic *Eros*," 183–187, for both the profundity of his account and this one elision. The elision shows up particularly on p. 187, when Halperin asks (but does not answer; his promised answers never, to the best of my knowledge, appeared) a remarkable set of questions about "what a properly Platonic love-affair [would] look like in practice. . . . How would it differ from what Plato's contemporaries considered normal in the way of erotic relations?" My reading, following in part G.R.F. Ferrari, hazards an answer to these questions. This point is crucial, in my view, for perceiving the Platonic affinities of late ancient thinking about sexuality. Halperin's account opens up, at the same time, other interesting points of contact (whether genetic or typological, I cannot yet say) between Platonic and rabbinic ways of thinking. In particular, I think we need a study in depth of the ways that

Platonic eros as creative force (Halperin, "Platonic *Eros*," especially 182) approaches rabbinic accounts of the *yeṣer*, on which see Rosen-zvi, "Evil Instinct." I am thinking particularly of accounts that describe the demise of the *yeṣer* (imagined as a daimon!) as the end of all human and animal creativity.

32. Benjamin Jowett, trans., *The Dialogues of Plato* (Oxford: Clarendon Press, 1875), 2:18.

33. Although, of course, the Stranger in the *Laws* would dearly like it to have been so (835c1–8); see the discussion in Seth Benardete, *Plato's "Laws": The Discovery of Being* (Chicago: University of Chicago Press, 2000), 239.

34. Cf. G.R.F. Ferrari, "Platonic Love," in *The Cambridge Companion to Plato*, ed. Richard Kraut (Cambridge: Cambridge University Press, 1992), 256: "the transition from the Lesser to Greater bears comparison, then, with the crucial shift of focus in the *Republic* from institutions grounded in the honor code (Books II–IV) to those derived from rule by philosopher-kings (Books V–VII)."

35. Boyarin, "What Do We Talk About."

36. Raw materials are not subject to ritual impurity, but finished implements or vessels are. The question that this text asks is, then, what constitutes the completion of production for these various weapons.

37. This sentence is not in the manuscripts and is clearly an addition in the text, but I cite it from the printed edition because it is very revealing of the meaning of the narrative as a whole, and indeed supportive of my reading. (It would seem to be an ancient gloss.) R.Y. is not made to say that he profited R.L. by providing him with a wife but only by having provided him with the spiritual female object of desire, the *Shekhina*.

38. That is, there is the class of the ignoranti (the *'ammei h'arasot*), but the Sages are enjoined not to separate themselves from this crowd. Much more can and will need to be said on this point, but it approximates my thinking at present.

39. A. A. Long and D. N. Sedley, *The Hellenistic Philosophers* (Cambridge: Cambridge University Press, 1987), 1:430.

40. Cf. "This movement [from family to polis] is recapitulated in the *Republic*, with its noble lie, myths, and bizarre sexual regulations, where first the family is annihilated in the name of the city, and then the philosophers, who are to be its rulers, do not want to turn away from their contemplations to descend to the city's cavelike darkness." Allan David Bloom, "The Ladder of Love," in *Plato's Symposium*, trans. Seth Benardete (Chicago: University of Chicago Press, 2001), 66.

41. Fascinatingly, however, when this same metaphor is used with reference to a non-Jewish male, Ahasuerosh, it seems that his pleasure in having sex with Esther was similar to that of the buck with the doe: "Rav Zeirah said [a parable]: For what Esther, [the person] was compared to a young female deer?—[It was done in order] to tell you that as the young female deer has a tiny vagina and her husband always loves [her] as if it would be their first time, so also [the king] Ahasuerosh always loved Esther as if it were their first time" (TB Yoma 29a).

42. Steven D. Fraade, "Ascetical Aspects of Ancient Judaism," in *Jewish Spirituality from the Bible through the Middle Ages*, ed. Arthur Green, World Spirituality: An Encyclopedic History of the Religious Quest (New York: Crossroad, 1986). My own work until recently had comprehended the apparent inner tensions of rabbinic literature as being the product of a contention between the Rabbis and

earlier/other Jewish groups on this issue (Boyarin, *Carnal Israel*, 61–76). At most, I allowed that an earlier and more Palestinian version of rabbinism had been closest to the ascetic ideals but that this shifted dramatically in Babylonian rabbinism (Boyarin, *Carnal Israel*, 46–57). Most recently, however, stimulated by the excellent scholarship of a new generation, I have concluded that the tensions and ambivalence over corporeality and sexuality were right at the heart of the rabbinic movement itself, and it is this that I wish to further document here, together with its implications for queer reading of those texts. What was once easier to see as an isogloss between the Rabbis and the Fathers now seems to be a complicated set of isoglosses within the rabbinic community as well.

43. Shlomo Naeh, "Freedom and Celibacy: A Talmudic Variation on Tales of Temptation and Fall in Genesis and Its Syrian Background," in *The Book of Genesis in Jewish and Oriental Christian Interpretation: A Collection of Essays*, ed. Judith Frishman and Lucas Van Rompay, Traditio Exegetica Graeca 5 (Louvain: Peeters, 1997), 73–89; Naomi Koltun-Fromm, "Yoke of the Holy-Ones: The Embodiment of a Christian Vocation," *Harvard Theological Review* 94, no. 2 (2001): 205–218; Michael Satlow, "And on the Earth You Shall Sleep: Talmud Torah and Rabbinic Asceticism," *Journal of Religion* 83 (2003): 204–225; Eliezer Diamond, *Holy Men and Hunger Artists: Fasting and Asceticism in Rabbinic Culture* (Oxford: Oxford University Press, 2004).

44. Daniel Boyarin, *Dying for God: Martyrdom and the Making of Christianity and Judaism*, The Lancaster/Yarnton Lectures in Judaism and Other Religions for 1998 (Stanford, CA: Stanford University Press, 1999), 56–58.

45. As pointed out already in Boyarin, *Carnal Israel*, 65, but with much greater clarity and power in Rosen-zvi, "Evil Instinct."

46. Let us not forget, then, that Socrates himself was married with children (perhaps his children were very naughty). Plato, most assuredly, was not.

47. Satlow points out a Pehlevi text from about the time of the redaction of the Babylonian Talmud that indicates that if a woman does not marry it is a "sin worthy of death; because for a woman there is no offspring except by intercourse with men, and no lineage proceeds from her; but for a man without a wife, when he shall recite the Avesta, as it is mentioned in the vendida, there may be a lineage which proceeds onwards to the future existence" (Satlow, *Jewish Marriage*, 33–34).

CHAPTER FIVE
Can I Really Count on You?

1. Congregation for the Doctrine of the Faith, *Considerations Regarding Proposals to Give Legal Recognition to Unions between Homosexual Persons* (June 3, 2003), in *Acta Apostolicæ Sedis* 100 (2004): §2, p. 42. "L'insegnamento della Chiesa sul matrimonio e sulla complementarità dei sessi ripropone una verità evidenziata dalla retta ragione e riconosciuta come tale da tutte le grandi culture del mondo."

2. John Paul II, Apostolic Letter *Mulieris Dignitatem* (August 15, 1988), in *Acta Apostolicæ Sedis* 80 (1984): §7, p. 1666. "Ex 'unitate duorum' vir et mulier inde

ab exordio vocati sunt non solum ut vivant 'alter apud alteram,' vel una sint, sed vocati sunt etiam ut *vicissim alter pro altero vivat.*" Emphasis is in the original.

3. Gen. 1:15–25.

4. Congregation for the Doctrine of the Faith, *Considerations Regarding Proposals to Give Legal Recognition to Unions between Homosexual Persons*, §1, p. 42. "La dignità del matrimonio, fondamento della famiglia, e la solidità della società."

5. Judith Butler, *Bodies That Matter: On the Discursive Limits of "Sex"* (London: Routledge, 1993), 54.

6. Ibid., 55.

7. Ibid., 72.

8. Judith Butler, *Gender Trouble: Feminism and the Subversion of Identity* (London: Routledge, 1990), 31. This position has been delightfully amplified in an unpublished paper by Ferdinand Knapp, "'Walk the Walk, Talk the Talk': Blokes, and Why It Doesn't Matter That They Think They Are Real" (Peterhouse Theory Group, Cambridge, UK, April 1998), which develops the notion of "heterosexual camp" to illustrate the phenomenon of the British "lad" culture, now with its parallel among women, or "ladettes."

9. For a fuller description of the heterosexual matrix as she understands it, see Butler, *Gender Trouble*, 35–78.

10. It is unsurprising, therefore, that Butler has continued to explore the effects of gender in the political. See her *Excitable Speech: A Politics of the Performative* (London: Routledge, 1997).

11. Martin Heidegger, *Sein und Zeit*, in his *Gesamtausgabe*, vol. 2, ed. Friedrich-Wilhelm von Herrmann (Frankfurt: Klostermann, 1977), especially §§25–27, pp. 153–173.

12. Martin Heidegger, *Metaphysische Anfangsgründe der Logik*, in his *Gesamtausgabe*, vol. 26, ed. Klaus Held (Frankfurt: Klostermann, 1990), 174ff.: "Das Dasein *Mitsein* mit Dasein ist. Dieses Mitsein mit . . . entsteht nicht aufgrund eines faktisches Zusammendaseins, es erklärt sich nicht nur auf dem Grunde eines vermeintlich ursprünglicheren gattungshaften Seins der geschlechtlich gespaltenen leiblichen Wesen, sondern dieses gattungshafte Zusammenstreben und die gattungshafte Einigung hat zur metaphysischen Voraussetzung die Zerstreuung des Daseins als solchen, d.h. das Mitsein überhaupt."

13. Heidegger, *Metaphysische Anfangsgründe der Logik*, 173: "Die Kennzeichnung der Mannigfaltigung (nicht 'Mannigfaltigkeit'), die je in jedem vereinzelten faktischen Dasein als solchem liegt."

14. Martin Heidegger, *Einleitung in die Philosophie*, in his *Gesamtausgabe*, vol. 27, ed. Otto Saame and Ima Saame-Speidel (Frankfurt: Klostermann, 1996), 145ff.: "Das Miteinander ist also nicht durch die Ich-Du-Beziehung und aus ihr zu erklären, sondern umgekehrt: Diese Ich-Du-Beziehung setzt für ihre innere Möglichkeit voraus, daß je schon das Dasein, sowohl das als Ich fungierende als auch das Du, als Miteinandersein bestimmt ist, ja noch mehr: Sogar die Selbsterfassung eines Ich und der Begriff von Ichheit erwächst erst auf dem Grunde des Miteinander, aber nicht als Ich-Du-Beziehung."

15. See, for instance, Hannah Arendt, *The Human Condition* (Chicago: University of Chicago Press, 1998), especially pp. 53ff.

16. Plato, *Symposium*, 189D: "ten anthropinen physin kai ta pathemata autes."

17. Plato, *Symposium*, 189D: "ton allon didaskaloi esesthe."

18. In contrast to the interpretation I have suggested, Leo Strauss notes the connection that this names with the original divinities, different from the Olympian gods. The three kinds of human already referred to each of the most primordial of divinities and corresponded to them. See Leo Strauss, *Leo Strauss on Plato's Symposium*, ed. Seth Bernadete (Chicago: University of Chicago Press, 2001), 74ff. The missing fourth element (in that the middle elements, water and air, are middle-up and middle-down) could be construed as present in terms of the missing fourth which I later indicate.

19. Cf. Plato, *Symposium*, 189E.

20. Plato, *Symposium*, 191 C–D: "esti de oun . . . ten anthropinen."

21. Plato, *Symposium*, 192 C: "oudeni gar an . . . sunousia."

22. The dictionaries often suggest that active and passive referred respectively to male and female but this is—to give it the kindest reading possible—disingenuous, since the passive form could be used with regard to men and, although with normally shameful implications, the active form with regard to women.

23. Cf. Plato, *Symposium*, 191C.

24. Hence the possibility of referring all the forms of the original human being to the elements.

25. It is actually this even more original relation to *logos*, or language that, one might argue, forms the basis of Aristotle's critique of Plato's relation of being to number.

26. Cf. Plato, *Symposium*, 190A: "kai prosopa dun ep' auchei kukloterei."

27. Plato, *Timaeus*, 33B: "panton teleotaton omoiotaton te autho e auto."

28. Although there are traces of a different tale in the reference to begetting in the manner of crickets (cf. Plato, *Symposium*, 191B).

29. Genesis Rabbah 8:1.

CHAPTER SIX
Contemplating a Jewish Ritual of Same-Sex Union

1. For the fuller exploration of the intersection between the halakhah and homosexuality, see Steven Greenberg, *Wrestling with God and Men: Homosexuality and the Jewish Tradition* (Madison: University of Wisconsin Press, 2004); and Chaim Rapoport, *Judaism and Homosexuality: An Authentic Orthodox View* (Ilford, U.K.: Valentine Mitchell, 2004).

2. My attempt at creating a same-sex Jewish marriage ritual is surely not the first. For other attempts, see Rachel Adler, *Engendering Judaism: An Inclusive Theology and Ethics* (Philadelphia: Jewish Publication Society, 1998); Elizabeth Resnick Levine, *A Ceremonies Sampler: New Rites, Celebrations, and Observances of Jewish Women* (San Diego: Woman's Institute for Continuing Jewish Education, 1991); Suzanne Sherman, *Lesbian and Gay Marriage: Private Commitments, Public Ceremonies* (Philadelphia: Temple University Press, 1992); Kittredge Cherry and Zalmon Sherwood, eds., *Equal Rites: Lesbian and Gay Worship, Ceremonies, and Celebrations* (Louisville: Westminster/John Knox Press, 1995); and Becky Butler, ed., *Ceremonies of the Heart: Celebrating Lesbian Unions* (Seattle: Seal Press, 1990).

3. Nonetheless, were the wedding to be canceled, a divorce bill (*get*) would still need to be served as in an ordinary marriage.

4. Some translate *erusin* as "betrothal," which is misleading because *erusin* is more than a promise to marry; it is a completed marital contract. Here I have followed Rachel Adler's good sense and have referred to *erusin* as "espousal." See Adler, *Engendering Judaism*, 251.

5. A variant blessing was preferred by the eleventh-century authority Rav Hai Gaon. His blessing ended with, "Blessed are you, O Lord, who sanctifies Israel," omitting the phrase, "by means of *huppah* and *kiddushin*." For Rav Hai, "the sanctity of Israel is not dependent upon this," i.e., on rituals of *huppah* and *kiddushin*. Rav Hai insisted on this difference because Jewish marriage was not considered a sacrament. See Isaiah M. Gafni, "The Institution of Marriage in Rabbinic Times," in *The Jewish Family*, ed. David Kraemer (New York: Oxford University Press, 1989), 14.

6. M *Kiddushin* 1:1.

7. BT *Kiddushin* 4b.

8. It is interesting that Jewish law does not give a person absolute rights in his own property. A person is not permitted to wantonly destroy his own property. The prohibition is derived from Deut. 20:19, which prohibits the destruction of fruit trees during a military siege. The rabbis derive from this text a prohibition against destroying or wasting one's own material resources. See Maimonides, Yad, Kings 6:10.

9. BT *Kiddushin* 2a, Tosafot d.h. d'asar.

10. The Ashkenazi ban was attributed to Rabeinu Gershom of the eleventh century, but Falk suggests that it was erroneously ascribed to R. Gershom but was developed in the twelfth century under pressure from the church, the government, and women themselves. See Zev Falk, *Jewish Matrimonial Law in the Middle Ages* (Oxford: Oxford University Press, 1966), 13. In Muslim lands, polygamy was formally permitted until the modern era. Where polygamy was practiced, an aristocratic family would often stipulate in their daughter's marriage contract that the husband not take on a co-wife in order to protect their daughter from the inevitable degradations a second wife would bring.

11. Adler, *Engendering Judaism*, 174–180.

12. Ibid., 192.

13. The language of lover as friend derives from the Song of Songs, which, according to Phyllis Trible, is itself a text of healing of all of the fractures of the Fall. See Phyllis Trible, *God and the Rhetoric of Sexuality* (Minneapolis: Fortress Press, 1978), 144–165.

14. BT *Hulin* 60b.

15. Halakhically speaking, *Kiddush Levanah* can be recited from seventy-two hours after the appearance of the new moon, referred to as the *molad*, until midmonth, which is fourteen days, eighteen hours, and twenty-two minutes after the *molad*.

16. BT Sanhedrin 42a.

17. In *Siddur Abodat Israel*, 338, Yehuda Baer suggests that this addition to the *Kiddush Levanah* is a tradition from the medieval German pietist R. Yehuda HaHasid. However, in the five-volume commentary on Jewish liturgy *Netiv Binah*, the author, Issachar Jacobson, admits not being able to find the origins of this prayer but believes that it derives from a mystical source. See *Netiv Bina*, 3:343.

18. Rashi on Megilah 22b, dh. *roshei hodashim*. I thank Rabbi Pinchas Klein for bringing this source to my attention.

CHAPTER SEVEN
Arguing Liturgical Genealogies

1. John Boswell, *Same-Sex Unions in Premodern Europe* (New York: Villard Books, 1994). Until otherwise noted, parenthetical citations will refer to the pages of this book. I have considered Boswell's book twice before, once in an extended book review and again in a constructive argument about rites for blessing same-sex unions. See Jordan, "A Romance of the Gay Couple," *GLQ* 3 (1996): 301–310, and *Blessing Same-Sex Unions: The Perils of Queer Romance and the Confusions of Christian Marriage* (Chicago: University of Chicago Press, 2005), 132–136. I repeat only some of my earlier points here, since the other pieces had quite different purposes—and audiences.

2. Jacobus Goar, comp., *Euchologion, sive rituale Graecorum* . . . (Venice: Bartholomaeus Javarina, 1730; reprint, Graz: Druck u. Verlagsanstalt, 1960).

3. Boswell's interpretation of the text in Grottaferrata MS Gamma.B.II (and from it to all other manuscripts) depends on ignoring a scribal line that would appear to mark off the marital ceremony of crowning from the rite of *adelphopoiesis*. Because I have not handled the manuscript myself, my sense that the reading may be doubtful comes from Boswell's strained arguments in support of it (296–297, n. 80).

4. *Codex iuris canonici* (1983), 1101 §2, in *Code of Canon Law: Latin-English Edition, New English Translation* (Washington, DC: Canon Law Society of America, 1999), 346. For one analysis of the kinds of "positive act of the will" that will invalidate marriage under this canon and the sorts of evidence needed to establish it, see Lawrence G. Wrenn, *The Invalid Marriage* (Washington, DC: Canon Law Society of America, 1998), 122–125.

5. Wrenn, *Invalid Marriage*, 90–91.

6. Gary Trudeau's comic strip *Doonesbury* ran a short series on Boswell's book beginning June 8, 1994. In the strip, the character Mark says that a Yale professor has written a book proving that "for 1,000 years the church sanctioned rituals for homosexual marriages."

7. Cf. Don E. Saliers, *Worship as Theology: Foretaste of Divine Glory* (Nashville: Abingdon, 1994), on the eschatological character of liturgy and its elements.

8. Compare Boswell's labored explanation for translating the various rites into something like the English of the 1928 *Book of Common Prayer* (*Same-Sex Unions*, 283–284).

9. Until otherwise noted, parenthetical citations will refer to the pages of Alan Bray, *The Friend* (Chicago: University of Chicago Press, 2003).

10. Leo Steinberg, *The Sexuality of Christ in Renaissance Art and in Modern Oblivion*, 2nd ed. (Chicago: University of Chicago Press, 1996).

11. Bray recounts a variety of ways for performing the ceremony before communion. See the summary in Bray, *Friend*, 242–243.

12. Bray's fullest explanation of these connections comes in his interpretation of the great east window at Holy Trinity, Goodramgate (*Friend*, 246–253).

13. Boswell had searched for something just like this rite, but somehow missed its publication by Zaninović in 1971; see Bray, 8–9, 316–317. Bray reprints and translates the *Ordo*, 130–133.

14. John Boswell, *Christianity, Social Tolerance, and Homosexuality* (Chicago: University of Chicago Press, 1980).

15. Derrick Sherwin Bailey, *Homosexuality and the Western Christian Tradition* (London: Longmans, Green & Co., 1955; reprint, Hamden, CT: Archon Books, 1975).

16. See, for example, Congregation for the Doctrine of the Faith, "Notification Concerning Certain Publications of Prof. Dr. Reinhard Messner" (November 30, 2000), *Acta Apostolicæ Sedis* 93 (2001): 385–403, especially proposition no. 9: "Between the magisterial forms of the definitions of the faith (Regula fidei, Symbolum, Dogma) and their actualization in the liturgy there cannot be any contradiction. The defined faith runs through every liturgy, through interpretation, and through new formulations of the liturgy."

17. Compare the ever-expanding notion of "juxtaposition" in Gordon W. Lathrop, *Holy Things: A Liturgical Theology* (Minneapolis: Fortress Press, 1993).

18. Michel Foucault, *Surveiller et punir: Naissance de la prison* (Paris: Gallimard, 1975).

19. See, for recent Catholic liturgies of engagement in France, Baptiste Coulmont, "'Politiques de l'alliance': Les créations d'un rite des fiançailles catholiques," *Archives de Science Sociale des Religions* 199 (2002): 5–27; and, more generally, Michael P. Foley, "Betrothals: Their Past, Present, and Future," *Studia Liturgica* 33 (2003): 37–61.

20. Michel de Montaigne, *Journal de Voyage en Italie par la Suisse et l'Allemagne en 1580 et 1581*, ed. Charles Dédéyan (Paris: Société des Belles Lettres, 1946), 231. Boswell takes this as evidence for the use in western Europe of a Latin liturgy of *adelphopoiesis* (*Same-Sex Unions*, 264–265); I read it rather as evidence of the appropriation for same-sex purposes of existing wedding rites.

21. Bray, *Friend*, especially 241–243.

22. See, for example, Rosemary Radford Ruether, *Women-Church: Theology and Practice of Feminist Liturgical Communities* (San Francisco: Harper & Row, 1985), 196–200; Kittredge Cherry and Zalmon Sherwood, eds., *Equal Rites: Lesbian and Gay Worship, Ceremonies, and Celebrations* (Louisville: Westminster/John Knox Press, 1995), 89–109; Becky Butler, ed., *Ceremonies of the Heart: Celebrating Lesbian Unions*, 2nd ed. (Washington, DC: Seal Press, 1997); Geoffrey Duncan, ed., *Courage to Love: Liturgies for the Lesbian, Gay, Bisexual, and Transgender Community* (Cleveland: Pilgrim Press, 2002), 286–306; William G. Storey, *A Book of Prayer: For Gay and Lesbian Christians* (New York: Crossroad, 2002), 80–86; and Diann L. Neu, *Women's Rites: Feminist Liturgies for Life's Journey* (Cleveland: Pilgrim Press, 2003), 106–120.

23. Compare Jean-Guy Nadeau and Manon Jourdenais, "La performativité des rites de la communauté gay confrontée au VIH/sida," in *Rites et ritualités: Actes du congrès de théologie pratique de Strasbourg*, ed. Bernard Kaempf (Paris: Éditions du Cerf, 2000), 27–43, especially p. 43.

24. See the remarkable analysis by Talal Asad, *Genealogies of Religion: Discipline and Reasons of Power in Christianity and Islam* (Baltimore: Johns Hopkins University Press, 1993), 55–79; and the exposition by Nathan D. Mitchell, *Liturgy and the Social Sciences*, American Essays in Liturgy (Collegeville, MN: Liturgical Press, 1999), 64–80.

CHAPTER EIGHT
Hooker and the New Puritans

1. For efforts similar to mine, see Don H. Compier, "Hooker on the Authority of Scripture in Matters of Morality," in *Richard Hooker and the Construction of Christian Community*, ed. Arthur Stephen McGrade (Tempe: Arizona State University, 1997), 251–259; and Stephen Sykes, "Richard Hooker and the Ordination of Women to the Priesthood," in his *Unashamed Anglicanism* (Nashville: Abingdon Press, 1995), 81–98.
2. See M.E.C. Perrott, "Richard Hooker and the Problem of Authority in the Elizabethan Church," *Journal of Ecclesiastical History* 49, no. 1 (1998): 36–39.
3. Parenthetical references in the rest of the essay will be to *Of the Laws of Ecclesiastical Polity*, citing book, chapter, and section, according to the most easily accessible edition, *The Works of . . . Mr. Richard Hooker*, ed. John Keble, R. W. Church, and F. Paget, 7th ed. (Oxford: Clarendon Press, 1888).
4. Francis Paget, *An Introduction to the Fifth Book of Hooker's Treatise of the Laws of Ecclesiastical Polity*, 2nd ed. (Oxford: Clarendon Press, 1907), 214.
5. "Issues in Human Sexuality: A Statement by the House of Bishops of the General Synod of the Church of England" (Harrisburg, PA: Morehouse Publishing, 1991), 2.28.

CHAPTER NINE
Ad Imaginem Dei

1. All quotations are taken from the presentation of February 13, 2003, as published on the Web site of the Canadian Conference of Catholic Bishops at www.cccb.ca.
2. "The Council proclaims man's high vocation, insists on a certain seed of divinity he carries within him." "Ideo sacra synodus, altissimam vocationem hominis profitens et divinum quoddam semen in eo insertum asseverans." *Gaudium et spes*, in *Decrees of the Ecumenical Councils*, vol. 2, ed. Norman P. Tanner, SJ (London: Sheed and Ward, 1990), no. 3.
3. *Gaudium et spes*, no. 9: "Men and women are becoming conscious of having to give direction to the powers which they have created, which can either enslave or serve them, and as a result are questioning themselves." "Praeterea, homo conscius fit ipsius esse recte dirigere vires, quas ipse suscitavit et quae eum opprimere aut ei servire possunt. Unde seipsum interrogat."
4. *Gaudium et spes*, no. 11: "The Council's first aim is to subject the values most highly regarded today to this light and to relate them to their divine source, since these values are very good insofar as they proceed from the God-given character

of the human person." "Concilium imprimis illos valores, qui hodie maxime æstimantur, sub hoc lumine diiudicare et ad fontem suum divinum referre intendit. Hi enim valores, prout ex hominis ingenio eidem divinitus collato procedunt, valde boni sunt."

5. *Gaudium et spes*, no. 12: "vera hominis condicio," "capacem suum creatorem cognoscendi et amandi."

6. *Gaudium et spes*, no. 15: "Recte iudicat homo, divinae mentis lumen participans, se intellectu suo universitatem rerum superare. . . . Intelligentia enim non ad sola phaenomena coarctatur, sed realitatem intelligibilem cum vera certitudine adipisci valet."

7. *Gaudium et spes*, no. 47: "Salus personae et societatis humanae ac christianae arcte cum fausta condicione communitatis coniugalis et familiaris connectitur."

8. *Gaudium et spes*, no. 48: "Ipse vero Deus est auctor matrimonii, variis bonis ac finibus praediti; quae omnia pro generis humani continuatione, pro singulorum familiae membrorum profectu personali ac sorte aeterna, pro dignitate, stabilitate, pace et prosperitate ipsius familiae totiusque humanae societatis maximi sunt momenti."

9. *Gaudium et spes*, no. 48: "e divino caritatis fonte exortae et ad exemplar suae cum ecclesia unionis constitutae, abundanter benedixit." "Germanus amor coniugalis in divinum amorem assumitur atque virtute redemptive Christi et salvifica actione ecclesiae regitur ac ditatur"; "magis et magis ad propriam suam perfectionem mutuamque sanctificationem, ideoque communiter ad Dei glorificationem accedunt."

10. *Gaudium et spes*, no. 49: "Hunc amorem Dominus, speciali gratiae et caritatis dono, sanare, perficere et elevare dignatus est. Talis amor, humana simul et divina consocians, coniuges ad liberum et mutuum sui ipsius donum, tenero affectu et opere probatum, conducit totamque vitam eorum pervadit; immo ipse generosa sua operositate perficitur et crescit."

11. *Gaudium et spes*, no. 52: "Ita familia . . . fundamentum societatis constituit"; "praesens tempus redimentes atque aeterna a mutabilibus formis discernentes"; "Ipse denique coniuges, ad imaginem Dei vivi facti et in vero ordine personarum constituti."

12. These have been collected into a single volume, along with *Humanae vitae* of Paul VI, *Mulieris dignitatem*, and *Evangelium vitae*, in John Paul II, *The Theology of the Body: Human Love in the Divine Plan*, reprinted from the English edition of *L'Osservatore Romano* (Boston: Pauline Books and Media, 1997).

13. Matt. 19:4: "He answered, 'Have you not read that he who made them from the beginning made them male and female?'" "ho de apokritheis eipen, ouk anegnote hoti ho ktisas ap arches arsen kai epoiesen autous." "qui respondens ait eis non legistis quia qui fecit ab initio masculum et feminam fecit eos."

14. John Paul II, "Original Unity of Man and Woman," in *Theology of the Body*, 29.

15. Ibid., 29.

16. Ibid., 32.

17. The discussion of this question begins at 506B and the connection is disclosed at 508E. "Touto toinun to ten aletheian parechon tois gignoskomenois kai toi gignoskonti ten dunamin apodidon ten tou agathou idean pathi einai."

18. John Paul II, "Original Unity," 35.

19. Ibid., 38.

20. Ibid., 94, n. 10.

21. Ibid., 38.

22. Ibid., 40–41.

23. Ibid., 38.

24. John Paul II, *Mulieris dignitatem* (Apostolic Letter of Pope John Paul II on the Dignity and Vocation of Women, August 15, 1988), no. 7, in *Theology of the Body*, 450.

25. "Ou kalon einai ton anthrôpon monon," "non est bonum esse hominem solum."

26. John Paul II, *Mulieris Dignitatem*, 450.

27. John Paul II, "The Sacramentality of Marriage," in *Theology of the Body*, 350.

28. Ibid., 406.

29. Ibid., 407.

30. John Paul II, *Mulieris Dignitatem*, 450–451.

31. Fergus Kerr, OP, *After Aquinas: Versions of Thomism* (Oxford: Blackwell, 2002), 124.

32. Aristotle, *Nicomachean Ethics*, book Z.

33. Thomas Aquinas, *Summa theologiae*, 1a–2ae, prologue.

34. 1 Cor. 7:14: "hegiastai gar ho aner ho apistos en tei gunaiki, kai hegiastai he gune he apistos en toi adelphoi."

35. 1 Cor. 7:29, 31: "touto de phemi, adelphoi, ho kairos sunestalmenos estin. To loipon hina kai hoi echontes gunaikas hos me echontes osin" and "paragei gar to schema tou kosmou toutou."

36. St. Catherine of Siena, *The Dialogue*, §13 (my translation): "Voglio dunque, e te lo dimando per grazia, che tu abbia misericordia del tuo popolo, per quella carità increata, che ti mosse a creare l'uomo a tua immagine e somiglianza, quando dicesti: 'Facciamo l'uomo a nostra immagine e somiglianza.' E questo lo facesti, perché volevi che l'uomo partecipasse di tutta Te, o alta ed eterna Trinità. . . . Chi fu cagione che tu ponessi l'uomo in tanta dignità? L'amore inestimabile col quale riguardasti in te medesimo la tua creatura, e ti innamorasti di lei; e però la creasti per amore, e le desti l'essere, acciochè ella gustasse e godesse il tuo eterno bene." From the modern Italian text, S. Caterina da Siena, *Il Dialogo della divina provvidenza* (Siena: Edizioni Cantagalli, 1998), 53.

CHAPTER TEN
Trinity, Marriage, Homosexuality

1. Eugene F. Rogers Jr., "Sanctification, Homosexuality, and God's Triune Life," in *Sexual Orientation and Human Rights in American Religious Discourse*, ed. Saul Olyan and Martha Nussbaum (New York: Oxford, 1998), 134–160; Rogers, *Sexuality and the Christian Body: Their Way into the Triune God* (Oxford: Blackwell Publishers, 1999); Rogers, "The Liturgical Body," *Modern Theology* 16 (2000): 365–376; Rogers, "Introduction," in *Theology and Sexuality: Classic and Contemporary Readings*, ed. Eugene F. Rogers Jr. (Oxford: Blackwell, 2002), xviii–xxii.

2. I owe my attention to the transformative perceptions of others to Thomas Nagel, "Sexual Perversion," and its application in Rowan Williams, "The Body's Grace," both in Rogers, *Theology and Sexuality*, 125–136, 309–321.

3. See the history in Adrian Thatcher, *Marriage after Modernity: Christian Marriage in Postmodern Times* (New York: New York University Press, 1999).

4. Judith Butler, "Contingent Foundations," in *Feminist Contentions: A Philosophical Exchange*, ed. Seyla Benhabib et al. (London: Routledge, 1995), 51–52, paragraph boundary elided; emphasis in the original.

5. For a classic discussion of white crows, see A. J. Ayer, *Language, Truth, and Logic* (New York: Dover, 1952).

6. For example, "The Order of Marriage, or of Crowning," in *Service Book of the Holy Orthodox-Catholic Apostolic Church*, ed. and trans. Isabel Florence Hapgood, 6th rev. ed. (Englewood, NJ: Antiochian Orthodox Christian Archdiocese, 1983), 293–305, especially 293–294.

7. Ibid., 297.

8. Paul Evdokimov, *The Sacrament of Love: The Nuptial Mystery in the Light of the Orthodox Tradition*, trans. Anthony P. Gythiel and Victoria Steadman (Crestwood, NY: St. Vladimir's Seminary Press, 1985), 65–84; for a shorter version, see the selection in Rogers, *Theology and Sexuality*, 179–193.

9. Clifford Kraus, "Free to Marry, Canada's Gays Say 'Do I?'" *New York Times*, August 31, 2003.

10. Kate Zernike, "The New Couples Next Door," *New York Times*, August 24, 2004.

11. Cf. Michel de Certeau, "The Weakness of Believing: From the Body to Writing, a Christian Transit," in *The Certeau Reader*, ed. Graham Ward (Oxford: Blackwell, 2000), 218.

12. See Sebastian Moore, "The Crisis of an Ethic without Desire," in *Jesus the Liberator of Desire* (New York: Crossroad, 1989), 89–107, reprinted in Rogers, *Theology and Sexuality*, 157–169.

13. For a longer account, see *Sexuality and the Christian Body*, 249–268; and Rogers, "Nature with Water and the Spirit: A Response to Rowan Williams," *Scottish Journal of Theology* 56 (2003): 89–100; especially 92–96.

14. Jacob of Serugh, translated as "Jacob of Serugh II," in Sebastian Brock, *The Syriac Fathers on Prayer and the Spiritual Life* (Kalamazoo, MI: Cistercian Publications, 1987), 287.

15. Jacob of Serugh, *Homily on the Veil of Moses*, ll. 141–151, translated in Sebastian Brock, *Studies in Syriac Spirituality*, Syrian Churches Series 13 (Poonah, India: Anita Printers, 1988), 95.

16. Jeffrey Stout, "How Charity Transcends the Culture Wars: Eugene Rogers and Others on Same-Sex Marriage," *Journal of Religious Ethics* 31 (2003): 169–180, quotation on 173–174.

17. Hosea 2:19a, 20. For argumentative context, see Rogers, *Sexuality and the Christian Body*, 219–236.

18. Matt. 22:2 (parallel Luke 14:16–24).

19. Luke 5:34.

20. Matt. 25:1 (parallel Luke 12:35, Mark 13:34).

21. Rev. 19:6–9.

22. Karl Barth, *Church Dogmatics* (Edinburgh: T. & T. Clark, 1961), vol. III, pt. 1:318.

23. Evdokimov, *Sacrament of Love*, 16–43. For this use of Evdokimov, cf. *Sexuality and the Christian Body*, 67–86.

24. Williams, "Body's Grace," 317.

25. Contrary to reviewers who have supposed that any means must be a means only.

26. David Matzko McCarthy, "The Relationship of Bodies: A Nuptial Hermeneutics of Same-Sex Unions," in *Theology and Sexuality*, ed. Rogers, 206.

27. For more on this topic, see Eugene F. Rogers Jr., *After the Spirit* (Grand Rapids, MI: Eerdmans, 2005).

28. These two sentences come from Rogers, "Nature with Water and the Spirit," 99, and depend on Sergei Bulgakov, *The Bride of the Lamb*, trans. Boris Jakim (Edinburgh: T. & T. Clark; Grand Rapids, MI: Eerdmans, 2002), 65–66. The exegesis can stand even without the conceptual context.

29. Thomas Aquinas, *Summa theologiae* I.47.1. For commentary, see Willis Jenkins, "Biodiversity and Salvation: Thomistic Roots for Environmental Ethics," *Journal of Religion* 83 (2003): 401–420.

30. Maximus the Confessor, *Ambiguum 7: On the Beginning and End of Rational Creatures*, in *On the Cosmic Mystery of Jesus Christ: Selected Writings from St Maximus the Confessor*, trans. Paul Blowers and Robert Louis Wilken (Crestwood, NY: St. Vladimir's Seminary Press, 2003), 54. Greek, *Patrologia Graeca* 91:1068D–1101C. For commentary, see Polycarp Sherwood, *The Earlier Ambigua of Saint Maximus the Confessor and His Refutation of Origenism*, Studia Anselmiana 36 (Rome: Herder, 1955), 155–180.

31. This sentence comes from Rogers, "With Water and the Spirit," 99–100. Among human beings, this diversity does not yield a common vocation for gay and lesbian people as a group, but one that demands discernment by each person if it is not to be washed out. So John of the Cross counsels the discernment of loves, if recent research is correct; see Christopher Hinkle, "A Delicate Knowledge: Epistemology, Homosexuality, and St. John of the Cross," *Modern Theology* 17 (2001): 436; for a critique of more prescriptive readings of John, see Sarah Coakley, "Traditions of Spiritual Guidance" in her *Powers and Submissions: Spirituality, Philosophy and Gender* (Oxford: Blackwell, 2002), 40–54. The vocation to sanctification, even on Catholic accounts, depends on individual discernment, so that it does not follow that homosexually oriented Catholics ipso facto have a call to priestly or religious celibacy.

32. Maximus the Confessor, *Ambiguum 7*, 59–60, pronouns modified.

33. Williams, "Body's Grace," 312.

34. Kendall Soulen, "YHWH the Triune God," *Modern Theology* 15 (1999): 25–54.

35. I owe this way of putting the matter to a similar formulation in ibid.

36. Peter Brown, *The Body and Society* (New York: Columbia University Press, 1988), 225–226, citing Athanasius, *Life of Anthony*, 67.

37. Susan Harvey, "The Stylite's Liturgy: Ritual and Religious Identity in Late Antiquity," *Journal of Early Christian Studies* 6 (1998): 523–539.

38. Barth, *Church Dogmatics*, vol. III, pt. 4.

39. *Nicomachean Ethics* IX.12, 1172a11–14; John 15:15.

40. *On the Lament of the Mother of God* 13, in *Kontakia on the Life of Christ*, by St. Romanos the Melodist, 148. I owe the insight that Christ is both physician and patient to Stephania Gianulis.

41. See Williams, "Body's Grace," for reflections on the positive moral possibilities of both.

42. McCarthy, "Relationship of Bodies," 212–213.

43. But see Stanley Hauerwas, "Why Gays (as a Group) Are Morally Superior to Christians (as a Group)," in *The Hauerwas Reader*, ed. John Berkman and Michael Cartwright (Durham, NC: Duke University Press, 2001), 519–521.

44. McCarthy, "Relationship of Bodies," 214, n. 12. See also Dale B. Martin, "Sex and the Single Savior," *Svensk exegetisk arsbok* 67 (2002): 47–60.

45. A shorter version of this essay appeared as "Sanctified Unions," *The Christian Century* 121, no. 12 (June 15, 2004): 26–29, with a response to a letter to the editor in *The Christian Century* 121, no. 17 (August 24, 2004): 42–43.

INDEX